PILLAR & TINDERBOX
The Greek Press and
the Dictatorship

The problem of the press is one of the most acute problems facing the free world. Press freedom is a great blessing and the pillar of the democratic way of life, but it can become a tinderbox threatening its own foundations if and when it degenerates into licence or becomes a means to serve obscure interests. – *George Georgalas*

A liar will not be believed even when he speaks the truth. – *Aesop*

PILLAR & TINDERBOX
The Greek Press and the Dictatorship

by Robert McDonald

Marion Boyars
New York . London

First published in the United States and Great Britain
in 1983 by
MARION BOYARS PUBLISHERS
457 Broome Street, New York, NY 10013
and
18 Brewer Street, London W1R 4AS.

Distributed in the United States by
The Scribner Book Companies, Inc.

Australian and New Zealand distribution by
Thomas C. Lothian Pty.
4-12 Tattersalls Lane, Melbourne, Victoria 3000.

Distributed in Canada by John Wiley & Sons Canada Limited

© by Writers and Scholars Educational Trust, 1983

Printed and bound in Great Britain at
The Camelot Press Ltd, Southampton

British Library Cataloguing in Publication Data

McDonald, Robert
Pillar & tinderbox: the Greek press and the dictatorship
1. Press – Greece – History – 20th century
I. Title
079'.495   PN5234

ISBN 0-7145-2781-5

Library of Congress Cataloguing in Publication Data

McDonald, Robert
Pillar & tinderbox

Bibliography: p.
Includes index
1. Government and the press – Greece – History – 20th century
2. Liberty of the press – Greece
3. Press law – Greece
I. Title
II. Title: Pillar and tinderbox
PN4748.G8M37   1982   323.44'5   82-14748

With thanks to all those
who helped me get the news.

In memoriam:
George Androulidakis
George Drossos

This book has been published with
the financial assistance of the Ford Foundation
and under the auspices of
the Writers and Scholars Educational Trust.

CONTENTS

PART THREE

FOREWORD AND ACKNOWLEDGEMENTS

A study of the press under the Greek dictatorship (1967–1974) may seem a rather narrow pursuit, particularly as no adequate general history of the period has yet been written. A regime's relations with the press, however, are an excellent symptom of its essential nature and, in the case of the colonels, the evolution of their attitudes closely mirrored their approach to society at large. In the beginning they were absolute, rigorously stifling all dissent and dictating the news. Later they tried to present a semblance of legality while maintaining control through covert, coercive means. Always, the aim of the Revolution was to create a guided political life, never to restore full democracy as was perpetually promised. Because the glasshouse effect exaggerated the general climate, it threw into sharp relief authoritarian attitudes which the colonels often successfully masked elsewhere.

There is a paradox at the heart of Greek scholarship in which, on the one hand, it is argued that only a Greek imbued with Greek culture (language, religion, family life and political heritage) can possibly understand Greek affairs, while on the other, it is claimed that anyone submerged in this culture is bound to be so partisan about one or other of its aspects as to make objectivity impossible. Although I am a Philhellene, my tradition is Anglo-Saxon and this is reflected in my appreciation of men and events. I hope that it has not been to the exclusion of an appreciation of the so-called Greek Reality.

One of the difficulties in doing research in Greece is lack of primary source material. The tradition is oral and memories for details are short. This necessitates collating numerous, often conflicting accounts and trying to draw what is common from them. Library facilities are limited and many archives are in private hands. The problem was compounded in this particular instance by the fact that the archives of the Secretariat General of Press and Information at the Ministry to the Prime Minister are said to have been removed by the military when they quit power. Efforts to obtain documentation from military archives have, with one exception, proved fruitless. The ephemeral nature of oral sources and the lack of documentation means that there has had to be a heavy reliance on secondary source material and here the problem is that an initial error can be compounded by repetition until such time as it assumes the force of veracity and even begins to be repeated by what are presumed to be primary oral sources. I have done what was possible to trace all information to its origin but, if I am responsible for continuing the perpetration of any error, I apologize in advance.

In writing this study, I am following a path already well marked out by two men: Armand Gaspard of the International Press Institute, who did more than any single individual to make the plight of the Greek press known to the outside world during the dictatorship, and Dominique Gazeau, whose doctoral thesis for the University of Paris constitutes an exhaustive collation of virtually all available secondary source materials. I wish here to acknowledge my thanks to the I.P.I. for giving me access to Gaspard's files, now in the library of the Institute at City University, London and to Gazeau for letting me read his unpublished typescript.

I also want to thank the many people who took time to help me in this project. Except for the late Nassos Botsis of *Acropolis* and *Apoyevmatini*, all publishers gave their full co-operation.

Mr. Botsis did provide cursory answers to a questionnaire but resisted repeated requests for a private meeting. When finally persuaded by intermediaries that he should see me, he was suspicious and aggressive. 'I do not know what use you want to make of this information. Other proprietors tell me you want to know about finances, balance sheets, profits, things like that. You are not my proprietor.' (Mr. Botsis' detractors have alleged that the implicit *quid pro quo* for large state-authorized loans contracted during the dictatorship was the support of his papers for the regime.) He entertained one general question but took umbrage at the second which was why his newspapers had supported a 'yes' vote in the 1973 referendum on the republic in which junta leader George Papadopoulos was endorsed as president. 'Because I chose to do so,' he shouted. Then, in a furious outburst, he screamed, 'You are not my judge. . . . You come here to accuse me . . . . Write that I said "No comment" and I will answer you in the newspaper.' And with that he strode from his office leaving me and my translator sitting in astonishment. We saw ourselves out.

Much of the material provided by the publishers did include details of such things as finances and court cases which, unfortunately, has had to be excluded for reasons of space. I realize it often took them a great deal of time to produce this information and can only hope they do not feel that their efforts have been wasted. Suffice it to say that it has all helped me to arrive at my general understanding.

This study was commissioned by Writers and Scholars Educational Trust, the London-based organization concerned with censorship and academic freedom. Its associated periodical, *Index on Censorship* has published numerous articles and notes on Greece and it was thought that a case study might provide useful insights which could be extrapolated and applied to other authoritarian regimes. The research was carried out under a grant generously provided by the Ford Foundation. My thanks to W.S.E.T. Council member Lord Sainsbury and to John Campbell of St. Antony's College Oxford, for having read the manuscript in an early draft.

Special thanks are due to George Krippas, head of the Legislative Co-ordination Office of the Secretariat General of

Press and Information for the long hours he spent explaining the intricacies of Greek press law and to George Aidinis, legal counsel of the Union of Proprietors of Daily Newspapers of Athens for the protracted sessions he spent explaining press practices. Dozens of other individuals have assisted in various ways and in varying degrees. Their contributions were appreciated. The principal translators deserve particular mention. They were George Apostolopoulos, Eleftherios Eleftheratos and Marion Sarafis. They donated much of their time and their interest in the research was often that of partners. Their help is appreciated more than they realize.

And finally thanks to Donna, my wife, for her patience during the writing, her intelligent criticisms during rewriting and her hard slog during the preparation of the manuscript for publication.

PART ONE

I THE COUP AND ITS PRELUDE

If you find me no job,
I'll open a newspaper
Nineteenth century political joke

The press in Greece is seen principally as a medium for the expression of political opinion. Newspapers are partisan and the notion of neutral, informational reporting is a recent one still not fully appreciated by many journalists and readers. This is a consequence of the history of the Greek press. Its inception coincided with the struggle for independence from the Turks and its development paralleled the growth of political life in the nascent state. Rival individuals and competing organizations each published journals to promote their causes and at one time in the nineteenth century there were as many as sixty newspapers appearing in Athens alone. The growth of the modern press coincided with the establishment, in the latter part of the last century, of political parties. Each had its own paper and in some instances the party leader was also the editor. Although gradually the parties and papers separated, an identity of interests was maintained.

In this century, newspapers have been inextricably caught up in the republican-royalist schism which literally split the country during World War I and which produced a republic in 1924 followed by a reversion to monarchy in 1935. Its antagonism infected all political life creating a profound gulf between conservatives and liberals and later contributing to both fascist dictatorship and communist insurrection. A number of contemporary newspapers were founded in the heat of these early divisions. The conservative and monarchist *Kathimerini* (Daily)[1] and *Vradyni* (Evening) appeared respectively in 1919 and 1923; the republican and liberal *Ethnos* (Nation) and *Vima* (Tribune) in 1913 and 1921. *Rizospastis* (Radical) became the official organ of the Greek Communist Party (K.K.E.) in 1924. The popular *Nea* (News) appeared in 1930 at a time when republican fortunes were flagging.

Factional feuding was suppressed during two decades of repression which began with the installation on August 4, 1936 of the fascist dictatorship of General Ioannis Metaxas. His government applied strict censorship until it could pass into law two comprehensive and rigid pieces of legislation: one on the operation of the press[2] governing every aspect from the reporting of the activities of the High Command to the coverage of divorce trials, and the other on its organization[3] covering everything from union structures to such petty details as what a newsvendor might lawfully shout while hawking his wares. This rigorous regime was followed by one of blanket censorship under the Nazi occupation. Some publishers were actually removed from their papers and replaced by collaborators. Liberation brought a brief respite in which *Eleftheria* (Freedom) emerged from the underground to become a daily. But almost immediately, the country was plunged into bitter civil war with the communists. Greeks boast how they got through it under a parliamentary regime and without censorship. However, the views of the communists were suppressed by measures which included the anti-constitutional requirements of prior authorization for both the publication and the circulation of printed matter.[4] *Rizospastis* was banned[5] and the Communist Party outlawed by legislation which made it a potential capital offence to propagate through the press 'ideas manifestly aiming at the overthrow by force of the regime or the prevailing social order. . . .'[6] Radio broadcasts were censored and the non-communist press published according to a tacit understanding of what was considered to be in the national interest.

There was something of a return to diversity after the civil strife. The truculently left-of-center *Athinaiki* (Athenian), appeared in 1949, and the arch-conservative *Apoyevmatini* (Afternoon) in 1954. *Avgi* (Dawn) began publishing in 1952 as the paper of the United Democratic Left (E.D.A.) which was the front party for the still-illegal communists. But domestic reaction to the civil war, coupled with the global cold war mentality, meant that fundamentally attitudes were still restrictive. The semi-dictatorial government of Field Marshal Alexander Papagos introduced amendments to the Penal Code in 1953 which severely increased penalties for press offences and, during the eight-year succession of conservative governments under Prime Minister Constantine Karamanlis and the National Radical Union (E.R.E.) party, official harassment of the opposition press was tolerated, if not promoted. Center-left papers faced repeated prosecutions for charges such as insulting public authorities: two crypto-communist publications were hounded into oblivion by this means. According to the director of *Avgi*, it was physically dangerous to read that paper in public. 'Readers are arrested because they buy our newspaper; some of them are manhandled at the police stations, while others are styled "anti-national" and deprived of their notorious "loyalty certificates" which are necessary in order to obtain all sorts of jobs. . . .'[7] Security forces interfered with the circulation of publications which they deemed undesirable. '. . . police agents carry out government orders requiring provincial distribution agencies not to circulate *Avgi*, (claiming that it has not arrived or that it has run out) and . . . not to send copies to small agencies or offices in the countryside. . . .'[8] While such action was usually directed at the left, the right also suffered. The circulation of the ultra-conservative *Estia* (Hearth) dropped by more than 40% between 1955 and 1962, the proprietor claims, because of interference by police and gendarmerie officers incensed by the paper's hostility to Karamanlis.

Real liberalization didn't come till the sixties when, reconstruction having ended, there was more time for politics and culture. It was a period of great ferment. There were strong pressures for a greater voice in public life from a large number of upwardly mobile young people. Among their leaders were graduates returned from universities abroad espousing social theories deemed revolutionary by the staid establishment. There was an artistic renaissance which took much of its inspiration from the humanity of the left. It endorsed no particular ideology but was nonetheless damned as politically propagandistic by the bourgeoisie. In 1961, Mrs. Helen Vlachou launched *Mesimvrini* (Noon) an upmarket afternoon paper aimed at the growing middle class. It was conservative but less so than traditional papers of the right, being inclined to cover a fairly broad spectrum of news and to confine its political views to the editorials. It rapidly became the top circulation conservative newspaper and its tautly sub-edited style, a novelty in Greece, was noted throughout the industry. The anticonstitutional press legislation passed during the civil war finally was abolished in 1962[9] and, while the Communist Party and its publications remained outlawed, E.D.A. flourished to such an extent that in 1963, *Dimokratiki Allagi* (Democratic Change) was founded as an afternoon stable-mate to *Avgi*.

The 1961 elections had returned Karamanlis for a third consecutive term but the opposition Centre Union (E.K.) party claimed that the victory was achieved by a fraud carried out with the connivance of the military. Party leader George Papandreou and his son, Andreas, who had recently returned from the University of California at Berkeley, launched the *anendotos agonas*, or unyielding struggle, to overturn the result. They were supported closely, sometimes seemingly led by, the mass circulation centrist papers *Nea* and *Vima* whose 27-year-old publisher, Christos Lambrakis, was a former student at the London School of Economics.

Karamanlis, harassed by this and embroiled in a constitutional wrangle with King Paul over an unrelated matter, retired from politics in 1963 and took himself off in dudgeon to self-exile in Paris. Elections later that year returned George Papandreou as the head of a minority government but gave the balance of power to the United Democratic Left. Papandreou, refusing to govern in coalition with them, immediately called fresh elections which gave the Centre Union a massive outright majority. King Paul died in March 1964 and was replaced by his 23-year-old son Constantine. For a period of months, a breath of fresh air blew through all walks of public life.

The Center Union, though, was a loose coalition of liberals and socialists and they quickly fell to squabbling among themselves. Eventually, Papandreou tried to remove his Defence Minister for not carrying through with sufficient vigour a political purge of the army. When he tried to appoint himself to this post, King Constantine demurred. Papandreou offered his resignation and the young monarch, poorly advised by conservative counsellors, peremptorily accepted. The country was plunged into twenty-one months of constitutional chaos. Throughout the summer of 1965, Athens was wracked with demonstrations and riots while successive senior members of the Center Union tried unsuccessfully to form a government which could win the confidence of parliament. Finally, a minority administration was created from a rump of the party under former deputy leader Stefanos Stefanopoulos. It was supported in the house by the National Radical Union. Lambrakis and his papers were deeply involved in backstage machinations to have Stefanopoulos form a caretaker government to conduct fresh elections. This was misconstrued by some party members as betrayal of Papandreou and, at one point, an infuriated mob seized and burned in the streets hundreds of copies of *Nea*. Once Stefanopoulos was installed as a mandated Prime Minister, it was Panos Kokkas' *Eleftheria* which became the mouthpiece of his Liberal Democratic Centre government. The Lambrakis group remained loyal to Papandreou.

The confrontation between Papandreou and the king reopened the old republican-royalist wound and the press lined up in two vituperative camps with *Kathimerini, Mesimvrini, Vradyni* and the two Botsis papers, *Acropolis* and *Apoyevmatini*, supporting the monarch and *Athinaiki, Ethnos* and the Lambrakis papers demanding fresh elections to vindicate Papandreou and his new slogan that 'The king reigns but the people rule.' *Avgi* and *Dimokratiki Allagi* sided with the centrists, leading to allegations of a popular front. Such suggestions were fuelled by Savvas Constandopoulos, a former communist turned extreme right-winger, who, in 1966, founded *Eleftheros Kosmos* (Free World), the paper that went on to become the mouthpiece of the colonels. Press behaviour degenerated into licence with the political coloration of reporting producing diametrically opposed accounts of the same events and calumnious characterizations of political figures which generally diminished respect for all those in public life.[10]

The Stefanopoulos administration, which had not been expected to last more than a few weeks at most, dragged on for eighteen months, sustained largely by the unwillingness of those who supported it to risk going to the polls. Because of the unusual amalgam of interests it represented, it was virtually paralyzed when it came to trying to implement policy, particularly where economic matters were concerned. There was mounting social unrest highlighted by almost daily strikes by everyone from taxi drivers to doctors. The administration gained a reputation for corruption; nepotism was rife. Constandopoulos, in a series of public lectures in July 1966, claimed that the situation was so anomalous that it brooked no normal political solution. He warned of 'the eventuality of an arbitrary dictatorship which will want to thwart the enforcement of one party over the other; it will separate them, stand above and beyond them and will wait for them to recover, to change ideas, to clear themselves of passion and [of the] the fanaticism of the moment so that it can once again put the institution of democracy into effect.'[11]

Finally, in December 1966, Papandreou and Panayotis Kanellopoulos, the successor to Karamanlis as leader of E.R.E., agreed that there should be new elections. Kanellopoulos withdrew his party's support from the minority administration, forcing its resignation, and a caretaker cabinet was installed to prepare for elections the following May. Kokkas published what purported to be an *aide memoire* from an alleged meeting between Kanellopoulos, *Kathimerini* publisher Helen Vlachou and an aide to the king in which several deals were apparently done about the future shape of political developments. The right was said to have obtained an undertaking from Papandreou not to make the monarchy an issue in the elections. According to some accounts, he had also agreed not to tamper with the military if victorious. The Lambrakis papers were said to tacitly concur with these arrangements. These claims were denied by the principals named but it seems likely that some understandings had been reached to allow the voting to go ahead. Otherwise, it was feared, senior royalist officers might intervene to protect the monarchy against a further confrontation with George Papandreou. Andreas, however, refused to abide by any undertakings and even threatened to break with the Center Union, taking a group of some forty deputies with him. In the event, this did not happen but it set the temper for the frenetic politicking which followed over the next few months.

The center repeatedly alleged that a junta waited in the wings to prevent their victory. Mrs. Vlachou lent credence to such charges with an editorial in *Kathimerini* in which she posited a scenario which might prompt military intervention:

. . . If, God forbid, the Center Union becomes the majority party or obtains the majority with E.D.A., these two parties in the course of the first night following the elections, mobilizing the revolutionary machine of E.D.A. and, under its protection, mounting demonstrations demanding power to the people, will abolish the regime [of crowned democracy] and become masters of the government or rather of power and it would be necessary to use the armed forces to oust them. . . .[12]

Vima countered, claiming that any action by the military would be met with a campaign of strikes and fighting demonstrations. Both sides seemed to be leap-frogging towards an inevitable fulfillment of their own predictions.

Andreas Papandreou's name was linked with *A.S.P.I.D.A.* (Shield), an alleged conspiracy to advance leftists in the army, uncovered in the aftermath of his father's attempted purge. Fifteen officers were sentenced to terms of up to eighteen years imprisonment for their part in the plot. As a deputy, Andreas had parliamentary immunity but as soon as the house was dissolved for the election he would lose this and might be arrested. The Center Union sought an amendment to the electoral law extending immunity throughout the campaign. E.R.E. refused and the caretaker government fell. On April 3, Constantine appointed Kanellopoulos prime minister with a mandate to dissolve parliament and to conduct elections on May 28. It was the antithesis of the last popular mandate and was denounced by the center as tantamount to a palace coup. The impending campaign promised to be furious and possibly bloody and apparently some royal advisers suggested that an E.R.E.-E.K. coalition should be formed to rule the country until tempers cooled. Both Papandreou and Kanellopoulos felt that the democratic process should prevail and so the preparations for the election forged ahead amid much acrimony. Royalist generals met to consider what action they should take and decided temporarily to bide their time.

The frenzied antics of the press during this period helped to generate an atmosphere of anxiety at what was already a time of anomaly and uncertainty. The papers helped to devalue politicians when what was needed was leadership of high moral stature. It has been suggested that many of the incidents which caused the press to behave so badly were purposely engineered by psychological warfare specialists in the Greek Central Intelligence Service (K.Y.P.) with a view to softening up society for a takeover. Be that as it may, it was the press which did the actual writing and which must bear a heavy burden of responsibility for creating the climate which allowed the *coup d'etat* to be so readily accepted by many ordinary citizens.

On April 21, 1967, the colonels short-circuited everybody's plans – the king's, the politicians' and the generals' – by declaring a state of emergency and activating a N.A.T.O. counter-insurgency plan which caused the army to seize control of the country. They did it in the name of Constantine, though he later disowned their action. As their tanks trundled into central Athens shortly after two a.m. Prime Minister Kanellopoulos was roughly arrested; so too were the Papandreous, father and son.

The troops assigned to deal with the press had three objectives: to stop that day's editions, to close *Avgi* and *Dimokratiki Allagi* and to arrest potentially hostile editors including Lambrakis, Kokkas and the two Center Union M.P.s who ran *Athinaiki*, Ioannis Papageorgiou and Emmanuel Baklatzis. The morning papers had already gone to bed when news of the troop movements started to trickle in. Helen Vlachou was awakened at home by staff and went immediately to the office to supervise the rewriting of a new lead. The material was all very tentative and *Kathimerini* set only one column reporting military movements and noting that soldiers had several times threatened to fire on inquiring reporters. 'We did not expect to circulate, but we made the change out of habit, in spite of still having little to say.'[13]

Foreign editor Michael Biotakis was the late man at *Avgi*. He opened a hole in the back page and inserted a short item saying there had been military movements giving the impression of a coup. He stuck a headline above the page-one logo and ordered the print run started immediately. A handful of these copies actually got to kiosks, because the military didn't close the central distribution agency until six a.m. The issues were, however, confiscated before any could be sold.

As the extent of the military movements began to become apparent, Christos Lambrakis left *Vima* together with editor-in-chief Leon Karapanayotis. They went to the home of a mutual friend where they spent the night trying to get information and debating what to do. According to Karapanayotis, 'We discussed mainly what was going on rather than the paper. No one knew what was happening. On that first night we had no understanding of what to do.' About dawn, it was agreed that Lambrakis should go underground until the situation was clarified while Karapanayotis would sound out the staff about whether to continue publishing. The decision, taken after much agonizing, was that the papers should remain open despite censorship in order to be able to fight another day. Lambrakis subsequently indicated that he concurred in this 'excruciating' choice.

Lambrakis stayed a week at this apartment which belonged to a friend who had been a member of the resistance during the occupation and who was skilled at clandestine activities. He then was transferred to the home of dance impressario Dora Stratou where he was eventually arrested on June 1. Held for several weeks in solitary confinement at a gendarmerie head-quarters in the Athens suburb of Goudi, he was later exiled to the island of Syros. At no time was he charged with anything except the vague assertion made by Public Order Minister Paul Totomis that he was a 'danger to the security of the state'. Lam-brakis was finally liberated in an amnesty at Christmas 1967 but refused to go to his office until after the lifting of prior censor-ship nearly two years later.

Panos Kokkas, publisher of *Eleftheria*, had been in court late on April 20 fighting a libel action brought against him by Kanellopoulos and Mrs. Vlachou over the publication of the *aide memoire*. Kokkas' sister, returning home about 1.30 a.m., spotted the tanks moving towards town and was able to alert him before telephone lines were cut. Kokkas had been expect-ing something like this and immediately went underground to avoid arrest. An hour later, a jeep with seven soldiers in it called at the Kokkas' home. When they could not find Panos, they took his seventy-six year old father as a hostage. At *Eleftheria's* printing works they found editor-in-chief, George Androu-lidakis, working on the stone and arrested him too. Kokkas remained inside Greece for nearly a month until arrangements were made for him to leave the country by means of a ship sailing from the west coast port of Patras. This he did in classic cloak and dagger fashion, kitted out in a disguise to get past military checkpoints. Kokkas' sister claims that during their first telephone call, even before he knew the political stripe of the junta, he asked her to announce to the staff that the paper would not publish so long as there was censorship. *Eleftheria* was closed down by the family and the staff were paid off at substantial cost. Kokkas remained abroad until 1973 when he returned following the lifting of martial law.

The *Athinaiki* publishers both managed to escape arrest and to go into hiding. Papageorgiou in Athens, Baklatzis in Crete. The paper continued to be brought out by a team of journalists, although, according to Papageorgiou, this was done 'without the permission of the publishers, who didn't want to publish under these conditions.' After two weeks, it closed and charges were preferred against Papageorgiou and Baklatzis for non-payment of Easter bonuses and a fortnight's wages. Baklatzis was tricked into giving himself up by a false radio news report which said that he was hiding unnecessarily as there were no charges outstanding against him. He returned to Athens and was arrested as he stepped off the boat in Piraeus. Papageorgiou emerged after the prosecutor of the Athens Extraordinary Court Martial declared that unless he presented himself for questioning within twenty-four hours, he would be considered a fugitive. He appeared before a very fat colonel.

'Why did you close the paper?'

'I didn't close the paper.'

'I'll teach you. You will go inside.'

'Why will I go to prison?'

'To teach you not to be insubordinate to the military authorities.'

'But I'm not being insubordinate. Once I got the summons I came straight away.'

'I'll teach you. You are going to prison for five years.'

The two publishers were remanded in custody for several months, a procedure unheard of on such charges. That it was only a pretext for incarceration on political grounds was amply demonstrated by the terms on which they were released. The newspaper was to shut down permanently but the government was not to be seen to have been the cause. The pair were to declare voluntary bankruptcy. Papageorgiou claimed that while the paper had debts, 'commercial debts with the agencies, with paper merchants, the usual type of debts,' nothing was owed to the bank and there was no need to wind up the business. He advised against accepting the terms and argued in favour of declaring *force majeure*, but it was Baklatzis who had ultimate financial authority for the paper and he, wanting out of prison, agreed to file the bankruptcy petition. They were released in September 1967. Baklatzis died of cancer three months later.

Leonidas Kyrkos and Manolis Glezos, respectively publisher and director of *Avgi*, were held on the military's list of proscribed persons and were among the first to be arrested.

Military police hustled Kyrkos from his house in his pyjamas while Glezos was snatched from sleep in his underwear. The editorial staff, putting the paper to bed at the *Ethnos* printing works, were not molested. After adding his insert, Biotakis and two colleagues repaired to a suburban apartment. En route, they were stopped by a policeman who asked for identification. They explained that they were journalists without producing their identity cards and were waved on their way with apologies. Only later, when they attempted to return to the paper and were turned back at a military roadblock, did they realize the full gravity of the situation. The three men went into hiding and were underground until September when they were arrested and interned.

Dimokratiki Allagi shared a printing plant with *Eleftheria* and editor-in-chief Harilaos Manos, together with two senior staff, were actually in the works when the soldiers barged in to arrest Androulidakis. The trio slipped out of a side door and alerted director Lefteris Voutsas at home. He later joined them in an all-night coffee shop. Like everyone else, these men did not know on whose part the military was moving but they assumed it was the right and that they should act defensively. Their first thought was to get at the office safe. April 21 should have been payday and it was full of made up wage packets. The men wanted to ensure that these funds could be saved for resistance action. Taking the newspaper's car and driver, they reconnoitred the office area but, as the premises were above a police station and across the street from a major telecommunications centre, they found the district alive with troops and so had to detour to avoid detection. When the first morning radio bulletins confirmed their suspicions about the political complexion of the coup, they proceeded to a safe house where they remained for four days before going underground. One of them escaped to Paris but two others were quickly arrested. Voutsas managed to avoid detection for three months, long enough for him to have set the wheels in motion for an underground *Avgi*. It later became *Rizospastis* (*Machitis*) (Radical Fighter), a monthly paper which appeared for sixty-five issues as the voice of the Greek Communist Party of the Interior (K.K.E.-E.s), a Eurocommunist splinter from the orthodox party. The K.K.E. published its own underground papers beginning with *Adouloti Athena* (Unenslaved Athens) and later its own version of *Rizospastis*. It appeared for sixty-seven issues until February 1974 when it was closed following a series of arrests of top level party leaders in the underground. There was a host of resistance publications produced during the dictatorship but it was only these communist papers which appeared regularly in printed form. They were produced at great risk and many people associated with them were arrested and tried for subversion. In the initial roundup of communists on April 21, some twenty regular working journalists were detained and interned, first at Yiaros and later at Leros prison camp. The property of *Avgi* and *Dimokratiki Allagi* was confiscated by the military and dispersed among state offices. Their printing plant and office facilities were rented and therefore could not be punitively seized in this way.

The conservative publishers were not bothered by the military but the greatest shock for the junta came from among right wing ranks when Helen Vlachou decided to close her prestigious papers rather than to publish under censorship. The colonels had expected *Kathimerini* and *Mesimvrini* to be the flagships of their revolution. Mrs. Vlachou had effectively endorsed military intervention in print and, had the coup been by the king and his generals (the so-called 'big junta'), *Kathimerini*, at least, would likely have continued to appear even under censorship. As it was a pre-emptive strike by junior officers, and, because the colonels dictated as well as censored the news, Mrs. Vlachou refused to publish. This position was not immediately made apparent as she feared the regime might find some means to force her to appear. 'We were ninety-nine per cent certain that we didn't want to publish but we didn't want that to come out too soon.' Under the Nazi occupation, her father had openly declared his intention to close *Kathimerini* and the Germans had thrown him out and put in their own people. 'This time we knew better. Unless we could publish a respectable paper, a newspaper that was free to inform and not obliged to misinform, we would not publish anything at all. But we were not going to advertize our decision.'[14]

Giving her staff temporary leave, Mrs. Vlachou retired to her villa in the suburb of Pendeli where she was barracked by other publishers. 'They were rather bitter with us. They said, "Why do you let us suffer this indignity and you don't share it?" ' The junta also sent emissaries to appeal for cooperation. She has cited Brigadier Pattakos as saying, 'There is not going to be any censorship for you. . . . We know you will write the right things. You will not be treated like the others. You will help us, guide us! We will create a new Greece together.'[15] But Mrs. Vlachou was adamant and on May 1 she issued redundancy notices, claiming *force majeure*. The action made her a symbol of resistance and she became a focus of attention for visiting foreign correspondents. She was placed under house arrest in October 1967 after giving an interview to *La Stampa* in which she referred to the colonels generally as mediocre men and to Brigadier Pattakos in particular as a clown. She managed to escape abroad to England in the confusion following the king's abortive counter-coup and settled there as a leading campaigner against the colonels.

The coup thus halved the number of national newspapers: *Kathimerini*, *Mesimvrini*, *Eleftheria*, *Athinaiki*, *Avgi* and *Dimokratiki Allagi* all disappeared. *Ethnos*, which was in severe financial difficulties tried to close in August 1967 but the government, smarting from its bad press abroad as a consequence of the other closures, ordered the paper to take a four million drachma loan to remain open. The owners boycotted the premises and the paper was run by a former city editor who thought the dictatorship a good thing. *Acropolis* and *Apoyevmatini*, the conservative papers of the Botsis brothers, did not endorse the colonels but neither in the beginning did they apparently go out of their way to oppose them. George Athanassiades' royalist *Vradyni* backed the regime while the king maintained his face of cooperation but when he turned against the colonels in his abortive counter-coup on December 13, 1967, *Vradyni* joined the opposition. The idiosyncratic *Estia* gave support so long as the colonels looked likely to restore political government but once their long term designs on power became evident, it too adopted a sniping posture. *Eleftheros Kosmos* founded, it has been alleged, with intelligence money in anticipation of the coup, became the sole mouthpiece of the regime.

NOTES

[1] *I-Avgi, I Kathimerini, Ta Nea, Ta Simerina, To Vima* and *I Vradyni* have definite articles in their titles. They have been omitted for brevity.

[2] Compulsory Law 1092, February 21–22, 1938, on 'The Press'.

[3] Compulsory Law 1093, February 9–22, 1938, on 'Journalistic Organizations'.

[4] Constitutional Resolution Gamma of 1946 as amended in October 1947.

[5] October 17, 1947.

[6] Law 509, December 27, 1947.

[7] Leonidas Kyrkos, Letter to the International Press Institute, April 22, 1960.

[8] *Ibid.*

[9] Legislative Decree 4234, July 1962.

[10] Demetrios Carmocolias, *Political Communication in Greece 1965–67*, Athens, National Centre of Social Research, 1974, 167 pp. This is a detailed study of the 'bellicosity' of the press in this period.

[11] As reprinted in *Eleftheros Kosmos*, April 23, 1967.

[12] *Kathimerini*, February 23, 1967.

[13] Helen Vlachou, *House Arrest*, London, Andre Deutsch, 1970, p. 20.

[14] *Ibid*, p. 37.

[15] *Ibid*, p. 41.

II THE ATTITUDE TO THE PRESS

The colonels mistrusted the press and were afraid of it. They had an image of publishers as ruthless, unscrupulous press barons prepared to do or to say anything to turn a profit and they believed newspapers to be manipulative instruments irresponsibly influencing public life from behind the scenes. It is not an uncommon attitude among the ilk of the junta who see themselves as little men, caught in the machinations of a system beyond their control and who are jealous of the press because of the power they imagine it enjoys. Among regime members, this view was not confined merely to the unsophisticated colonels but also found expression among more worldly figures such as Foreign Minister Panayotis Pipinellis. In a bizarre speech to a colloquy of ambassadors, in which he attacked Greece's 'so-called democratic allies' in the Council of Europe, Pipinellis claimed: '. . . I am firmly convinced that these countries are only nominally democratic and that they are ruled by a regime of hypocritical and secret oligarchy which is worse than any other oligarchy since it is irresponsible. Instead of being the oligarchy of Hitler and his company, which at least was bearing its historic responsibilities . . . the western countries have the oligarchy of different, irresponsible profiteering journalists. . . .'[1]

The junta's first policy statement, broadcast on the night of the coup, pledged to restore the press to its 'national mission':

Impelled by its belief in the serious mission of the press within the framework of a true democracy, the government will endeavour to create appropriate conditions under which the entire press will be able and obliged to respond to its national mission. Freedom of the press does not mean irresponsibility, shamelessness, 'yellow' press writing and the betrayal of all national values.

The colonels believed that the press should perform 'a public function', a concept enshrined both in the 1968 constitution and in the 1969 Press Law. In essence, it was a vision of the press as an extension of government which would disseminate executive thought, criticize administrative action, shape public opinion and monitor state activity. It permitted no attack on either the legitimacy or the legality of the authoritarian regime. It was a difficult notion to come to grips with because, while the concept ran counter to traditional ideas of a free press, pronouncements about it were couched in a democratic vocabulary, the ordinary connotations of which were quite contrary to the colonels' meaning. Junta leader George Papadopoulos contributed substantially to the confusion with two speeches in which he obviously felt he'd made the definitive statement on 'the function'. It was a mark of his simplistic arrogance that he seemed genuinely pained when the press did not whole-heartedly embrace it. It was difficult enough to understand, let alone to accept.

In his impenetrably convoluted style, with its heavy use of metaphor, Papadopoulos spoke of the press variously as the digestive system of the body politic and as a regiment on the attack on behalf of the Revolution. But his foremost allusion was religious with the intimation that journalism was a sacred vocation. The very word function, *litourgima*, is related to liturgy and religious rites. *Litourgi* are functionaries in a social sense but ministrants in a religious context. 'Journalism,' said Papadopoulos, 'is, without doubt, a function and journalists its functionaries.'[2] It seemed tautological nonsense until viewed from the religious perspective. Then, translated roughly, he had said, 'Journalism is a calling and journalists its votaries.' On various other occasions Papadopoulos referred to the head-quarters of the journalists' union and to newspaper premises as temples. The colonels' dogma envisioned a 'Greece of Christian Greeks' with a national identity of interests comprised of history in the form of the Greek heritage, nationalism in the spirit of duty to the motherland, morality in the shape of the precepts of the Orthodox Church and a social order based on the traditional hierarchical structure of the family. This sense of purpose had been lost in the pre-coup political maelstrom and it was one of the main 'Aims of the Revolution' to restore it and to make the individual aware of his proper relationship to society.

> We are struggling for the progress of individuals in society and of society as groups of individuals. Such progress pre-supposes a mutual recognition of obligations to the group and by the social group towards the individual. If this under-standing is lacking there can be no society, no progress, no civilization.

The regime, like the church of the Inquisition, was the repository of this received truth. Salvation depended upon mandatory acceptance. Miscreants were sick and the torturers believed themselves physicians who had to steel themselves to the agonies of their patients for the sake of their ailing souls.

Journalists were not to be captious members of some autonomous fourth estate but priests in the Church of State; preaching the Revolutionary gospel, administering its sacra-ments, hearing confession, castigating wrongdoers and carrying on militant missionary work on behalf of the faith. 'The press is not a purpose in itself nor its freedom an aim in itself. Freedom of the press is [merely] one means of the functioning of democracy.' In one of his grosser corporeal similies, resonat-ing with the image of the priest spooning out a gruel of host and wine to eager, kneeling supplicants, Papadopoulos said the journalist must make a pablum of revolutionary ideas so that they would be more easily assimilable by the public:

As the individual's digestive system functions as a consequence of mastication which prepares the digestible material for the stomach, so you as journalists, as social functionaries, must understand your duty to prepare the intellectually digestible material for suitable absorption . . . by the individual members of society so that they may be able to constitute a developed society with an understanding of both individuals and groups.

It was not enough to sit idly by and hope to wait out the revolutionary interlude. He exhorted journalists to show missionary zeal and, although the metaphor changed from an ecclesiastical to a military one, he still called on journalists to fight for the faith.

You must abandon this position of biding your time as if you did not know what situation you were facing. . . . There are positions in the front line for the progress of our nation for everyone. . . . I am sure that I may regard myself as a colonel in active service with the Journalists' Regiment in the attack for the taking of our immediate objective which is called development and progress.

Press criticism was to be limited to pointing up the errors of their ways to those faithful who might imperfectly understand regime teachings or to denouncing reprobates who deliberately disobeyed them.

I might say that such and such should be done but those who take the instructions in order to carry them out might misunderstand. They translate the order and he who gave it is not able to ascertain if it was faithfully carried out. Thus mistakes are made, unknown to the Revolution and things done which the Revolution does not wish. So I say that everyone must resume their responsibilities and develop the courage necessary to denounce the sinners, those who err and those who transgress the law and it is for this reason that the press is given the right of criticism in good faith.

Criticism of the regime *per se* was heresy. 'If you write against the Greek government,' said Papadopoulos' colleague

Brigadier Stylianos Pattakos, 'then you are an enemy.'

In case Papadopoulos' language should create any ambiguity about the subservient role foreseen for the press as an extension of the administration, it is worth examining briefly how the newspapers were used in the charade of public participation in the drafting of the 1968 constitution. Revision of the constitution had been one of the principal points of contention between King Constantine and the junta. The colonels wanted to curb the powers of the monarch and to vest his functions as arbiter of the constitution in a special court. They sought to halve the size of parliament, to separate the legislature from the executive by insisting that no one who had ever been a deputy could become a cabinet minister and generally, to introduce limitations on civil and individual liberties. These proposals were formulated as early as summer 1967[3] and probably before the junta seized power. Constantine, however, was prepared to accept only limited changes, particularly as regards the royal prerogatives. A revision commission approved by him produced a draft constitution which, while it introduced some of the changes the colonels wanted, stopped far short of their full demands.

After the king's departure from the scene, the colonels set about devising a method of making their design acceptable and hit upon the idea of making the modifications appear to be a manifestation of popular will. Beginning in March 1968, newspapers were required to print daily cutout sections containing extracts from the revision committee's draft. Space was provided for comment by the public. The cutouts were then sent, post free, to a special committee at the Ministry to the Prime Minister where, it was implied, they were collated and the recommendations taken into consideration in the preparation of the final draft.

Some newspapers were allowed to carry editorial critiques provided they confined themselves to the proposed modifications and did not question the validity of the amending process or the right of the regime to undertake it. With one exception, no comments by former politicians were permitted as they had adopted the attitude that unless they were free to make political comments, they would say nothing at all. They argued that, by participating in the debate on the colonels' terms, they would be indirectly recognizing the regime. The committee collecting the constitutional cutouts claimed to have received more than five million submissions, but the amendments eventually produced by the colonels were for all intents those decided upon over a year earlier. The entire exercise had been nothing more than a diversion to distract attention from the dictatorial manner of their imposition. A referendum was set for September 29, 1968 but, in further revisions, announced at the eleventh hour, the colonels included a provision which allowed them to implement vital clauses concerning individual and political liberties at their discretion. Acceptance of this, they said, would constitute a popular mandate. Rejection, however, would not lead to their resignation: they would simply draft another constitution. The ballot, which was interfered with, produced a 92% 'yes' vote although there was a $22\frac{1}{2}$% abstention rate; telling in a country where it is illegal not to vote.

This 'mandate' crowned an ineluctable shift in emphasis in presentation of the regime. No longer was it a 'parenthesis' holding out the prospect of an early return to the former style of parliamentary democracy; increasingly it was the National Revolution to create the New Democracy of New Men and New Ideas. Aware that this did not catch popular imagination, the colonels embarked upon a programme of political re-education. Papadopoulos indefatigably stumped round the country preaching 'a new democratic order' in which Greeks would 'socialize' their interests for the good of the nation. He urged journalists to create 'social attitudes for improving the operation of the state citizen system'[4] and berated publishers who were unprepared to co-operate in the effort. If they continued to be unhelpful, he threatened to 'shut down their newspapers because one cannot allow this conglomerate called press to become richer and not be helping Greek realities.'[5]

As part of the re-education process, Papadopoulos' speeches were collected in seven volumes as *To Pistevo Mas* (Our Credo) and distributed free to teachers and opinion-makers. A civics text, *Politiki Agogi* (Political Education), was commissioned from former press minister Theofyllaktos Papaconstantinou and disseminated in tens of thousands of copies to students, public servants and opinion makers. Finally, *I Ideologia tis Epanastaseos* (The Ideology of the Revolution) was set down in pamphlet form by the man then responsible for the press, Undersecretary at the Ministry to the Prime Minister, George Georgalas, and distributed free to all those who would take time to decipher it. Georgalas' thesis was that the regime was not a dictatorship but a true Revolution which expressed the deep-seated, unspoken aspirations of the Greek people. The Revolution embraced all facets of public life – social, economic and political – and it required that citizens submerge their individualism in a new polity. This was the fundamental Aim of the Revolution and it was only when it had been achieved that political life could be restored. But it would not be a return to the *ancien regime*; the new democracy would involve new men and new parties. It would be 'the legitimate child of the Revolution.'

Georgalas was a professional propagandist. As a youthful communist, he had been trained by Agitprop to work among Greek refugees in Eastern Europe but after the downfall of Stalin he defected and became 'a special adviser to the Greek Army High Command on National and Political Education.'[6] He likened his conversion to that of St. Paul on the road to Damascus. Georgalas viewed journalists as an integral part of the machinery of state, 'an ethical element, an instrument for instilling ethics into society.'[7] He detailed this attitude in a keynote address some months after taking office. 'Before, it was the press that created public opinion and public opinion created governments. Today the Revolution, as a huge regenerating surge of Hellenism, is moulding a new *public opinion*. . . . The press in turn *informs* the people and *controls* authority.'[8] The conception was a secular gloss on Papadopoulos' sacred function and reeked of the authoritarian ideal in which the ruling power is the sole repository of received wisdom, informing the public via the press about what it should and should not believe. Georgalas contended that the average individual could not pick his way intelligently through the plethora of news available in the modern, information-saturated world and, thus, it was the responsibility of the press to filter the requisite facts which would allow him or her to become a responsible citizen. He argued that an 'informative' press must be an 'interpretive' press. 'Whether the journalist uses a pen, a camera, a microphone or *a conductor's baton*, he is always and everywhere a social worker with a public mission and a sense of public responsibility.'[9]

Georgalas urged development of a National Propaganda Service 'directly dependent on the Prime Minister to plan national enlightenment as a totality....'[10] It would have involved recruitment of two hundred young people, 'cultured, talented, gifted, enterprising and idealistic,' who would have been given systematic training at a specially established public relations school. They were to form the spine of a team of professionals styled as press or public relations officers and operating from local government offices, ministries and embassies.' They should, he said, be specially committed people who could rise above the bureaucratic mentality of ordinary civil servants to become specialists in a new 'political' war:

> In this war we do not use bullets or bombs as much as ideas and emotions. This is a war for the human being and especially for the young. Whoever loses the human soul and the young, loses the war, and this loss of his will be a million times more definite and final than any military loss. ... We have reached a strange situation where the Ministers of Education and Information are even more responsible for the defense of a country than the Minister of Defense. In this war, we have all the possibilities of winning ... provided that all of us will enlist *to influence by any means* public opinion, all of us that have contact with the soul of the Greeks and especially the young. If we do this, we win, because we, the soldiers of the Greek idea, from the tradition of the humanitarian civilization, we have this flame in us. Our enemy has got but its frozen ashes.[12]

In addition to such overt action, Georgalas recommended the creation of a variety of covert organizations 'as private purveyors of information free from the bonds that shackle all official information [such as] diplomatic relations, public accountability [and] bureaucracy.' He did not elaborate upon this scheme but presumably meant the establishment of apparently innocuous social and cultural organizations which could be used for insidious indoctrination or manipulation.

Georgalas suggested government funding of commercial publishing houses to produce pro-regime books. He also recommended the establishment of a revolutionary newspaper, an afternoon daily 'modern and popular in character,' and a monthly theoretical outlet. A pro-regime morning paper, *Nea Politeia* (New State), had been founded on September 17, 1968, just twelve days before the constitutional referendum. It provided a regular forum for Georgalas and a handful of other 'socialists' who had embraced the regime, but its tacky style and relentless diet of the new dogma meant that it had low circulation and limited influence. There was already a pro-government periodical called *Theseis kai Ideai* (Tenets and Ideas) but, according to Georgalas, it was 'slow to appear and is of academic, pedantic character.' His criteria for the new publication were that it should have 'urgency, radical audacity and revolutionary vision.'

Georgalas opposed censorship as such. It 'muzzles but does not cure and its protracted use is destructive.' Instead, he argued the need for rendering the press 'healthy . . . cleaning it up.' The regime's draft press legislation, if not his handiwork, certainly reflected his ideals. It would have purged the press of all who opposed the regime, leaving only its adherents to spread the word. If Papadopoulos saw himself as the Saviour of Greece, then Georgalas was his chief disciple and all the more dangerous for being a professional in his field.

NOTES

[1] Panayotis Pipinellis, address to a meeting of Greek ambassadors to western Europe in Bad Schninznach, Switzerland, August 26, 1969, cited in Max van der Stoel, *Report on the Situation in Greece,* Doc. 2719, Strasbourg, Council of Europe, January 23, 1970, p. 12.

[2] This and all subsequent quotes from Papadopoulos in this chapter are taken, unless otherwise indicated, from two complementary addresses made

to journalists on June 26 and July 2, 1967. The full texts may be found in the collected speeches, *To Pistevo Mas* (Our Credo), Vol. Alpha, Athens, Directorate General of Press [and Information], April 1968, pp. 54–64.

[3] Brigadier Pattakos outlined them to me in a private interview July 20, 1967.

[4] Press conference on January 4, 1969, the full text is in *To Pistevo Mas*, Vol. Gamma, pp. 168–173.

[5] *Ibid.*

[6] Official biography.

[7] Speech to representatives of press organizations, December 17, 1970.

[8] *Ibid*, his italics.

[9] *Ibid*, my italics.

[10] This and all subsequent quotes from Georgalas in this chapter, unless otherwise indicated, come from a volume which appeared after the dictatorship called *To Elliniko Provilima kai i Lysis tou* (The Greek Problem and its Solution), Athens 1975.

[11] Steps were taken to this end in legislation to establish a school of journalism, Compulsory Law 248/67, Article 16, and in a law to re-organize the Directorate General of Press and Information, Legislative Decree 744/70, but the Propaganda Service as such was never formally established.

[12] Lecture to a seminar at Air Force headquarters, Athens, as reported in *Nea Politeia*, July 11, 1970, my italics.

III THE COLONELS' FIRST YEAR

The colonels expected the full support of King Constantine in carrying out their coup and were taken aback when he refused to sign the takeover decree implementing martial law or to publicly endorse a military government. Constantine held out instead for a largely civilian cabinet of non-political men under Chief Prosecutor of the Supreme Court, Constantine Kollias. Only five military men took office: Lieutenant General Gregory Spantidakis as Deputy Prime Minister and Minister of Defense, and Lieutenant General George Zoitakis as Undersecretary of Defense, together with three members of the junta, Brigadier General Stylianos Pattakos as Minister of the Interior, Colonel Nicholas Makarezos as Minister of Economic Co-ordination and Colonel George Papadopoulos as Minister to the Prime Minister. This last is an umbrella ministry designed to secure for the head of government powers of patronage, propaganda and security. It was then responsible for, among other things, the Civil Service, the Greek Central Intelligence Service (K.Y.P.), the Directorate General for Press and Information and the National Broadcasting Institute. Because of the influence that can be wielded through the ministry it is usually filled by someone in whom the Prime Minister has the utmost confidence. (George Papandreou named his son Andreas for the post and in the delicate days immediately after the restoration of representative government, Karamanlis assigned it to his brother Achilles.) Papadopoulos used the position to monitor and manipulate the activities of Prime Minister Kollias until he was himself elevated as Prime Minister following King Constantine's unsuccessful counter coup. Papadopoulos prudently retained the Ministry for five of the six years he was in office, naming two of his brothers[1] to key posts there to watch out for his interests. This meant that for the majority of the dictatorship he was the ultimate authority for all matters relating to the press and media. He delegated the day by day responsibility to a succession of individuals each of whom, for his brief span, became influential as the chief government spokesman, though none of them ever spoke as the true voice of the revolutionaries. The first of these was Nicholas Farmakis, an ultra-conservative former M.P. with business connections in Washington, whose name has been linked with C.I.A. activities although the allegations have never been proven. According to Farmakis, there was dissension within the junta from the outset about who should be responsible for the press. Papadopoulos considered it his preserve but Pattakos apparently believed that both censorship and the provision of official information fell within the purview of the Ministry of the Interior. The two men rowed over the issue, leaving Farmakis caught in the middle. For example, on April 22 at noon, Farmakis convened political correspondents to explain to them how censorship would operate. That evening, Pattakos called in publishers to give them the same briefing. Farmakis says the first censorship committee was an informal body organized in haphazard fashion. 'It was made up in my ante room by the people that were there. A couple of them were ministry personnel. The others were two or three young people. Someone took initiatives and they all went off into the next room and started censoring.' He claims that it was Pattakos' office which produced the official takeover communiques imposed upon the newspapers.

When they resumed publication on the morning of Sunday, April 23, the papers were pathetic specimens. Only four pages long, they all carried identical texts including the government policy statement, the Prime Minister's message to the country and lists of the new cabinet. A similar uniformity seized the Monday afternoon editions, all of which ran the officially dictated version of what had prompted the coup. It was that large numbers of communists had been gathering in the northern capital of Salonika in order to cause disturbances in conjunction with the opening of Papandreou's electoral campaign. It was false but a necessary lie in order to satisfy the constitutional requirement that there had been a 'manifest threat to public order' before application of the Law on the State of Siege. Thus it was mandatorily published.

This procedure of requiring newspapers to publish official communiques regardless of their accuracy or authenticity was one of the more noxious features of the new regime. By it, the colonels exceeded even their extraordinary martial law powers which permitted them to ban publication of information deemed to present a threat to security but did not authorize them to force-feed the press. It was this factor which finally confirmed Mrs. Vlachou in her decision not to publish. It was one thing, she said, to be told how not to worry the government but quite another to be obliged 'to give under your own by-line, false information, libellous things, barrack-style propaganda.'

Farmakis' second function at the Ministry was to control the foreign press. For the first 24 hours, all telephone, telex and air links were interrupted although Farmakis admits that he helped certain correspondents get their copy out. Once Hellenikon airport opened, a horde of international correspondents descended, few speaking the language but all anxious for quotes to make up their copy. For four days, Farmakis obliged with a nightly press briefing in English. Greek journalists could publish nothing save the government handouts but foreign correspondents were free to file whatever they wanted. Everything was monitored as it left the country. Some stories deemed too hostile were simply plucked off the wire never to reach their destination and 'phone calls were erratically interrupted by monitors with an obviously imperfect command of the language on which they were eavesdropping but the majority of reports got through. The policy, says Farmakis, was undertaken on Papadopoulos' personal responsibility in the teeth of fierce opposition from other junta members. Papadopoulos wanted to 'improve our assessment of our reception abroad.'[2] Obviously the regime didn't like what it heard for, on April 26, what limited amount of information had been forthcoming was abruptly interrupted. Farmakis was in full flow at his regular briefing when a green-bereted major of the Special Forces strode into the room and whispered something in his ear which caused him to excuse himself and leave. There was much speculation about the incident at the time since Farmakis effectively dropped from public view thereafter. He now claims that it was a *coup de théâtre*. Papadopoulos had decided he no longer wanted foreign correspondents 'hanging around' and figured that if information dried up, they'd move on some place else. The following day, April 27, Papadopoulos made his first appearance at a press conference which was also to be his last for two months. It was a chaotic meeting in which his clumsy efforts to explain the aims of the Revolution ended in confusion as a result of bad translation and his penchant for obscure metaphor. The session did serve, however, to round off the first week of coverage and allow foreign editors to shift gear and concentrate on the next story breaking in the area which was the build up of tensions in the Middle East prior to the Six Day War. The visiting correspondents left. For the resident foreign press community there was no further contact with the government for two weeks until May 8 when Brigadier Pattakos began a series of nightly briefings of Greek journalists which foreign correspondents were permitted to attend. These continued for some months.

Whether Farmakis' version of events is to be believed or whether he was squeezed out as a consequence of a dispute between Papadopoulos and Pattakos remains an open question. In any case, he was replaced by Colonel Constantine Karydas who, while not an actual member of the junta, was a close associate. Records show that Karydas officially assumed the title of Director General of Press and Information on May 29, although Farmakis recollects that he handed over to him informally on April 27 with 'a chat to bring him up to date'. On April 29, the informal censorship committee was transformed

into an official Press Control Service headed by an officer of
the Military Justice Department, Colonel Elias Papapoulos with
a brief to 'take instructions from and be responsible to us
[Papadopoulos] for every oversight or omission in the preventive control of every sort of published printed matter.'³ The Ministerial Decision set out General Instructions (see Appendix A)
which gave the Service absolute control over all aspects of
newspapers including copy, headlines, pictures, make-up and
even the alleged opinions contained in editorial comment. The
Service handouts comprised incessant, tedious accounts of
formal official functions coupled with interminable texts of
banal ministerial speeches. There was no news sense. The day
the Arab-Israeli war broke out, the censors consigned the story
to half a column on the back page, while the lead for the day
was the 'triumphal' tour of Crete by Deputy Premier Spantidakis. Occasionally, the Service made absurd mistakes like
insisting on typefaces for headlines too large for the space
designated. The leeway of newspapers for personal expression
was so circumscribed that they resorted to little tricks like
putting front page stories below the fold where they wouldn't
show while on display at kiosks. The censors retaliated by
dictating layout as well.⁴   The most sinister feature was the
way in which the regime dictated lies about former politicians in
order to discredit them. For example, all papers were ordered
to publish documents said to prove the links between Andreas
Papandreou and A.S.P.I.D.A. which also implicated the elder
Papandreou. They were later proved to be forgeries but there
was no possibility of reply or redress for the injured parties.
Moreover, newspapers were forced to appear to endorse the
lies they propagated through dictated editorials. The tone is
typified by this page one commentary imposed on *Vima* which,
prior to the coup, was a pro-Papandreou paper.

> For two years this country has been shaken by the affair of
> the communist organization A.S.P.I.D.A. and for two years
> Mr. Papandreou and those shouting with him have waged
> with tenacity the dirty battle of corrupting facts and strang-
> ling truth and slandering every institution, their only objective
> being to save from the people's verdict the persons who bear

the greatest guilt for this inner undermining of Greece, namely himself and his son. Already, with a large crashing sound, with an earthquake, with country-wide denunciation, the unstable construction of the 'defense' of Papandreou has collapsed.[5]

In a text smuggled from jail, Lambrakis complained about the dictation of these 'imbecile commentaries' which he said 'violated' the Greek press.[6]

Such blatant propaganda eventually proved counterproductive for the public stopped buying newspapers. Circulation dropped nearly 40% between April and July, from a daily average sale of 834,111 to 509,554. The closure of so many newspapers was partly responsible; their sales comprised a potential two-thirds of the lost copies. Equally, readers who lost their regular paper didn't bother to change to another. Not only was the news the same from one to the next, it was identical to that which could be heard on the radio.

To try to get round the problem, the colonels sought to have newspapers publish on their own responsibility. In late May, soundings were taken among the pro-regime papers, *Eleftheros Kosmos, Estia* and *Vradyni*, but their reaction was that, as long as martial law remained in force, they preferred prior censorship because of the legal protection it afforded. So, a tactic was adopted whereby on some stories, the Press Control Service, instead of issuing complete texts, issued detailed notes, requiring the newspapers to rewrite them. This got round the problem of uniformity of style while retaining control over substance. It gave newspapers a fractional margin for opposition. The situation is best illustrated by example. On June 21, 1967, Richard Nixon, passing through Athens on a fact-finding tour, held a brief airport press conference. The Press Control Service issued the following guidelines.

A NOTE FOR THE STATEMENTS OF NIXON

It is mandatory that the leading paragraphs of the Nixon story and headlines for the article shall include:

1. Nixon: there existed serious reasons for a certain change.
2. The need of a new Greek constitution was great.
3. The old situation led to government instability.

4. His [Nixon's] talks with the king and the government were extremely fruitful.

5. I know that the American press, among other things has dealt widely with the virtues of the revolution and whether it was correct or not for the present government to stay in power.

ATTENTION: Not to be included in the headlines are Nixon's comments about a rapid return to parliamentary democracy, etc. The remarks can, however, be mentioned in the text.

Vima's version of this story ran as follows.

THE FORMER U.S. VICE PRESIDENT ON THE 21st APRIL REVOLUTION
NIXON: THERE WERE GOOD REASONS FOR SOME ACTION
HE HOPES THAT THE PARLIAMENTARY FORM OF REGIME WILL BE RESTORED
HIS TALKS WITH THE GOVERNMENT AND THE KING VERY FRUITFUL.

The old political situation would lead to government instability and the need was felt for a new constitution, former United States Vice President Richard Nixon said yesterday.

'I know,' he added, 'that the American press has dealt at length with the virtues of the revolution and with the correctness of the present government remaining in office. There were strong reasons for some action,' he concluded. . . .

'During my short visit here I had the opportunity of talking with the Prime Minister, the Ministers of Foreign Affairs and Interior and other Greek leaders in public and private life. I had the honor of being received by the king. . . .
I found the talks highly fruitful. Naturally in all of my discussions the issue came up of the present government, when the new constitution will come into effect and when elections will be held. It is my general impression that all the people I talked with strongly indicated that they are in favor of the principle of representative democracy and that they wish to restore it as soon as possible. On this issue, the king was

specially forthright and decisive. . . .'

The obvious headline for this story was something like KING SEEKS DEMOCRACY 'AS SOON AS POSSIBLE' – NIXON but the best *Vima* could get away with – and then only by bending the censor's guidelines – was the inclusion in the subordinate headline of the reference to restoration of a parliamentary government. Since the colonels were still saying their regime was a 'parenthesis' and that there would be an eventual return to democracy, this was only just politically acceptable. *Vima* was unable to add the all important rider 'as soon as possible' and this reference was dutifully buried deep in the story. Other papers didn't even attempt this tentative critique instead stressing the serious reasons for change and the need for constitutional reform.

Needless to say, newsmen found such practices frustrating although they were nothing to the difficulty they had trying to work with Director General Karydas. An officer of undoubted courage but little intelligence, he was rigid and unbending and expected absolute obedience. Crossed by one editor, he threatened to 'fry his brains' and, flouted by another, he threatened to shoot him on the spot. Relations between press and government plumbed abysmal depths. To try to alleviate matters, the junta appointed as Under-secretary at the Ministry to the Prime Minister a senior journalist, Theofyllaktos Papaconstantinou. A former trotskyite who had grown conservative with age, Papaconstantinou had, since 1963, been a leader writer on *Mesimvrini*. He was well-regarded in the profession and, in a statement on taking office, he promised that 'shortly, the temporarily suspended freedom of the press will be restored' and 'a special effort will be made for the uplifting of the journalistic profession.'[7] The appointment fleetingly generated much optimism but this quickly soured as Papconstantinou failed to introduce any material change in censorship controls.

Just what he thought he might achieve and even his motives in taking on the job have since been called into question. Papaconstantinou told the International Press Institute that the government planned before the end of 1967 to restore the suspended Article 14 of the Constitution which guaranteed press freedoms. He said a royal decree would stipulate that press offenses were to be heard by civilian courts although military tribunals would continue to try other crimes. Papaconstantinou said that this measure would not be tied to the process of drafting new press legislation. That was a separate matter in the hands of a committee. Papaconstantinou claimed a draft already existed but said that it remained confidential. Elaboration of the final law would be a 'question of long and exacting labor.'[8] Such a policy would have constituted a major change, freeing the press from prior censorship and the fear of the harsh sentences meted out by military justice. It left open the possibility of a restrictive press law to be introduced at some later date but that, by Papaconstantinou's phrasing, seemed to be well in the future.

A second account suggests, however, that the colonels intended that Papaconstantinou should introduce only limited reforms designed to give the semblance but not the substance of press freedom and that these eventually were applied in January 1968 after Papaconstantinou had left the ministry. The whole episode, according to this version, was bound up with the government's efforts to get Mrs. Vlachou to republish. On the day he was appointed, Papaconstantinou called on his former boss claiming, according to her account of the meeting, to have accepted the post on two conditions, namely that 'censorship would be lifted and that a new, acceptable press law would be drafted by him.'[9] This he said was 'very nearly ready.'[10] This is not fundamentally different from the policy outlined to the I.P.I. except in the implication that the press law would be introduced sooner rather than later. There was, however, an important rider in the Vlachou version. As the *quid pro quo,* she was to recommence publishing before censorship was lifted. The regime, he explained, could not, for reasons of face, be seen to have bowed to her opposition. She quotes Papaconstantinou as saying, 'The whole future of the Greek press now lies in your hands.'[11]

Mrs. Vlachou refused. She says she told Papaconstantinou that while she might trust his intentions, she did not trust the colonels' and, while he might resign from the government if promises were not kept, she would be prevented by the martial law from closing her papers again, once they had reappeared. 'First you announce that the press is free, then we shall see [about publication].'[12] The colonels put it about that Mrs. Vlachou was responsible for the continuation in force of censorship. Speaking to the rapporteur of the Council of Europe in December 1967, Papadopoulos commented that 'press conditions would have improved three months ago but for the action of Mrs. Vlachou.'[13]

Another course of developments seems more likely. Once Mrs. Vlachou's papers had begun to reappear, a committee would have been established to revise press regulations. There would have been a purposeful public blurring of its brief as to whether it was to deal with censorship or the press law. Within a couple of months, a package of nominal censorship relaxation measures would have been produced in the committee's name and this would have been hailed by the colonels as the restoration of freedom of the press, Mrs. Vlachou's resumption of publication being cited as proof thereof.

When she failed to cooperate, it seems the program was introduced anyway but over a longer period. On August 26, a seven-man committee of academics and jurists, which had been sitting prior to the coup to consider revision of the Press Law, was reconstituted. The former head of the Press Control Service, Colonel Papapoulos, was added to its ranks. The committee was described as having been convened to draft a press law but its nebulous brief was to consider measures for 'the improvement of the press.' It was given sixty days to report. This time-scale is consistent with Papadopoulos' assertion to the Council of Europe that changes would have been introduced in September had Mrs. Vlachou cooperated in July.[14] She, however, proved intractable and eventually was placed under house arrest. A further effort was made to get her to publish in late October when she was brought from detention for a meeting with Public Order Minister Totomis who urged her to reconsider her intransigence. She reiterated that if the regime were to produce a press law and abandon the obligation to publish 'all the propaganda rubbish and lies issued by the Ministry,'[15] she would consider reappearing. She says

Totomis indicated that her position and that of the government were not irreconcilable but she was returned to house arrest and there was no follow-up to the meeting.

The committee never actually met although a public announcement was made in November, at the height of the struggle with the King over the constitution, that its reporting mandate had been extended by four months. Coincidentally, Papaconstantinou was transferred to become Minister of Education. Whether he was party to the regime's apparent attempt at deception, or whether he quit his ministry when he realized that all was not as it seemed to be, remains unclear. He had, however, prevaricated in outlining his programme to the I.P.I. The draft which he claimed the committee had prepared was one which had been being worked on at the time of the coup – none had been drafted since the advent of the colonels – and, in the end, Papaconstantinou did not actually leave the government but merely moved to another ministry. Evangelos Vlachos, a professional civil servant, took over briefly as acting Under-secretary.

Ultimately, the development of press affairs was overtaken by events. During the last three months of 1967, relations between the junta and the king deteriorated rapidly as the monarch, first, resisted efforts by the colonels to retire many senior army officers loyal to the crown and, second, insisted on his own shape and timetable for the new constitution. The situation was complicated by the near war with Turkey over Cyprus. One of the colonels' main aims in seizing power had been to achieve *enosis* or union of Cyprus with the mainland. It was a nationalist ideal which, had they been successful, might just have won them sufficient popular support to secure their regime in power. When they botched diplomatic endeavours to achieve their ends, a clumsy attempt was made at force. This involved Greek troops which had been illegally infiltrated onto the island. Turkey mobilized and imminent war was only averted by top-level international mediation and a humiliating withdrawal by Greece.

This occasioned the first major press revolt. From his exile in Paris, former conservative Prime Minister Constantine Karamanlis issued a statement challenging the colonels to 'put an end to their experiment ... [to] open the way for the re-establishment of legality.' The Press Control Service forbade publication and issued a rebuttal decrying Karamanlis' 'provocation of anarchy' and 'lack of all sense of national responsibility.' *Vradyni* and *Apoyevmatini* refused to publish the reply without Karamanlis' original. Their editions of December 5, 1967 failed to appear, according to the Press Control Service because they had 'not complied with existing instructions regarding the circulation of papers.' The publishers held out for thirty-six hours and finally the government caved in. It was a significant blow to the colonels' authority at a time when they were already backsliding and it was one of the factors which contributed to King Constantine's decision to go ahead with his widely anticipated counter coup.

It was a disastrous failure and he fled into exile in Rome, together with his family and Prime Minister Kollias. They were later joined there by Deputy Prime Minister and Defense Minister Spantidakis who'd been abroad at the time of the attempt. The press remained firmly in the hands of the colonels, lavishing praise upon the regime for 'the salvation of the nation from the adventurers who had misled the monarch.' A telegram to Papadopoulos, demanded from the journalists' union and distributed by the Press Control Service for mandatory publication in all papers, was typical of what passed for news copy at the time.

We congratulate you, for – by a successful and decisive action of the government, the armed forces, and the people [together] – you succeeded in saving the country from brotherly bloodshed and the disaster accruing from it. ... Believing in the necessity of the nation's unity and the avoidance by every means of a new division, we wish for a happy end to the efforts of the government and the foundation of peace and the security of progress of Greece and the people.

In the monarch's absence, Lieutenant General Zoitakis was sworn in as Regent, while Papadopoulos was elevated to the posts of Prime Minister and Minister of Defense.

NOTES

[1] Haralambos Papadopoulos, a former civil servant in the Ministry of Agriculture, was named director of the Prime Minister's Political Bureau on December 7, 1967, only six days before Constantine's counter coup. Constantine Papadopoulos, colonel of army aviation and a member of the inner junta, was named Secretary General of the entire ministry on January 23, 1968. In the beginning he was largely occupied with the committee drafting legislation but he was able to keep an eye on the press. Later he appears to have been closely involved in the drafting of the regime's press laws.

[2] Foreign language newspapers continued to be sold in Athens although for some weeks after the coup the Greek news was carefully scissored out. This soon ended and all western publications, including some which were consistently hostile such as *The Guardian* and *Der Spiegel*, were allowed to be sold. This was a clever maneuver. Repeatedly foreigners would say, 'Well, if they'll allow this kind of thing, I can't see that censorship can be all that bad.' This was particularly true of travellers coming to Greece via Communist countries where no western papers were on sale. What they failed to observe was that there were no critical Greek language publications available. Cypriot newspapers, for example, were forbidden. The only sources of uncensored news available to the average Greek citizen who spoke only his native tongue were the Greek broadcasts of foreign radio stations such as the British Broadcasting Corporation, Deutsche Welle and Radio Moscow.

[3] Ministerial Decision 19603/Gamma, April 29, 1967.

[4] An excellent analysis of this is found in Armand Gaspard, 'A free press vanishes,' *I.P.I. Report*, vol. 16, no. 8, December 1967, pp. 4–10.

[5] *Vima*, May 7, 1967.

[6] Christos Lambrakis, 'The Big Lie Crumbles,' *Observer Foreign News Service*, No. 24367, October 13, 1967.

[7] *Athens News Agency*, July 24, 1967.

[8] Armand Gaspard, 'Mission to Athens, October 16–24, 1967.' Confidential memorandum to Per Monsen, secretary general of I.P.I., November 1, 1967.

[9] Helen Vlachou, *House Arrest*, p. 43.

[10] *Ibid*, p. 44.

[11] *Ibid*, p. 45.

[12] Helen Vlachou, Interview in *La Stampa*, September 24, 1967, p. 3.

[13] W. A. Siegmann, *Report on the Situation in Greece*, Strasbourg, Council of Europe, Doc. 2322, January 22, 1968, p. 64.

[14] Perhaps some light could be shed on this situation by circular order of the Ministry to the Prime Minister E.P. 1787/Zita of July 11, 1967 which apparently referred to the relaxation of censorship. But neither the press ministry nor the archives of the military justice department could produce a copy, nor could the individual with probably the most complete personal library of press materials in the country.

[15] Helen Vlachou, *House Arrest*, p. 74.

IV THE COUNCIL OF EUROPE AND PRESS LEGISLATION

Constantine's departure stripped the colonels of their facade of constitutional legality and, despite the international practice of governments affording recognition to an administration holding effective control of a country, regardless of the nature of the regime, there was an hiatus of several weeks before it was forthcoming for the colonels. In an effort at ingratiation and in order to mollify domestic public opinion, the junta undertook a number of measures designed to democratize its image. Just before Christmas 1967 the triumvirate, Papadopoulos, Pattakos and Makarezos, resigned their army commissions. The disputed draft constitution was published and an amnesty was granted to non-communist political prisoners, including Christos Lambrakis and several other prominent journalists who had been arrested during the counter coup. In the early weeks of 1968, the majority of the remaining members of the junta also resigned from the forces and entered the administration at the level of Secretary General, the Greek equivalent of permanent under-secretary. Papadopoulos' brother Constantine went to the Ministry to the Prime Minister and the much loathed Karydas was replaced as

Director General by a career civil servant, Ioannis Apostolides.

The new Under-secretary, Michael Sideratos, dusted off the proposals for reform of press legislation which had been under consideration at the time of the coup and sent them to publishers and journalists asking them for their views. He then established two committees to draft laws on the functioning of the press and the organization of the profession of journalism.[1] They were given thirty days to report with a public commitment that once the legislation was approved, press controls would be lifted. In the interim, measures were taken to relax censorship. A ministerial decision, issued in Sideratos' name,[2] detailed the new regime at great length (see Appendix B). Basically it meant that newspapers were to be free to exercise a degree of news judgment in the selection and presentation of their copy. Prior censorship was to remain and the Press Control Service retained an 'absolute right' to dictate news, although the amount of mandatory material was supposed to be much reduced. Newspapers could present government policy state-ments 'according to the editors' judgment and under the newspaper's responsibilities.' This meant that, within circum-scribed limits, ministerial speeches and government handouts could be summarized and placed in the paper where editors thought appropriate. Free use of news agency wire copy from abroad was again permitted, although the Press Control Service maintained 'complete control' over copy concerning foreign policy. Letters to the editor could be published on the joint responsibility of the newspaper and author. Editorial criticism was to be allowed provided it was 'responsible, bona fide and constructive.' Newspapers would be held accountable for both their facts and their sources when making such comments. Politics remained completely taboo. On no account was there to be any reference to 'the former political parties or their leaders either in a critical or a complimentary manner or even in connection with their participation in society life (sic).'

The argument that these were the measures that the regime had intended to introduce the previous summer is reinforced by internal evidence from the text of the Ministerial Decision. The definition of bona fide criticism was a direct quote from Papadopoulos' press policy speech of the previous June about the need to 'denounce errors not known to the Revolutionary authorities.' The preamble contained a further quotation from that same address which said newspapers should commence their criticism 'at this very moment.' The quotation stressed the need 'to break the monotonous aspect' of newspapers, another concern of the previous summer. What effect such relaxation would have had, had it been introduced six months earlier, must remain a matter for conjecture, but it is fair to say that while the measures left no scope for substantive criticism on political grounds, they nonetheless allowed newspapers the possibility of conducting a form of guerrilla warfare which the colonels found unsettling. Perhaps opposition forces could have capitalized on this more successfully when the regime was not so entrenched.

The leeway was limited when viewed with hindsight but it seemed significant at the time if only for the reason that it allowed journalists to employ their wits in a tactical manner which made them feel as though they were doing something to oppose the regime. This boosted morale. The devices were often little more than pranks such as printing mandatory communiques next to death notices or in the same type as the advertisements, although some, such as playing up foreign news stories with a democratic bias, had real impact. For instance, Robert Kennedy made an offhand remark during his presidential campaign that, if elected, his administration would press for the restoration of democracy in Greece. Reporting of the remark itself was forbidden but thereafter Kennedy's campaign was banner headline news every day until, finally, the censors issued directives ordering Kennedy coverage onto inside pages so that regime leaders could get a look in on page one again.

Retaliation, if a paper stepped too far out of line, was heavy handed. After *Apoyevmatini* published an editorial which claimed the draft constitution would produce an 'armored democracy,' the publishers and the chief editor were arrested and questioned, ostensibly for publishing an edition with more than the legally permitted number of pages. When they wrote an editorial which cunningly mocked the definition of *bona-fide* criticism by producing a fatuous argument to demonstrate that new boxes from the state match monopoly, bearing a revolutionary symbol, were illegal, they were again arrested. This time they were detained for 24 hours and warned that they could be prosecuted under martial law. After some weeks of the experiment, Papadopoulos complained irritably to journalists, using his notorious image of Greece as a patient for whom he was the doctor.

> You have so far not been a help to me. Since you are the nervous system and since it is possible that you would disturb my patient emotionally in the course of the operation and since I am unshakeably determined to make the patient well with this operation, although I displease you, I shall not yet do you the favor of letting you free to act as you please.... Possibly if you calm down without my having to resort to the use of barbituates, we can discuss the matter again.[3]

In the wake of the matchbox affair, the civilian censors were temporarily sacked and replaced by military men, although the decision was quickly reversed as the servicemen proved more maladroit than their predecessors in coping with the wiles of the journalists. Papadopoulos himself assumed direct control of the Directorate General, naming two former journalists as his eyes and ears there. The hapless Apostolides was replaced as Director General by Byron Stamatopoulos, a freelance journalist who ultimately became one of Papadopoulos' most slavish adherents, and later, Sideratos' post as Under-secretary was taken by Constantine Vovolinis, a journalist who during the Civil War had edited *Ellenikon Aima* (Greek Blood), the newspaper of the white terrorist organization.

Despite such skirmishing, the regime sought to make political capital out of the press' supposed new right of criticism, vaunting it at home and abroad as a major step towards democracy. They were particularly anxious that the world should believe that the press had been free to discuss the constitution, though as the *Apoyevmatini* case proved, the bounds were strictly circumscribed. They were equally limited as regards the press' allotted role as public watchdog. The point is best illustrated by an incident involving the pro-regime newspaper *Eleftheros Kosmos*.

After leaving the press ministry, Papaconstantinou had gone on to Education. *Eleftheros Kosmos* thought that, because of his communist background, he was unsuited for the post and sought to demonstrate its dissatisfaction in an editorial alleging that under his administration, ministry officials were being high handed in their dealings with the public. The paper prefaced its critique with a scornful denunciation of opposition publishers who had failed to take up their new prerogative of criticism. 'The government has given newspapers the right to exercise criticism of public affairs as a first step towards full restoration of freedom of the press. Those of bad faith have denied in advance any value in this measure. ... They are not right. The government has agreed to be subject to control provided [the criticism] is based on facts and aims at the public interest.'[4] The paper then launched into its attack on Papaconstantinou.

We have been informed that the three Deans of Salonika University tried persistently for two weeks to see the Education Minister on official business. They were given the answer that the Minister was busy. Is that true? We have been informed that, following this, they decided to come to Athens, but once more the Minister was unapproachable. They then asked to see the competent Director of Higher Education, but were told that they could not enter the Ministry because admission was forbidden to all and, if they had a document, they might hand it over to the Ministry messenger. In fact, that is what the Deans did. Is that true? We have been informed that the Salonika Deans asked to see the Premier [who] although being much busier than the Education Minister, working eighteen hours daily, received them on the same day. Is that true? We fully undertake the responsibility for the accuracy of our reports. We directly attack the stand of the Education Minister and we are certain George Papadopoulos, with the intelligence and despatch which characterize him, will reach the necessary conclusions.

The same day, Papaconstantinou answered with a communique which the Press Control Service ordered compulsorily published in all papers.

> The allegation of the newspaper *Eleftheros Kosmos* is not
> correct in saying that to those who have asked to visit the
> Ministry of Education the reply was given 'entry is forbidden
> for everyone.' A board which is at the entrance to the
> building says clearly that the public is accepted every
> Tuesday and Friday from twelve to two p.m. and bishops . . .
> professors of Higher Educational Foundations and lawyers
> every Monday, Wednesday and Thursday from twelve noon
> till one p.m. It is untrue that the Dean and the Deputy Dean
> of the Salonika University were asking insistently for fifteen
> days to meet the Minister of Education on official business.
> No such application has been written in the special book
> kept by the Office of the Minister.

The reply continued with a point by point refutation, concluding '. . . it appears that what has been published in this connection by the newspaper *Eleftheros Kosmos* was not responsible.'

The obsequious editorial, fawning as it did on the Prime
Minister, was typical of the sort of toothless critique the regime
was prepared to tolerate; the self-justifying, mandatorily
imposed response of the Ministry inevitable. The irony which
escaped no one in the know, was that behind the incidents
referred to lay a much more serious issue. The regime had just
purged 54 university professors by means of a Constitutent Act
which had temporarily suspended academic tenure. The
Deans had been seeking access to the Ministry to protest
against this arbitrary interference in university affairs. The only
way in which the press could report these much more substantive matters was merely to reprint the text of the relevant acts as
they appeared in the *Government Gazette*. The right to reprint
such official information was one of the 'freedoms' granted
under the new rules.

The regime had another reason to promote the semblance
of a free press. This was in order to placate the Council of
Europe in a dispute over individual liberties. Immediately
following the coup, the colonels had attempted to derogate
Greece's obligations under the European Convention on
Human Rights, claiming that an emergency existed 'threatening the life of the nation.' The Consultative Assembly

demurred, demanding compliance with the Council's statutes and recommending that, if this was not forthcoming, formal complaints be lodged against Greece before the European Commission on Human Rights with a view to prosecution before the European Court. When the Greeks did not respond, complaints were filed in September 1967 by the governments of Denmark, Norway, Sweden and the Netherlands, charging the colonels with the elimination of civil and political liberties including suppression of freedom of expression through the application of censorship. Under the guidance of Foreign Minister Panayotis Pipinellis, the colonels decided to ride out the process of dealing with the charges. They calculated that the Commission's report would take several years to draft and to prosecute and gambled that the Council would be unlikely to take interim action for expulsion, this being a political decision requiring action by the Council of Ministers who, Pipinellis felt, would be less disposed to adopt radical postures than their parliamentary colleagues of the Consultative Assembly.

The regime adopted relaxation of press controls as its symbol for the restoration of constitutional government, although at every step along the way the liberalization claimed fell short of the reality as, in the end, did the colonels' guided democracy when compared with truly free political life. Examination of the regime's tactics in manipulating the press issue before the Council is illustrative of just how cynical it could be.

In the wake of the counter coup, Council rapporteur W. A. Siegmann had arrived in Athens to prepare a report for the January 1968 Assembly sessions. He was told by Pipinellis that '... there would be a new press law which would come into existence even before a new constitution was in existence.'[5] At this time, the colonels were still committed to introduction of a constitution by August 1968. Pipinellis promised Siegmann that the IPI would be asked to advise on formulation of the legislation.

The Consultative Assembly was to hear Siegmann's report on January 22, the Human Rights Commission was to rule on whether it could consider the formal complaints on January 24

and the Consultative Assembly was then to vote on possible
further action on January 31. On January 18, the Greek
government announced the formation of the two committees
to draft the press laws with their instructions to report within 30
days. On January 24,[6] the committees were briefed on the need
for completion of their work 'with all despatch', on January 25,
the measures of relaxation of prior censorship were introduced
and on January 31, Sideratos held a public briefing of editors
to outline their new freedoms.

The ploy did not work. The Human Rights Commission
ruled regardless that it could hear the Scandinavian and Dutch
complaints, while the Assembly adopted a further resolution
calling for the expulsion of Greece from the Council by Spring
1969 unless there was a new press law, a new constitution and
the restoration of acceptable parliamentary democracy. The
Assembly appointed Max van der Stoel of the Netherlands as
its new rapporteur. He travelled to Greece at the time of the
first anniversary of the coup to prepare a follow-up report but,
in that brief space of three months, all the earlier promises had
evaporated. Instead of legislative drafts in thirty days with the
lifting of censorship to follow soon after, Sideratos now told van
der Stoel that 'although [the] committees were working night
and day, they were finding it physically impossible to complete
their work within the time limits specified.'[7] This was despite the
fact that he had in hand a report from the chairman of the law
drafting committees[8] advising that a finished press law and a
detailed outline of companion legislation on the practice of the
profession could be ready by the end of June.

The regime had adopted a new tack. Affording van der Stoel
the minimum of courtesy, it began instead to address itself
directly to the permanent representatives of the Council, a
diplomatic level of the hierarchy less moved by political
concerns than the parliamentarians of the Assembly. In a series
of letters addressed to the Secretary General between May and
July 1968, the regime argued that, following the revised
measures of censorship, press offenses were once again
covered by the Penal Code. The press '. . . can exercise its
activities freely, subject only to such restrictions as are imposed
by the criminal law already in force before the Revolution. The

only obligation is to respect the country's foreign policy and *publish the government communiques.*'[9] It was claimed that by July 1968, 265 publications, including *Eleftheros Kosmos* and *Vradyni* were appearing without prior censorship. The implication of these letters was that the prosecution of press offenses was now a matter for the civilian courts, although this was not the case. Press offenses under the Penal Code continued to be subject to prosecution by military tribunals and those newspapers which had agreed to publish on their own responsibility were still required to submit proofs to the censors for vetting after the fact. Because of the risk of post-publication prosecution, those publishers who appeared without prior control practiced rigorous self-censorship, a point not lost on van de Stoel who remarked in his second report to the Assembly that 'preventive control has to a certain extent been replaced by the fear of prosecution under martial law.'[10]

The problem is illustrated by the case of *Vradyni*. Although the paper was nominally pro-regime, proprietor George Athanassiades had, following the colonels' confrontations with Karamanlis and the king, become an opponent. His mode of resistance was cunning. He struck a bargain with the Press Directorate whereby he would employ a commentator who, of his own volition, would sing the praises of the Revolution in exchange for which *Vradyni* would not have to carry the editorials provided by the Press Control Service. The commentator's articles were not to be subject to prior censorship; Athanassiades would publish them on his own responsibility. The deal was agreed. A retired general, Nicholas Ventiris, was hired. The regime was able to declare to the Council of Europe that *Vradyni* was now publishing without prior censorship and Athanassiades was able, as he put it, 'to take profit of their confidence: take all the articles of Ventiris and, without wasting time to take in all the story, read the last two paragraphs. These included all the mines.' He admits that one or two paragraphs was not much but 'it was the only means we had at the time' and even these brought reprisals. The paper had constantly complained about the fact that rehabilitated communists were allowed to take posts in state services. When, in November 1968, Ventiris specifically challenged Papaconstantinou about his leftist background, the regime clamped down. Ventiris was forced to resign and Athanassiades was convicted on a charge concerning failure to comply with the technical requirements governing right of reply[11] with regard to a letter from Papaconstantinou. This was an offense which could be heard by a civilian court and which could be bought off with a fine, but it put Athanassiades and other publishers on notice.

Some journalists didn't even have the benefit of such spurious legal process when they fell foul of the colonels. Three of them were personally assaulted by the thuggish Secretary General of the Ministry of Public Order, Ioannis Ladas, after they'd published an article which offended his sense of history. This bizarre incident involved Panayotis Lambrias, Constantine Psychas and Ioannis Lampsas, three former employees of Mrs. Vlachou, who bought the title of her magazine *Ikones* (Pictures) and began to reissue it in March 1968. It appeared until late July when the public prosecutor ordered confiscation of an edition containing an article by Lampsas called 'The Dark World of the Third Sex' which discussed the problems of homosexuals. The article included an historical reference which noted that Demosthenes, Zeno, Aeschylus, Sophocles and Phidias had all been pederasts. The three journalists were charged with obscenity. While their case was awaiting trial, Ladas issued a press statement fulminating first against the article, which, he said, 'spat filthily in the face of Greek history and trod on the holy memory of brave men,' and then against the journalists, whom he described as 'vile insulters of the creators of Greek national grandeur.' The Revolution, he concluded, 'will never abandon the holy to the dogs.'

It wasn't enough, however, for Ladas to pre-empt justice in this way. He had the three men brought before him at the Ministry where he proceeded personally to beat up each in turn. Lambrias, in testimony before the Council of Europe, said that as Ladas rained blows on him he screamed, 'Go and join your friend Helen, that arch whore. If you don't bugger off, I'll kill you with my own hands.' When the three men were finally brought to trial in October they were acquitted after reading in their defense extracts from an encyclopedia entry written by Education Minister Papaconstantinou in which he said that pederasty was widespread among ancient Greeks. 'It was considered a natural desire ... and was not despised by public opinion.'[12]

I myself became obliquely involved in this incident when, in a commentary for the B.B.C. Greek Program, I quoted Ladas' statement and remarked that in most countries, comments such as his, while a trial was pending would constitute contempt of court. The next day the Press Control Service issued as a mandatory page one item for all newspapers, the following statement from Ladas.

The commentator of the B.B.C. has taken it upon himself to defend the persons responsible for *Ikones* magazine and has despatched with ironic emphasis my statements concerning insult against the holy memory of national personalities. Taking into consideration that, according to the pornographic article, homosexuals support each other, we think that we may be able to explain this voluntary intervention of the B.B.C.

It was typical of the way a calumny could be perpetrated through the press without any hope of reply or redress.

Following the constitutional referendum, the colonels put it to the Council of Europe that they now had a mandate to continue the suspension of individual liberties. The Council reiterated its demands for the restoration of representative government and, when the Ministerial Committee met in May 1969, it promised to take action against Greece before the year was out unless there had been demonstrable progress. This was a significantly tougher response than the colonels had expected. They nonetheless decided to participate in the procedures in the hopes of somehow deflecting or postponing definitive action by the Council. During that summer, they entered into secret negotiations for a so-called 'friendly settlement agreement.' They proposed a program for implementation of suspended elements of the constitution which would have meant that by the end of 1970 most civil liberties would have been restored but political life would remain in abeyance. Martial law would have remained in force, although much reduced in scope. The centrepiece of the proposals was a three-stage plan to further relax press controls. First, martial law restrictions would be eased and control exercised for a time by executive decision. By November 15, 1969, there would be a press law. Finally, in September 1970, the extent of the application of martial law would be further reduced. 'The internal legislation will be organised in [such] a manner that the full freedom of the press is re-established with the exception of those publications which, by calling up past events that preceded April 21, 1967, aim at stirring up political passions and thereby threaten the public order.'[13] This program, only made public months later, made perfect sense of otherwise Delphic comments by Papadopoulos. In late July 1969, he told Greek journalists that he was 'uncertain as to what should be done with regard to the extent and timing of the return to press freedom. . . . I shall do so on a trial basis. I shall publish the law. I shall give freedom, not by legislation but by decisions and I shall give you the opportunity of applying it with my full personal backing. I am afraid, however, that you yourselves will soon ask that we should not return to that state of affairs.'[14]

As proof of its good intentions, the government published a Draft Press Code five days before submitting the liberalization timetable to Strasbourg. Nothing could have better illustrated the authoritarian nature of the regime. Implementation of its provisions would have given the state the sort of controls over the press one might expect it to exercise over a public corporation. It proposed a government audit of press finances, a register of journalists with entry to the list vetted by the government and supervision of press unions by the press minister. Not surprisingly, the text was rejected by journalists as 'inadmissible.' What prompted the regime to publish the obviously illiberal draft at a time when it was allegedly trying to demonstrate its democratic intentions has never been properly explained. It obviously was a major factor in the decision of the plaintiff governments to reject the Greek settlement proposals.

The regime nevertheless proceeded to implement its program. On October 3, 1969, modifications were made to the way in which martial law was applied to the press and three days later, Papadopoulos issued his administrative strictures in a lengthy memorandum outlining subjects still prohibited (see

Appendix C). Although originally the intention had been to sustain prior censorship during the interim period before the Press Law was introduced,[15] orders were given for its abolition on October 7. This had an immediate, dramatic effect on the appearance of the papers as they were now free for the first time in nearly $2\frac{1}{2}$ years to select their own stories and pictures and to write their own headlines. On November 15, 1969, a much modified version of the Press Law was introduced to become applicable from the beginning of the following year. This was three weeks after the Council's next session and the general feeling was that the delay made the legislation a hostage to its decisions.

Pleading the Greek case before the Council on December 12, 1969, Foreign Minister Pipinellis stressed how the regime had adhered strictly to its timetable on press matters and implied that it would act similarly in the introduction of other measures which the regime deemed necessary before representative government could be restored. But there was no hint of a date for possible elections and this lack of commitment to political evolution, coupled with the leakage of the report of the Human Rights Subcommission which revealed that the regime sanctioned torture as a matter of administrative policy, decided the Council upon expulsion. Before this could happen, Pipinellis walked out and Greece withdrew from the Council of Europe. This renewed concern that the regime would not apply the Press Law, but it did, and the legislation came into force, as had been promised, on January 1, 1970.

NOTES

[1] Legislative Decree 2622, January 18, 1968.

[2] Ministerial Decision E.P. 579/Lambda, January 25, 1968.

[3] Press Conference, March 1, 1968, the full text is in *To Pistevo Mas*, Vol. Beta, pp. 10-17.

[4] February 6, 1968. The version published here is a precis.

[5] Siegmann, *Report on the Situation in Greece*, p. 59.

[6] This is the date given by the committees' chairman, Constantine Roubanis, in an unpublished report to Under-secretary Sideratos in April 1968. Press reports at the time spoke only of the January 31 briefing.

[7] Max van de Stoel, *Report on the Situation in Greece*, Strasbourg, Council of Europe, May 4, 1968, para. 55.

[8] Constantine Roubanis, 'A Report [on] the Progress of the Work of the Press Committees,' April 24, 1968.

[9] Letter of the Greek permanent representative at the Council of Europe to the Secretary General of the Council, April 29, 1968, cited in *The Greek Case*, Vol. 1, Part 2, Strasbourg, Council of Europe, 1970, p. 152. My italics.

[10] Max van der Stoel, *Report to the Consultative Assembly*, Doc. 2467, Strasbourg, Council of Europe, September 25, 1968, p. 12.

[11] Ventiris' article had appeared in its entirety on page one. Papaconstantinou's reply began on page one but carried over to page seven. The law said a reply should appear in the same place and the same type size as the original.

[12] Papaconstantinou resigned from government on June 22, 1969 claiming exhaustion.

[13] Submission of the Greek Government to delegates of the Human Rights Commission, August 25, 1969, *The Greek Case*, Document 42, Athens, Ministry of Foreign Affairs, 1970, pp. 138–141.

[14] *Speech*, July 21, 1969.

[15] *The Greek Case*, Document 43, para. 4, p. 142.

V LIBERALIZATION MEASURES

If evidence were needed of just how little sympathy the colonels commanded after $2\frac{1}{2}$ years in office, the reaction of the press to the abolition of prior censorship provided a dramatic demonstration. Overnight, the perpetual promotion of the regime gave way to hard news coverage, much of it implicitly critical. It was far from full press freedom, for the prohibition remained against attacking the present regime or promoting the former, but the new system did allow the reporting of a wide range of subjects that had previously been suppressed. In essence, it permitted factual accounts of most events, provided that neither their subject matter nor the manner of their recounting constituted a direct political attack on the regime. Thus, for example, it was possible to cover a resistance bomb attack, provided the story confined itself to the facts of the detonation of the explosive device, the damage, the injured, etc., without saying who claimed responsibility for it or what their motives were. However it was not permitted to report resistance tracts because of the tenor of their contents. Transcripts of the trials of resistance workers with their horrific allegations of torture were permissible but examination of the political rationale for the defendants' actions or editorial demands for official inquiries into the claims of maltreatment were not. Statements critical of the regime, either by individuals or institutions could not be reported but complaints about specific acts of the administration occurring as a consequence of the dictatorial nature of the regime could be, provided that no derogatory conclusions were drawn from the facts.

It was a situation fraught with pitfalls for journalists because of the multitudinous ambiguities, but it was one from which they were able to make much mileage because of the subtlety of political appreciation of their readers who took volumes from every nuance. Opposition was expressed obliquely by playing up the activities of groups opposing dictatorships abroad in Iberia and Latin America. American reverses in the Vietnam war featured prominently because, as the United States was deemed to be responsible for the colonels, anything seen to diminish American prowess was construed as a blow against the dictatorship. Liberation struggles, urban terrorist activities, hi-jackings all got good play, not because they were condoned but because of the political upheaval they implied. Constantine's every move was chronicled; two papers even ran extensive accounts of the events of the counter coup. After months of official silence about the increasingly troubled situation in Cyprus, there was now extensive coverage.

The papers constantly strained at their limitations. One favorite device was the trick headline, such as eight columns of screaming woodtype declaring, 'The dictatorship is rapidly receding' coupled with a tiny kicker reading 'in Spain'. Another was to reprint critical comments by foreign political figures. This could be done only in those instances where it was nicely judged that the diplomatic embarrassment to the regime of being seen to suppress the remarks would be greater than the domestic political damage of allowing them to appear. France, for instance, was, for pragmatic reasons of trade, one of the few western European countries not overtly critical of the colonels. Thus, when receiving a new ambassador, French president Georges Pompidou made a one-line passing reference to possible political developments in Greece, it was bannered in Athens next day as 'Insinuations by Pompidou on evolution.'

Similarly a transcript of U.S. Congressional hearings urging restoration of parliamentary government appeared because at the time the colonels were working to end an American arms embargo and to have intervened would have been counterproductive. Regular denunciations of the regime by British, German and Scandinavian parliamentarians went unreported.

The Lambrakis papers indicated their opposition by refusing to publish editorial commentary. To abide by the rules and to criticize administrative actions without drawing political conclusions, they argued, was only to give comfort to the regime. In a boxed item on the front page of *Vima* the day that prior censorship was lifted, Lambrakis wrote, 'We consider that there is not the scope permitting us to write political articles. We will thus abstain from all political commentary until the lifting of the state of siege re-establishes all political and individual liberties.' *Vima* and *Nea* did, however, become masters of the art of critique through reportage. For example, one day they would report that certain individuals were denied passports; the next they would publish the relevant legislation setting out the legal criteria for them to be granted. Soon there would be letters from others who had been refused papers. The reports never stated that the action was political but it was obvious and very quickly the papers could create what amounted to a campaign of complaint without a viewpoint ever having been expressed.

Eventually *Vradyni* encroached on the forbidden territory of political commentary when it offered a forum to retired Colonel Dimitrios Stamatelopoulos, a former member of the junta who had broken with his colleagues over their efforts to create a new political order. He favored quick refurbishment of democratic institutions and restoration of a purified parliamentary government. Athanassiades gave Stamatelopoulos *carte blanche* to write an article for the Saturday paper whenever he wished on the subject of his choosing and at whatever length he liked (each one was worth an additional 30,000 copies in circulation). They were rambling, turgid texts which reiterated Stamatelopoulos' fears that 'a chapter might become a tome.' They had an unnerving effect on the regime because they represented a worm in the bud. More importantly, his association with the paper gave it an immunity from overt persecution and afforded protection to other, intelligent commentators, such as political and diplomatic editor Vassos Vassileiou who made sophisticated critiques. Vass. Vass., as he was known, regularly wrote subtle front-page editorials in which he would analyze the discrepancies between government policies and pronouncements and regime practice. He was particularly adept in detailing how statutes produced to flesh out the constitution frequently curtailed in their details liberties set out in the general principles of the larger law. Vassileiou probably did more than any other single individual to destroy the regime's efforts to create a veneer of democratic respectability.

The colonels retaliated against the press by using covert measures of economic punishment. Circulation was interrupted. Newsprint taxes were applied in proportion to circulation which hit hardest at the popular opposition papers. State advertising was placed selectively and loan facilities which required government authorization were denied to opposition publishers. The revenue department was used to make harassing inspections and to levy punitive sums of tax. But the colonels hadn't counted on *Ethnos,* a paper which was effectively bankrupt and which, as a consequence, decided that it could afford to risk its all in political defiance of the regime.

Founded in 1913, *Ethnos* was a family business owned 50% by Constantine Nicolopoulos, son of the founder, 30% and 20% respectively by his first cousins Constantine and Achilles Kyriazis. Nicolopoulos was a businessman, Achilles a translator. Constantine Kyriazis was the journalist, active in the day-to-day operation of the publication. The newspaper was liberal by tradition and in the early days of the dictatorship was one of those papers which it was politically unwise to be seen reading. Its circulation dropped by more than half between April and May 1967 and the paper lost so much money that in August that year the partners agreed that they should cut their losses by declaring bankruptcy. The regime, however, forced *Ethnos* to take a four million drachma loan from the National Bank of Greece and to accept a government nominee to oversee publication. This was former city editor Andonis Andonikakis, a man described by Kyriazis as 'an ex-communist who had become an addict of the dictatorship.' Kyriazis boycotted his own office for nearly two years as a sign of protest. Under Andonikakis' guidance, the paper staggered on in undistinguished fashion gradually losing more and more money until, by the time censorship was lifted, the paper was once again on the brink of collapse. Kyriazis says the government would have provided more funds had the paper been prepared to 'genuflect' but the partners refused and again contemplated bankruptcy. This time, however, Kyriazis argued that they should see whether they might reverse their fortunes by taking what advantage there was to be had from the limited freedom of expression. He returned to the paper on November 1, 1969. Finding staff that had not been paid their salaries for two weeks, he told them there was 'no money, only the will to fight the dictatorship.' Everyone, he claims, agreed to work on.

In the beginning the approach was tentative, with opposition confined to reprinting the texts of others such as Council of Europe deliberations on Greece. But, by the new year, the newspaper was itself generating opposition material. It openly challenged the regime's press policy in a bold page one editorial on January 10, 1970. 'We call on the government to decide. If it thinks it feasible and expedient, let it go ahead with its experiment on press freedom – courageously, sincerely and without hesitation. If not, let it reimpose preventive censorship. It would be preferable and braver.' In February, it launched a series of hostile features, one serious, involving well-known writers being interviewed about the degree of freedom of expression then current in Greece, another lighter, in which public figures were asked to say what they could do 'If I were a dictator.' The paper dredged up and ran an Athenian law from 335 B.C. which urged citizens to slay all tyrants.

The government reacted by diverse means. There were private threats that they would close the paper and there was interference with provincial circulation so extensive that in some places it was impossible to buy the paper for days on end. In one town at least, readers were told the paper had ceased publication. Overall, the rise in *Ethnos'* circulation was inexorable, climbing 139% in the short space of seven months. Then, the government called its imposed loan. The first installment of

700,000 drachmas was declared due on March 14, 1970 and a court order was obtained saying that equipment could be auctioned if payment was not made. Only minutes before the auctioneers were due to move in, it was met with the proceeds of a whip-round among the publishers' wealthier friends. Finally, the Internal Revenue Service was called in to do a detailed audit following which it was alleged that the paper had practiced a number of administrative irregularities. It was assessed back taxes totalling some fourteen million drachmas. From that moment on *Ethnos* was financially lost and effectively dead. In such hopeless straits, it became reckless and the regime finally resorted to the naked force of martial law, although not without further warnings. The Athens Military Commander called in first the paper's editor, Ioannis Kapsis, and then the senior partner, Constantine Nicolopoulos, and told them that if they did not cease their opposition forthwith, they would be brought before a military tribunal and be found guilty of press offenses which would carry the maximum five-year sentence. When the paper continued, the threat was methodically carried out.

The pretext for the prosecution was an interview with the former Center Union politician, John Zigdis, which the paper published on March 24, 1970. It recommended the formation of a government of national unity in Greece to deal with the burgeoning political crisis in Cyprus. In the weeks immediately preceding, there had been an attempt to assassinate President Makarios, in the wake of which Cyprus Interior and Defense Minister Polycarpos Georgadjis had been murdered. It was widely rumored that the colonels were hatching a coup. Zigdis had called for the formation in Greece of 'a political government, fully trusted by the Greek people. ... A government of national unity should face this critical time.' It was the sort of open challenge to the regime which was absolutely forbidden. The three proprietors; the editor, Zigdis and 82-year-old Constantine Economides, honorary director of the paper, were arrested and charged under an article of the Penal Code which fell under the aegis of the martial law. This was Penal Code Article 191 concerning the dissemination of false information liable to cause anxiety to the public. They were also charged with breaching martial law orders by making 'anti-national propaganda.'

The trial, on March 31 and April 1, was a legal farce. The prosecution made no serious effort to mount a case and, as the charge was a political one, the defense treated it as such, calling twenty leading figures of the former political world, headed by deposed Premier Panayotis Kanellopoulos and centrist George Mavros. The confrontation turned into a political slanging match at one stage of which an officer of the military tribunal leaned forward and barked, 'Zigdis and the others won't live long enough to see elections again.' At two a.m. on April 2, the tribunal handed down its verdicts: Kapsis five years, Zigdis four and a half years, Constantine Kyriazis four years, Nicolopoulos and Achilles Kyriazis three years and Economides thirteen months, these to be accompanied by fines ranging between 100,000 and 200,000 drachmas. It spelled the end. From their prison cells on April 3, the proprietors announced the closure of *Ethnos*. That this had been the intention of the regime from the outset was reinforced by the substantial reduction of the sentences when appeals were heard the following September: Kapsis twenty months, Constantine Kyriazis fourteen months, Nicolopoulos and Achilles Kyriazis thirteen months, and Economides acquitted. The appeal hearing was highlighted by an incident which epitomized the farcical tone of the entire affair. One of the prosecution witnesses, a trade union official, told how he had read the report in Athens at 8.30 a.m. before setting out for Patras. He said that when he arrived there, he found a number of people anguishing over the article. *Ethnos* was an afternoon paper which did not come out till noon.

With time off for good behavior, the four jailed newspapermen were free by May 1971. Zigdis, however, refused to recognize the court's right to have tried him in the first place and would not appeal. He stayed in jail until January 1972 when the regime released him, without an appeal, on the grounds of ill health.

Kyriazis says that, while imprisoned, the partners were approached by an employee of long standing, acting as an emissary of the colonels, with a new offer of a loan if only the paper would re-appear without attacking the regime. This was refused. The proprietors were determined that if the paper couldn't operate on their terms, it wouldn't open again. By the time they were released from prison, staggering debts of twenty-seven million drachmas had accumulated and so, finally, in June 1971, *Ethnos* was put into liquidation.

The treatment of *Ethnos* served as an object lesson for the rest of the press, demonstrating just how ruthless the regime was prepared to be if it felt threatened. Editors took the message and cautiously curbed their criticism. The tone of the papers for a while after was one of grudging sullenness. To chivvy them along, Papadopoulos introduced as Under-secretary the propagandist, George Georgalas. In his capacity as a psychological warfare specialist prior to the coup, he had been associated with Papadopoulos at the Greek Central Intelligence Service (K.Y.P.) and probably advised the junta on how to prepare public attitudes for the takeover. His approach to the press was coldly calculating. Using classical tactics of divide and rule, he crooned a siren song designed to persuade journalists to abandon their loyalty to their proprietors and to ally their interests with the Revolution. 'I believe that the press problem in Greece is mainly a publishers' problem and it is my conviction that a way must be found to draw a distinction between the responsibility of journalists and owners.'

Prior to the coup, he said, publishers had been able to make and unmake governments. Their opposition to the Revolution was founded in their desire to reassert that influence. In this, they exploited their employees. The Revolution wanted a 'true democracy which means that no individual or group will wield as much power as that wielded by the press before the Revolution.' In the beginning, he said, the regime had made a mistake; it had tended 'to identify journalists with press enterprises some of which had played a negative role.' Now it realized that 'a free, responsible and conscientious journalist cannot but agree with the great national and regenerating endeavour of the Revolution.' The government was therefore 'studying ways to prevent publishers from dismissing journalists who refuse to act against their consciences.'

To induce journalists to travel the pro-regime road, Georgalas offered cash prizes and medals for 'national and social' reporting and said the state would provide scholarships for selected individuals to undertake foreign study and assistance for those wanting to take time off to write books. These measures were, he said, only 'the first instalment;' if journalists co-operated, 'we shall think of other things as well.' His approach revealed a fundamental contempt for the press which he thought could be bought by such mean commerce. It permeated all his thinking about journalism. Asked why newsmen were not allowed to buy off prison sentences, even for petty offenses, he railed about sensationalism and distortion and replied, 'if a merchant can be jailed for selling shoddy goods, why should a journalist not be jailed for selling shoddy ideas.'

His alternative, spelled out in draft legislation on the profession of journalism published in August 1971, would have made journalists as dependent upon the state as he contended they now were upon their employers. It called for them to sign loyalty oaths similar to those required of civil servants, laid down a code of ethics which said that journalists should 'serve the interests of the nation' and made them subject to discipline administered by government appointed committees. Georgalas argued that this code of ethics, by being enshrined in law, gave journalists for the first time a legal means with which to confront their employers.

In a further effort to curb the hegemony of the Athenian publishers, Georgalas produced legislation to strengthen provincial publications. It provided for indirect central government subsidies to regional daily newspapers and the establishment of a regular news service for the provinces to be provided by the government controlled Athens News Agency. The wire service was inaugurated on June 1, 1971, but, although the legislation to provide the financial aid was actually gazetted,[1] the decision of the Prime Minister necessary for its implementation was never forthcoming.

During Georgalas' tenure, pressures on the press showed scant respect for the rule of law. The Lambrakis group was particularly hard hit. George Romaios, editor-in-chief of *Vima*, disappeared on March 19, 1971 and was missing without trace for several days before the military police admitted that they were holding him on suspicion of being a member of Andreas Papandreou's Panhellenic Liberation Movement. Romaios claims that 90% of the questions asked during his interrogation had nothing to do with his alleged resistance but with stories he had run.[2] According to *Vima's* publisher, Leon Karapanayotis, 'It was the perception of everyone in the office at the time that Romaios was being held hostage for our good behaviour.' He was released after five months detention without charge the day after Georgalas left office. Other *Vima* and *Nea* personnel were periodically called in by the Military Police (E.S.A.) and had Romaios' example to contemplate while awaiting interrogation. Karapanayotis suffered the experience several times. 'You would be brought in and Theofylloyannakos would scream and shout at you. Then you'd be locked in a room for a couple of hours until you thought you were under arrest when, suddenly, they'd let you go. The next time you'd be put in a room and curious characters would be brought in to stare at you. Hadjizisis would say, 'You don't know Mr. Mallios? Mr. Babalis? Let me introduce you,' and then they'd all go away again.' (Theofylloyannakos and Hadjizisis were both Military Police officers with public reputations as torturers: Mallios and Babalis were similarly notorious security police officers.) Ministers would telephone the paper 'to make sinister noises' about the way specific stories had been played and anonymous threats were made to individual journalists. Court reporter Nikos Kakaounakis was threatened with arrest and torture for his coverage of resistance trials. There were niggling persecutions in which the charges were so transparently manufactured as to make a mockery of the judicial process. In the spring of 1971, there were three cases in as many months.

Lambrakis and Karapanayotis were prosecuted for publishing stories which could 'mislead public opinion and do harm to Greece's foreign relations.' The charges arose out of articles concerning a sixteenth century Roman Catholic church in Crete which the government had demolished despite protests by archaeologists and architects. *Vima's* stories, it was alleged, threatened to damage relations with the Vatican and other Catholic nations, a charge so ludicrous that when the case came to court, even the prosecutor suggested that the two men should be acquitted. In a second case, a week later, the publisher and editor of *Nea*, Costas Nitsos and Vassilios Varikas, were charged with obscenity for having published a photo of a nude dancer at Paris' Crazy Horse Saloon. Again by the end of the hearing the prosecutor recommended the defendants' acquittal.

The third charge was more substantial. *Nea* had published an article on western intellectuals by a Soviet professor but had changed the by-line. *Eleftheros Kosmos* ran a series of editorials accusing them of publishing 'contraband communist ideas.' Nitsos and Varikas were convicted of a breach of the press law and each sentenced to four months' imprisonment. Varikas' testimony before the court spoke eloquently of the strain.

> We live with the nightmare of being brought before a military tribunal for a phrase, a word, a slip of the pen, a mere nothing. We have constant recourse to our lawyer who has become a sort of super-editor ... without this always being effectual, as our present hearing proves. In these conditions, the management of the newspaper has given a very strict order to all levels of the editorial staff to be specially careful. We must cut out of our texts anything which has even the slightest chance of getting us involved in judicial adventures.[3]

The day after the two men were convicted, Lambrakis and Karapanayotis both published signed articles on political subjects for the first time since the lifting of prior censorship. Karapanayotis insists that it was mere coincidence but it has been suggested that this was the *quid pro quo* for a subsequent successful appeal in which the verdict against the *Nea* editors was overturned.

Georgalas left the Ministry to the Prime Minister in a cabinet shuffle on August 26, 1971 after a furore over the draft legislation on the profession. Papadopoulos regularly renewed personnel but the wholesale changeover at the Ministry to the Prime Minister on this occasion suggested that he realized that the draughtsmen of the bill had so incensed the press that they could no longer have any influence with them. Minister without

Portfolio Loukas Patras, one of the main authors of the draft, was dropped from the government altogether; Georgalas was replaced as Under-secretary by Byron Stamatopoulos (who had resigned as Director of Press and Information in 1969 apparently over the earlier draft law on the practice of journalism); and Secretary General Ioannis Anastassopoulos was transferred and his place taken by Loukas Papangelis, a lawyer newly associated with the regime.

The cabinet reshuffle was meant to mark the beginning of a process of transformation from a revolutionary to a guided political regime. Pattakos and Makarezos were kicked upstairs from their vital posts at the Ministries of the Interior and of Economic Co-ordination to become largely titular Deputy Ministers, and senior civilians who had proven particularly loyal to the regime were elevated to their ministerial positions. Other former junta members were sent off to become governors of recently created regional administrations, being replaced in cabinet with new men, some of whom came from the Advisory Committee on Legislation, the so-called mini-parliament. This was a body of 56 members selected by the Prime Minister following a preliminary balloting procedure carried out by a college of 1,240 state-nominated electors. It met in the old parliament building and discussed draft laws presented to it by the government although its opinions were in no way binding and it had no power to generate legislation. It was designed primarily to give public exposure to 'new personalities' for the New Democracy.

In a cabinet reshuffle in 1972, Papadopoulos included a number of minor former politicians, but none of these people were the sort who could appeal to the public to command widespread support. The end result of these moves was that, contrary to the intention of broadening the base of government, all significant powers were consolidated in Papadopoulos' hands, producing a one-man dictatorship of the Latin American style. He became Prime Minister, Defense Minister, Foreign Minister and Minister of Government Policy. On March 22, 1972, after a row with Zoitakis, he also became Regent. The regime was stagnant. Gradually, it began to crumble under the weight of its own inertia.

NOTES

[1] Legislative Decree 1263, November 4/8, 1972.
[2] Dominique Gazeau, 'La Presse Sous La Dictature Militaire Grecque,' University of Paris, 1976, p. 244.
[3] *Nea*, June 22, 1971.

VI DECLINE AND DEMISE

On April 21, 1972, the fifth anniversary of the coup, students staged their first demonstration. There were only a hundred of them sitting on the steps of the Athens University chanting 'Long live Democracy' and singing the national anthem. They were brutally dispersed by a baton charge of massed police and five cautionary arrests were made. The incident in itself was innocuous but it represented the germ of a student protest movement which burgeoned rapidly over the next 19 months until it culminated in the occupation of the Athens Polytechnic and the bloody incidents which led to Papadopoulos' downfall.

The pretense at first was that the students' actions were not politically motivated but concerned rather with practical matters such as poor teaching standards. Gradually the focus began to shift, starting with complaints about lack of freedom to elect student union leaders and eventually turning into overt opposition to the colonels. The newspapers played a significant role in sustaining the movement's momentum. Coverage required great delicacy because the regime's reaction to the press in this period was inconsistent. On the one hand, Papadopoulos, in the throes of his efforts at politicization, sought to allow sufficient leeway to give potential collaborators a sense of evolution. On the other, he had to ensure that any relaxation neither jeopardized the regime nor outstripped the sensitivities of hardline supporters under the leadership of Brigadier Dimitrios Ioannides, head of the Military Police (E.S.A.). It led a virtually autonomous existence and constituted both a mailed fist in Papadopoulos' velvet glove and a latent threat to his authority. He could disown E.S.A.'s actions to potential collaborators but could not divorce himself from the unit for fear of being overthrown.

The erratic reactions kept newspapers constantly off balance. For example, in March 1972, the English language daily, *Athens News*, published a joint statement on Cyprus by the former Prime Minister Panayotis Kanellopoulos, the leader of the Center Union Party, George Mavros and Ioannis Zigdis who had recently been released from prison on grounds of ill health.

No action was taken either against the politicians or the newspaper although the challenge which the statement represented was comparable to that which had led to the closure of *Ethnos* only two years earlier. Three months later, however, when Christos Papoutsakis, an intellectual of the new left, tried to launch a periodical called *anti*, with ex-*Ethnos* editor Ioannis Kapsis in charge, he was arrested by the Military Police and subjected to prolonged, brutal beatings which forced him to close the publication. A year later, a different periodical, financed by the same printing concern and published by a group which included a leading communist, was allowed to appear without incident. Stamatopoulos promised that no journalist would be tried before a military tribunal. However at least one publisher was subjected to questioning by military investigators. The government repeatedly said it would amend penal procedures so that journalists could buy off sentences for misdemeanours but no such legislation was forthcoming.

Inevitably in such circumstances, newspapers continued to be circumspect, although gradually their coverage of the student unrest became openly antagonistic until, finally, in February 1973, the regime clamped down. At the time, students of the Polytechnic were on strike demanding greater participation in education policy. The government responded by passing legislation to lift the draft deferment of any student abstaining from studies. Thirty-seven ringleaders of the protest were immediately inducted into the army, a move which touched off violent clashes between students and police. Former members of parliament took up the student cause and issued public statements denouncing both regime policies and tactics. Some newspapers, led by *Vradyni*, went out on a limb and published these alongside photographs of policemen savagely assaulting demonstrators. The government adopted the line that the protests were the work of a tiny group of left-wingers and did not represent the general sympathies of students. It claimed that the politicians were making a 'popular front' with these agitators. Newspapers were warned off the story. When they failed to respond voluntarily they were ordered to cease their coverage. Pattakos called in all editors on February 22 and told them they were to publish nothing about the student situation except official government communiques. All the papers except *Vradyni* and the *Athens News* complied. For Christos Lambrakis of *Nea* and *Vima* it was a tactical decision. 'It was not a question of being intimidated. It was more a sense of not knowing what would come out of it. Ioannides and all that party of extremists existed already and there was a possibility of them acting. I think the possibilities of bloodshed at that moment were rather more important to me.' *Vradyni's* independent coverage lasted only four days. During that time it was subjected to all the pressures that the regime could bring to bear short of actual prosecution. Athanassiades was called before Pattakos and Makarezos and given a tongue lashing. Later he was summoned before a prosecutor who interrogated him at length about possible press offenses. Several employees of the paper were questioned by the security authorities. Tax men raided both the paper and Athanassiades' home, removing reams of business and personal correspondence. Finally, *Vradyni* conformed, but only after Athanassiades had run a page one editorial outlining the pressures to which he'd been subjected, together with a letter of support signed by a dozen of the leading political figures from the last parliament.

The student demonstrations continued and gradually coverage crept back into the papers. Several weeks later Lambrakis wrote in *Vima* that the ban had only served to demonstrate that the newspapers were not, as the government contended, responsible for generating the unrest; all it had proved was that the maintenance of martial law constituted an effective means of 'hushing up' the press. Athanassiades got his own back in April. On the sixth anniversary of the coup, Papadopoulos made a speech describing Greece as an oasis of peace in a troubled world but said it was not yet ready for democracy. From Paris, Karamanlis produced a statement in reply saying that, in the light of the ever-increasing student unrest, such pronouncements were obviously false. He called upon the colonels to make way for a 'strong' and 'experienced' government, adding that one led by him would offer 'protection from revenge.' The statement was brought to *Vradyni* by Karamanlis' brother Achilles and surreptitiously set on April 22. The following day an ordinary front page was printed for the first run which went to the press secretariat and various ministries; then, immediately, there was a replate which splashed the Karamanlis text all over page one. By this device, 100,000 copies of a print run of 180,000 were distributed before the authorities realized the ruse and were able to confiscate the issue. Two other publications the *Athens News* and *Thessaloniki*, an independent paper from the northern capital, picked up and reprinted the text. They too were confiscated.

Athanassiades managed to avoid summary prosecution by going underground for three days. (He claims he received a telephone call from a friendly officer saying 'Get lost. I am coming to arrest you.') But he was still faced with the daunting prospect of fighting legal battles before 67 courts up and down the country on charges ranging from incitement to rebellion to creating defeatism, for which he could have faced imprisonment of up to twenty years. In the event, the government decided the cases were not to be pursued after Karamanlis indicated that he would return to Greece to stand trial alongside Athanassiades. The Ministers of Justice and the Interior resigned two days later.

This inability of the colonels to cope with conservative

opposition at a time when they were already backsliding before the student pressure, opened press floodgates and, when the Navy mutinied on May 24, coverage of the event was almost as detailed within the country as without. Perhaps, however, the regime had an ulterior motive in permitting this, as the mutiny became Papadopoulos' excuse for declaring a republic on June 1, 1973.

The next five months constituted a false spring. A referendum to ratify the republic was declared for July 29. Papadopoulos put himself forward as the sole candidate for president together with former chief of the Armed Forces General Odysseus Anghelis as vice-president. He hinted strongly that, if voted into office, he would rapidly develop a form of political government. During the campaign a simulacrum of politicking was allowed. Two incipient parties made statements on behalf of the new order. These were the Greek Cultural Movement (E.P.O.K.), of which the spokesman was Chris Bitsides head of the Athens News Agency, and the Social Union of Scientists, headed by former Press Under-secretary, Michael Sideratos. The former politicians organized themselves into an illegal cross-party Committee for the Restoration of Democratic Legality to campaign for a "no" vote. It could have been broken up at any moment but the regime chose to allow it an ineffectual existence. It was unable to put up posters or to hold rallies although it did succeed in staging one surreptitiously organized press conference. Newspapers, taking heart from the failure to act against the Committee, published some statements from its individual members.

The papers were also able to present something approaching a political editorial line. The Lambrakis group, although traditionally republican, embraced the "no" campaign on the grounds that the referendum was just another device to maintain Papadopoulos in power. (Proposed amendments to be added to the republican constitution gave the President continuing responsibility for Defense and Security, Foreign Affairs and Public Order, as well as for the office of Prime Minister although all these functions could be delegated.) Athanassiades campaigned in favor of the monarchy. Though he published nothing from the king, he did carry with impunity a Karamanlis text urging rejection of the republic. On the day of the ballot, the whole of *Vradyni's* front page above the fold was taken up with a Stamatelopoulos editorial overprinted with a giant *Oxi* (no) in nationalistic blue. The Botsis papers, on the other hand, endorsed Papadopoulos. 'A "yes" vote in this referendum is, under the present circumstances, the only way out, the only door that opens a road to the future and substantial democracy.'[1] Botsis apparently feared the hard men waiting in the wings and the tenor of his editorials was that the choice lay between Papadopoulos and the tanks. Better the devil you know than the one you don't, he concluded.

On the eve of the referendum, Papadopoulos announced that regardless of the outcome, he would not resign. If approved, he would lift martial law and appoint a political government to prepare elections which would be held during 1974; if not, he would continue to govern as in the past. Needless to say, he won with a 78.4 per cent "yes" vote.[2] Immediately after the balloting there were fears that he would renege on his undertakings. The disquiet was caused by proceedings instigated against several newspapers under martial law for their behavior during the referendum campaign. On August 19, before the cases could be heard, the martial law was lifted and all outstanding prosecutions were annulled. The 1968 constitution was finally implemented and an amnesty declared for all political prisoners. Several members of cabinet, including Under-secretary Byron Stamatopoulos, resigned with a view to entering political life. Stamatopoulos was reported to be planning 'to take the leadership of a political party imbued with the principles of the revolution.'[3]

Newspapers generally gave a cautious welcome to the developments. *Vradyni* allowed, for example, that 'the president has opened the door to hope,'[4] but it took Papadopoulos a full two months first to appoint the Constitutional Court which would oversee political life and then to nominate a prime minister. His eventual choice, Spyros Markezinis, was an intelligent and seasoned politician but a man whose arch-conservative views had little popular following. In the last parliament his extreme right-wing Progressive Party had held only eight of the three hundred seats. *Estia* was ecstatic but the rest of the press disappointed and the Lambrakis group openly hostile. Some politicians, including a number on the left, argued for accommodation with Markezinis in order to use him as a wedge to prise more democratic freedom at a later date. The Lambrakis policy was that '. . . it should be a dictatorship for all to see rather than a qualified democratic process that would bastardize everything.' Freed from the constraints of martial law, the Lambrakis papers came out sharply against the entire artificial edifice that Papadopoulos had created. Their harsh tone did much to engender the turbulent climate which led to the Polytechnic uprising.

On November 3, some 20,000 people, taking advantage of the restored freedom of assembly, staged a demonstration in Athens to mark the fifth anniversary of the death of George Papandreou. They were attacked by rightists and, in the ensuing mêlée, police intervened, injuring 60 people and arresting 17. The press leapt on the police behavior, denouncing it as barbaric. Students mounted mass demonstrations every night outside the court where the 17 were on trial. When five of the accused were convicted 2,000 protestors peeled off to occupy the precincts of the Polytechnic. Food and medical supplies were brought in in anticipation of a long siege. The Senate asked government authorities to respect university sanctuary and not to invade the campus to which Markezinis agreed. But, when a pirate radio station began broadcasting from the school, calling for the overthrow of the regime and, when associated demonstrations erupted into pitched street battles between laborers and riot police, Papadopoulos reimposed martial law. On the night of November 16–17, tanks and troops were brought in to clear the Polytechnic. Thirty-four people died and more than a thousand were injured in a long night of officially sanctioned carnage. Newspapers under renewed censorship were required to report an official version of events saying that nine people had been killed and 148 injured. *Vradyni* ran it but risked the rider 'Publication of our own news is forbidden.' *Vima* refused and instead ran a front page editorial calling for 'the restoration of unadulterated popular sovereignty.' It was temporarily shut down as a consequence.

The manner in which this was accomplished was typical of the sort of arms-length controls that Papadopoulos had always exercised and that he undoubtedly would have continued to try to apply even under his guided democracy. Press under-secretary Spyridon Zournatzis called in Lambrakis and delivered an ultimatum: either the paper published the government version or it would be closed. When Lambrakis refused, the paper was struck. The secretary general of the typographer's union, a regime man who sat in the mini-parliament, arrived at *Vima* saying, 'This is it. Now you learn to behave. There is going to be a little strike here.'

Unlikely as it might seem, it is widely held among Greeks that the Polytechnic riots were the work of *agents provocateurs* and had been engineered by Papadopoulos' henchmen in the Intelligence Service in order to give him an excuse to restore martial law and thereby pervert the promised elections. If so, the convoluted plot backfired totally for, on November 25, Brigadier Ioannides used the tanks which had been brought to Athens to quell the students to overthrow Papadopoulos. Ioannides was the sole member of the original junta who had refused to resign his commission. He had become the effective leader of a rump of purist revolutionaries of junior rank who disliked the politicization process. In one respect this had always served Papadopoulos' interests. He was able to argue that he could not move precipitately for fear of provoking these hardliners, but Papadopoulos made the fatal mistake of having no countervailing force. He kept in touch with Intelligence and liaised with specialist counter insurgency units but no longer exercised direct command as Ioannides did. Thus, when Ioannides finally turned against Papadopoulos, the president was defenseless.

The counter-revolutionaries had viewed askance the promise of elections, realizing that they could not be won without coercion and that the army would yet again have to be the agents. The bloodbath at the Polytechnic suggested that this time round it might not be such an easy task. The new group's takeover statement denounced Papadopoulos' co-operation with Markezinis as 'an agreement of political cynicism between one interested in preserving at all cost what he had gained and another who, having lost all in the past, sought at the cost of any concession or compromise, to gain anything at all.'

Ioannides took no post in the new administration but he was decidedly in command. He was an austere presence haunting the corridors of the Armed Forces Headquarters, issuing orders which he expected a country to answer with the alacrity of a regiment. On the night of the coup, all the Athenian publishers (including one plucked from his hospital bed) were picked up in military staff cars and brought to the Pentagon. Not knowing whether or not they were under arrest, the men were ushered into Ioannides' presence and informed that they could publish without censorship but that if they appeared, 'You'll have to support us.'[5] If they disagreed, they would have to close down. George Athanassiades recalls Ioannides saying there would be no tribunals for insubordination. 'It is I who will judge you and I who will condemn you.'[6]

Athanassiades was the first victim of that threat. The new administration had said in its policy statement that it did not want to 'perpetuate the state of emergency' or 'to establish a regime.' That was all well and good wrote *Vradyni* in an editorial but what about a commitment to the restoration of political life? On December 1, 1973, a group of Military Police, acting, they said, on orders from 'the chief,' chained and padlocked the front door of the newspaper. There were no written orders, no judicial warrants, just the jailer's mentality of lock and key. Athanassiades filed suit in the courts blaming 'persons unknown' for having closed his paper. Forty days later, this elicited a judicial response saying that the paper had been closed on the orders of the Military Governor of Athens under the provisions of martial law. At the time of the closure Athanassiades had approached this officer seeking an explanation and the man had assured him that he had no knowledge of the affair.

A similar fate awaited the biweekly publication *Christianiki*, a one-man operation which had gained notoriety for its outspoken criticism of Papadopoulos. Following the counter-coup, the paper appeared with a blazing editorial headlined, 'The tyrant has fallen, let the tyranny fall too.' The paper was summarily closed and its front door was also chained. Proprietor Nikolaos Psaroudakis sent out Christmas cards bearing a photo of the padlocks and noting ironically that one was made in America, the other in Hungary. On January 4, he was arrested and deported for a year to the re-opened prison island of Yiaros on the grounds that he was 'extremely dangerous to public order and security.'

The seven months of the Ioannides dictatorship were a time of desolation for the press. The staff at the Ministry to the Prime Minister were little better off. Like the editors, Constantine Rallis, a minor former politician had been picked up from his home by a staff car on the day of the counter-coup and taken to the Pentagon. Instead of being arrested, as he anticipated, he was named the new Under-secretary at the Ministry to the Prime Minister. Dimitrios Karakostas was appointed as secretary general. The pair gave virtually no press conferences, only infrequently issued communiques and essentially were unprepared to assume the responsibility of acting as government spokesmen. The little information which was made available tended to be attributed to 'authorized sources.' The problem was that they were scarcely more privy to the thinking or activities of the ruling clique than were the journalists. For example, when it was announced that the police had ordered the expulsion of two foreign correspondents in July 1974, Karakostas claimed to be totally ignorant of the action. When, after 24 hours, he was able to confirm the information, he told protesting members of the Foreign Press Association that he would endeavor to have the police reverse the decision.

It was the nadir of the dictatorship. Rumors abounded and there were no means of checking them. Journalists practiced rigorous self-censorship and still went in fear of reprisals. Lambrakis was the victim of a mock assassination. 'I was kidnapped in the street, hurled into a car where both my mouth and eyes were bandaged and what seemed to be a gun held to my temple. Transferred from car to car, I was finally brought to the "place of execution"; I was charged with having an uncooperative attitude and acting against the regime and finally thrown out of the car on the highway from Ekali to Athens. The whole procedure lasted for about five hours. . . .' Newspapers did what they could, in their foreign coverage, to play up the restoration of democratic government in Portugal and, in their domestic news, to milk for its anti-dictatorial implications the scandal of former junta member Michael Balopoulos who was tried for being party to a Rhodesian sanctions busting operation. In the main, however, newspapers were decidedly non-political and there was a proliferation of stories about the weather.

The law required Athanassiades to keep on his staff at *Vradyni* for at least two months after the forced closure but he retained them for the duration of the six months suspension in anticipation of re-opening. In the late days of May, 1974, he spent a million and a half drachmas papering Athens with posters announcing republication. He made arrangements for an initial print run of half a million copies. Then on May 27, Ioannides' hatchet man, Major Anastassios Spanos, called and unofficially advised him that he'd wasted his money. He was told that he'd obviously not learnt his lesson because he was still known to be consorting with Karamanlis. The Military Governor renewed the suspension for a further six months on the grounds that the paper constituted a threat to public order. On June 5, Athanassiades declared *Vradyni* closed. He perfunctorily went through the motions of appealing the banning order but was cited as saying that the paper would not appear again unless there was an 'evolution from the present situation. . . .'[7]

He did not have to wait long. On July 15, 1974, Ioannides sought to realize the aim of the original junta to install a pro *enosis* government in Cyprus. The Cypriot National Guard which is commanded by Greek officers, together with the irregular forces of E.O.K.A-B (the successor to the guerrilla organization which wrested independence from the British, staged a coup which overthrew Archbishop Makarios and installed as president, Nikos Sampson, a particularly thuggish right-wing politician). The move brought swift retaliation from Turkey who, acting in her constitutional role as guarantor of the rights of the minority Turkish Cypriot community, invaded and occupied the fertile northern sector of the island. Hundreds of Greek Cypriots were killed, thousands wounded and a quarter of a million were made homeless. In the face of this fiasco, the Greek government evaporated. In the final hours of the dictatorship, foreign intermediaries trying to arrange a ceasefire simply could not locate the Greek Prime Minister, Foreign Minister or, for that matter, anyone else in authority. The Greek Armed Forces, acting through the President, General Phaedon Ghizikis, decided to hand back power to a civilian administration. A meeting of senior political figures was convoked at which it was agreed to recall Constantine Karamanlis. Before it was officially announced, *Vradyni* was on the streets with a massive one-word headline *ERXETAI!* – he is coming! No one needed to ask who.

The squares of Athens filled with jubilant citizens and the scenes, as Karamanlis touched down aboard a private jet at Hellenikon airport at 2 a.m. on July 24, bordered on delirium. The press changed character overnight. After seven years of being muzzled, it became unbridled.

NOTES

[1] *Acropolis*, July 27, 1973.

[2] There were allegations of extensive ballot rigging. I watched civil servants at one polling station being given special ballot papers which, because of scrutineering procedures, would have put pressure on them to cast a 'yes' vote.

[3] Agence France Presse in *Le Monde*, August 17, 1973.

[4] *Vradyni*, August 20, 1973.

[5] 'Athens is placed under curfew,' *Times*, London, November 26, 1973.

[6] Gazeau, 'La Presse . . .,' p. 314.

[7] Agence France Presse, 'Le Quotidien "Vradyni" se saborde,' *Le Monde*, June 7, 1974.

PART TWO

VII PRESS LAW

The Greek press is governed by three legal instruments: the Constitution, the Penal Code and the Press Law. A general statement of their relationship is that the Greek press enjoys a constitutional guarantee of freedom under law but that specific governing legislation is allowed. The Constitutions of 1952 and 1968 and the current Constitution of 1975 each contained an Article 14 of broadly similar construction which says that the press was free and censorship forbidden although post-publication confiscation was permitted for obscenity, blasphemy, insult to the head of state, revelation of military secrets and the instigation of treason, secession or rebellion. These last were a legacy of the civil war which the colonels' Constitution reinforced with several measures directed specifically against communist publications.

The Constitutions have recognized the concept of a press crime; that is to say, the notion that an offense committed through the press is particularly grave and thus must be prosecuted more quickly than other crimes. The ordinary procedure for the prosecution of press offenses is much foreshortened relative to that for other crimes and if those accused of a press offense are apprehended within 24 hours of its commission, they are considered to have been taken *in flagrante* and are tried summarily. On the other hand, the statute of limitations for press offenses is also reduced: to eighteen months compared to five years in the case of most other crimes punished with the same penalties. In the case of offenses in which no individual is involved – such as offenses against the state and its institutions – prosecutors act *ex officio* and, in these instances, their position and role becomes rather ambiguous because, while considered part of the autonomous judiciary, they are ultimately legally responsible to the Minister of Justice and their perceptions of political offenses tend to be finely attuned to those of the government of the day.

The Constitutions have provided that press offenses should be heard by mixed courts, consisting of judges and jurors sitting together so that the accused may be said to have had a hearing by his peers while, at the same time, not to have been mis-judged on a point of law because of a jury being confounded by the legal and procedural niceties involved in press crimes. The 1952 Constitution provided that jurors should predominate whereas the colonels reversed this. The preponderance of judges was maintained in the 1975 Constitution and currently press offenses bearing a potential sentence of up to five years are heard by three-member Courts of Misdemeanors while felonies, where the sentence might be five years or more, are heard by five-member Courts of Appeal.

The courts may suspend temporarily or permanently a publication convicted of offenses constitutionally admitting of seizure. In the case of the 1952 Constitution, a publication was suspended after three convictions over any time span; in the 1968, after two convictions in five years; and, in the 1975, after three convictions within five years. The courts are also empowered in the case of serious offenses to prohibit an individual from practicing journalism. The Constitutions have also guaranteed both the individual's right of reply and his right to compensation in the event of being done 'a moral injury' through the press. The 1975 Constitution drops the stipulation regarding restitution but it is provided for in law.

Further to these general exceptions, freedom of expression

is subject to due adherence to law. Some thirty-eight articles of the Penal Code apply to the press although the exact number is a matter of contention among jurists. The Penal Code was the product of twenty years elaboration by a commission of experts which reported in 1949. It was passed into law by the centrist government of retired General Nicholas Plastiras on August 17, 1950 and took effect on January 1, 1951. As far as the press is concerned, it covers crimes against the state, the church, the individual and public order, but protects fair comment and the right to publish information of general interest. Sentences for press offenses include both imprisonment and fines. Modifications introduced by the demi-dictatorial Papagos government in 1953[1] made it incumbent on the courts, when passing sentence for political insult, criminal incitement or personal libel, to both suspend a newspaper's right to duty free newsprint and to prohibit a journalist's translation of a term of imprisonment into a fine.

Generally the Penal Code cannot be said to have any political bias but a number of articles do have political connotations. For example, Article 168 makes it a crime to libel or to defame the Head of State. While constitutionally the president is not a party figure, he is one in practice and it is possible to imagine criticisms levelled against the individual on political grounds forming the basis of a prosecution for an attack on the office. Similarly Articles 153–155 make it a crime to libel the government, diplomatic representatives or symbols of a country with which Greece is at peace, provisions which might afford grounds for a government to prosecute political opponents critical of foreign policy. Such tenuous applications of the law have not been a problem under democratic governments but the junta was notably expansive in its interpretation of how laws could be applied.

Two articles, however, have been used extensively against the press by both dictatorial and elected governments: Article 181 on insulting authority and Article 191 on the dissemination of false information. They are ill-defined and could be adapted to fit almost any circumstance. The original formulation of Article 181 made it an offense, punishable by up to three years imprisonment, to insult state, municipal or communal authorities. Insult of an individual (covered by Article 361) required that the injured party bring an action, whereas the wording of Article 181 implied hostility towards an institution and a prosecutor had the right to file suit *ex officio*. The 1953 amendments added to the article the offense of insulting a party leader, making it a cobbled up instrument embracing both institutions and individuals. The provision against insulting a party leader has virtually never been invoked but that of insulting authority has been frequently applied in cases involving comment on the security services, the courts, public corporations and all levels of government. It is not necessary for the prosecution to prove malice aforethought to obtain conviction. It is sufficient that the court deem that whatever was said was insulting. The determining factor is whether the comments are considered to diminish the stature of the institution in the eyes of the public. It is a highly subjective judgment, particularly if the alleged insult arises out of an over-vigorous statement of strongly held political convictions.

Article 191 on the spreading of false information is even more vague in its conception and thus more catholic in its potential application. It has been applied both to press speculation and to oral 'rumor-mongering' and was particularly favored by the colonels who used it to kill *Ethnos* and generally to keep a check on so-called 'whispers.' The original text of Article 191 reads.

> Whoever in any way knowingly[2] disseminates false news or rumors capable of causing concern or fear to the citizens or of disturbing public faith[3] or of shaking the public's trust in the national currency or in the Armed Forces of the country is punished by a prison sentence of up to one year or a fine.

The Papagos amendments extended the catalog of offenses making it a crime 'to disturb the country's international relations' and appended a paragraph making dissemination of false news an offense even if committed through negligence. this addition fundamentally altered the intention and made it a means not only of curbing false rumors but also of persecuting unwitting purveyors of incorrect information. Papagos stiffened the penalties so that when committed intentionally a first offense was punishable by imprisonment of from three months to five years and a fine and subsequent offenses by a minimum sentence of six months and a 200,000 metallic drachmas fine.[4] The courts could not suspend sentence nor could a convicted person be freed pending appeal; moreover, the sentence could not be bought off. If the offense was committed through negligence, the sentence was imprisonment for a maximum of one year or a fine and, while a first conviction could be bought off, a second could not.

The junta repeatedly modified Article 191 to extend its scope and further strengthen its provisions. Amendments in 1967 made it a crime to 'disturb the public confidence in the state power securing common peace' and changed the provision concerning fiduciary trust so that it referred instead to government fiscal and economic policy. It thus became an offense to 'disturb the public's confidence in ... the economic or public finances policy in general pursued by the state....'[5] This legislation made the penalties for commission of an offense through negligence the same as those for perpetration with intent. Again in 1969, the law was modified to further tighten up on economic reporting. This time it was made an offense to disseminate 'inaccurate news concerning government policy regarding economic investment from Greece and abroad.'[6] Penalties were increased to make the minimum sentence one year's imprisonment and a fine: in the event of subsequent convictions, these doubled. Finally, in November 1970, yet another law was passed which said that the provisions of Article 191 were to be applicable to all publications about Greece whether written by Greek or foreign journalists either inside or outside the country.[7] This caused uproar among the international press community and the regime immediately claimed that there had been an error in the printing of the text. Justice Minister Angelos Tsoukalas said that the new measure aimed 'exclusively and only at Greeks who indulge in anti-national activity abroad.' The legality of such extra-territorial jurisdiction, even over Greeks, was questionable and there seems to have been no use made of this provision.

Another act illustrating the regime's hostility to journalists was its refusal to allow them to buy off prison sentences. Penal

Code Article 82 allows that in the case of a sentence of imprisonment of not more than one year the court may, when it is persuaded that a crime is not dangerous to society, allow the translation of the term of imprisonment into payment of a sum of money. The court assesses an amount ranging between 200 and 20,000 drachmas per day depending upon the seriousness of the offense and the circumstances of the individual. Upon payment, the condemned is set free. The Papagos amendments had revoked this right for certain crimes but the colonels enacted a law[8] which refused the right to journalists altogether, thus putting them on a par with spies, dope peddlars, procurers, smugglers, rustlers, tax evaders and white slavers. The legislation was not published for some weeks after its enactment and when it appeared it caused a furore in the journalistic community. Georgalas responded contemptuously, 'The criterion in this case is the social impact of the offense. . . . Just as the trader in narcotics poisons the body of young persons, so a journalist or a bad paper can poison the mind.' The measure constituted not only an affront but also a danger to journalists and there was constant behind the scenes lobbying to have it rescinded. When Stamatopoulos became Under-secretary he promised to rectify the situation. In October 1971, he said publicly that legislation would be passed 'shortly' and, according to some reports, a bill was actually drafted but held in abeyance. Again in December 1972, Stamatopoulos was cited in an interview as saying that the regime was 'drawing up plans' to change the law. He was not, however, able to prevail upon his more repressively-minded ministerial colleagues and the right of a journalist to buy off his sentence remained suspended until the change of regime.

Two pieces of emergency legislation with potential application to the press also were on the statute books throughout the dictatorship. These were Compulsory Law 375/36 and Law 509/47. The former, passed by the Metaxas dictatorship, made it a crime punishable by a maximum of one year's imprisonment to publish any confidential military information including maps, plans, diagrams, documents and codes. It remained dormant during the colonels' rule but surprisingly was resurrected under the restored political administration in a

1976 case brought by a military prosecutor against the new left periodical *anti*. Law 509/47 which outlawed the Greek Communist Party made it a 'particularly serious' offense punishable by 5–20 years imprisonment to propagate its ideology through the press. This law was used indiscriminately by the colonels against all their resistance opponents whether or not they were communist and thus was employed in every prosecution of the underground press. It was not, however, used in any case involving a national daily. Law 509 was rescinded in September 1974, thus legalizing the Communist Party and permitting its publications to appear once more. Some concern was expressed by left-wing organizations that an anti-terrorism law passed in April 1978[9] effectively replaced the rigors of Law 509. Article 4 of the new law made it an offense punishable by a minimum of two years imprisonment to provoke or to incite terrorist actions – hijacking, kidnapping, arson, etc. – or to 'praise any such committed act thus endangering public security. . . .' Jurists argued, however, that so far as the press was concerned such offenses were more than adequately covered by the provisions of the Penal Code and that the anti-terrorism law was therefore inapplicable.

Many nations feel the role of the press in society is so unique and the implications of its actions of such consequence that peculiar legislation is necessary to define and delimit its activities. Greece is among them. Therefore, in addition to being subject to the legal constraints applicable to society at large, newspapers have been subject to a special Press Law. It has two strands: administrative and criminal. Sanctions attached to both including fines for breaches of regulations and jail sentences for offenses. The law reiterates the civil liability of the press and the individuals' right of redress as guaranteed by the constitution but, because of the general nature of the legislation, it is considered part of the criminal law.[10]

The Press Law prior to the coup was a confused body of Standing Legislation comprising elements of a relatively liberal law passed in 1931 by the Venizelos republican administration,[11] restrictive legislation imposed in 1938 by the

Metaxas dictatorship,[12] detailed administrative measures, governing the importation and use of newsprint brought into force in 1944–45 by the succession of governments which followed the liberation[13] and Papagos' 1953 modifications to the Penal Code which elaborated upon and, in some instances, superseded provisions of previous legislation. One of the first acts of the centrist government of George Papandreou in December 1963 had been to establish a commission to try to rationalize this tangle. It was also 'to revise press laws in a more democratic spirit' but before the commission could report, the government was overturned. Another attempt was made in 1966, when a seven-man commission of experts was established with three sub-committees each headed by a publisher. They were to formulate a constitutional charter for the press which would embrace a code of ethics, a permanent press council and a freedom of information act requiring public authorities to yield information to the press. Their work too was unfinished when it was interrupted by the coup. On August 20, 1969, the colonels produced a comprehensive 180-article Draft Press Code which sought to impose state control over the press. It met with such bitter opposition from all levels of the journalistic community that it was withdrawn. It was subsequently remodeled as two laws, one on the operation of the press[14] and another on the practice of the profession.[15]. This brace governed the press until the restoration of political government when the Standing Legislation was restored. At the same time Penal Code Article 191 was restored to its 1953 formulation and journalists were given the right to buy off sentences for minor infractions.[16] The journalists' union asked that the colonels' law on the profession be retained for a time as it gave them certain advantages in working conditions which had been added by the regime to offset measures of interference in union affairs. Eventually, the union negotiated the advantages bilaterally with publishers and revised its own constitution and bye-laws to get rid of the interferences and, in 1978, the dictatorship law on the profession was also abolished.[17]

Two attempts at press law reform under political governments, first by Under-secretary at the Ministry to the Prime Minister, Panayotis Lambrias, in 1975 and later by his successor, Athanassios Tsaldaris, in 1979, both encountered professional opposition and, at the time of writing, the Standing Legislation with its legal criteria introduced over the course of half a century continued to apply.

All the laws and drafts, both those of political governments and those of the dictatorship, have had a number of common concerns. These include regulations about the disbursement of duty free newsprint and the licensing and practices of distributors and vendors[18] and definitions of matters such as who may call himself a journalist. The fundamental criteria in every instance have been that the individual should be a Greek, enjoying his civil rights and not protected from assuming responsibility before the law through any parliamentary, diplomatic or other form of immunity. The laws carefully defined who was responsible when an offense was committed. By and large, this was shared collectively by the author, the publisher and the editor and, in some instances, the print room foreman and the distributor. Civil liability rests with the publisher and it is his responsibility to indemnify an individual or institution insulted or libelled. The laws stipulated the damages to be paid for 'moral injury.' The Standing Legislation set these at between 2,500 and 150,000 drachmas while the dictatorship's law, which sought to crack down on slights against the honor of the individual, upped them to 50,000 to 500,000 drachmas.

There were provisions guaranteeing public servants and government departments the right of denial, refutation or rectification and the ordinary citizen the right of reply regardless of whether a newspaper could demonstrate the accuracy of its facts. This right of reply guaranteed an offended individual or corporation the insertion of a text of equal length provided it was signed and 'free of punishable content.' If an editor deemed a reply to be legally unacceptable according to either the Press Law or the Penal Code, the burden of responsibility rested with him to demonstrate to a prosecutor or to a justice of the peace why it should not appear. It was then incumbent on the prosecutor to make the reply conform to the law so that it might be published. A prosecutor's ruling that a text should appear made its publication mandatory. The colonels effectively abolished the right of reply for former politicians but provided that 'the replies or contradictions of the Government and the Ministers ... are published irrespective of their length.'

A catalog of offenses has been common to all the laws and drafts. Obscene publications have been defined as anything offending 'common sentiment.' Forgery included both false texts or apparently genuine documents the contents of which have been altered. The colonels said that editing a text in such a way as to distort its meaning constituted forgery. Blackmail has been defined as a threat to publish something against a demand for a preferment, concession or emolument.

There has been concern to protect against invasion of privacy and constraints placed on the coverage of the reporting of court cases involving adultery, divorce, paternity, and other matters of morality. Publication has been prohibited of coroners' reports the contents of which 'might be offensive to good morals' (such things as rape and child molestation), the 'manner and execution' of suicides and the names of minors involved in court proceedings. The press has been forbidden to publish case documents before they have been presented in court and to report on *in camera* hearings or the deliberations of jurors. A contentious issue introduced by Metaxas and retained in all subsequent laws allowed that once an inquiry was underway and until there was an irrevocable order of committal, a prosecutor could ban all reporting of a case if he felt that publicity would hinder investigations. Theoretically this was a reasonable stricture designed to prevent the press from contributing to the escape of a criminal by providing him with vital information or from causing a miscarriage of justice by publishing details of the investigation of an individual later proved to be innocent. It has, however, been politically abused, even by elected governments. For example, in 1975 it was applied to coverage of the assassination of the C.I.A. station chief in Athens[19] and later it was invoked during investigations into a neo-fascist terrorist group agitating for restoration of the junta in which some of the individuals eventually arrested had Greek and American military connections.

Generally, there have been restrictions on military reporting in order to avoid breaches of security. Thus all unauthorized accounts of the composition and armament of the Forces have been forbidden together with unofficial reports about mobilization plans or details about intelligence gathering.

The dictatorship, however, was not satisfied with these constraints. It sought to realise Papadopoulos' concept of the 'function' by introducing legislation which would literally have made journalists an extension of the administration. While this was being prepared, blanket censorship was imposed and, even once a Press Law was in force, a range of Penal Code provisions continued to fall within the aegis of the martial law. This meant that for all but three months of the seven years that the dictatorship was in power there was always the possibility that journalists might be referred for trial before an extraordinary military tribunal with the especially severe penalties that entailed. Thus, journalists always practiced some degree of self censorship.

The actual mechanics of preventive censorship were founded in a tortuous web of legal measures. Article 91 of the 1952 Constitution allowed that in the event of a 'manifest threat to public order and to the security of the country from internal danger,' the king, on the recommendation of parliament, was empowered to suspend ten articles of the Constitution and to implement the Law on the State of Siege, commonly known as the martial law.[20] These articles governed civil liberties and included Article 14, together with three others ensuring that the individual be tried by his natural judges.[21] At 0643 on April 21, 1967, Armed Forces Central Radio announced that a Royal Decree[22] had been promulgated implementing the suspension procedure. The statement was fraudulent. The king had signed no decree and most of the cabinet who were supposed to have proposed it, including Prime Minister Panayotis Kanellopoulos, were under arrest.

The decree nonetheless triggered application of the Law on the State of Siege. Article 9 entitled the military 'to ban the announcement or publication of information in any way,' and 'to seize newspapers or printed matter either before or after publication, as well as to suspend newspapers for a certain period. . . .' The ban was instigated by means of a military proclamation broadcast by radio. It said simply, 'The announcement or publication of reports in any manner what-soever . . . without prior censorship is prohibited.' Article 10 made disobedience of such military proclamations an offense punishable 'by imprisonment imposed by military courts.' Fur-thermore, Article 5 said civilians could be brought before military tribunals for any offense 'against the security of the state, the regime or public order and peace.' This was principally designed to curb resistance activity but the law said the press was particularly liable to prosecution before courts martial if deemed to be involved in such activity. The formula-tion was sufficiently loose to allow wide latitude of interpreta-tion.

The Constitution required that the prorogued parliament be reconvened to ratify the decision within ten days and provided that the effect of the Royal Decree should terminate within two months unless extended by the Assembly. The colonels did neither. Instead, they indefinitely extended the martial law by means of two constituent acts.[23]

The censorship foreseen by Article 9 was to be carried out by a Press Control Service established by a decision[24] of the Minister to the Prime Minister, Col. George Papadopoulos. Its brief was 'the prevention of publication in the newspapers . . . and in all forms of printed matter of all general information or any comment or illustration or cartoon intended in any way to defame the general policy of the National Government or con-stitutional institutions, or to harm the internal or external security of the country.' It was also to enforce a set of General Instructions (see Appendix A) which compelled newspapers to publish government communiqués and Athens News Agency bulletins which included both factual information and editorial comment. Technically, such dictation exceeded the martial law mandate to ban information and seize newspapers which failed to comply but the colonels argued that a Revolution makes its own law.[25]

The Press Control Service was headed briefly by Papadopoulos' close associate Colonel Elias Papapoulos of the Military Judicial Branch. The task was taken over during the summer of 1967 by Colonel Constantine Vryonis, an expert in psychological warfare, who remained in the job until prior censorship was lifted. The Service had a staff of twenty civilians led by an elderly man who had obtained his training working as a censor for the Metaxas dictatorship. Its procedures were cumbersome. Each day newspapers were circulated with a list of banned topics together with the official texts of the articles and commentaries to be compulsorily printed. Once these were set, editors were required to present the Service with duplicate copies of page proofs. These were scrutinized minutely, right down to the classified ads and the crosswords, blue-pencilled as the censor saw fit and then one copy was returned to the paper so that it might 'conform completely with any excisions.' Blank spaces were forbidden. Because of the pressure of deadlines most newspapers assigned senior staff with editorial responsibility to this job in order to be able to negotiate changes with the censors on the spot. Once the paper had been put to bed, two printed copies had to be presented for final approval. When this was given, the representative of the newspaper would initial one copy for the ministry files and the Press Control Service would stamp the other for presentation to the distributors. Circulation was only authorized on presentation of this officially sanctioned copy. If, in the course of the print run, the Press Control Service changed its mind about something previously authorized, the entire elephantine procedure had to be gone through again and the original copies earmarked for pulping. Colonel Vryonis was notoriously indecisive, some editors believed consciously so as a form of harassment.

The Service supplemented the General Instructions with occasional additional written regulations. These concerned social as well as political issues. For example Number 314/H June 5, 1967 said, 'Newspapers should abide by the Greek Christian principles of the national government and abstain from publishing reports and photos referring to sexual crimes, photos of criminals and other persons of the underworld, as well as indecent photos under cover of presenting Greek and foreign artists.' More politically, on October 13, 1967, instructions were issued which said: 'Do not publish articles which show life in the Soviet Union or other Eastern Countries in a favorable light. Write nothing on the war in Vietnam which could be interpreted as anti-American. Refrain from any commentary on Greek political parties or their leaders.'

The majority of such *ad hoc* directives were communicated orally, either by the phone or during personal confrontations between Colonel Vryonis and editors. Every editor has a host of anecdotes about specific, unreasonable demands that were made but two prohibitions which applied to all papers are illustrative of the way in which the regime employed censorship to further its political ends. In mid-October 1967, the press was forbidden to publish news of the government's declared intention of holding a referendum on a new Constitution by August 1968. A statement to this effect had been made to the United States government by the Greek ambassador to Washington and had been published around the world in news agency accounts. Details of the ambassador's remarks were available in Athens through United States Information Service bulletins but, because the colonels were locked in a struggle with the king over the form of the Constitution, the domestic press was not allowed to carry the story in order that the regime might have greater flexibility of action than if publicly tied to a timetable. In the event , the referendum was held on September 29, 1968. The second example occurred in November 1967 when editors were told they could not publish texts from the Government Gazette unless they were also contained in official communiqués. This was designed to mask the extensive purge of royalists then going on in the military which would have become immediately apparent had newspapers been able to publish the regularly gazetted lists of early retirements.

The new ministerial instructions issued in the wake of the king's counter coup[26] (see Appendix B) reduced the amount of dictated material newspapers were required to publish but did nothing to change the legal regimen. Neither did application of the Constitution on November 15, 1968. Article 138, a special transitional provision, suspended the twelve Constitutional articles governing civil and political liberties, including Article 14 on the freedom of the press. Eleven paragraphs were implemented but the three vital ones guaranteeing freedom of expression, a free press and prohibition of censorship remained suspended. The Constitutional articles securing natural justice were also held in abeyance which meant there continued to be no protection against trial of civilians by court martial.[27] These suspended provisions were to be implemented at the discretion of 'the National Revolutionary Government' following the passage of eighteen Institutional Laws which would supplement by statute certain matters only adumbrated in the Constitution.

It was implied that the Press Law would be one of these, although a close reading of Papadopoulos' various pronouncements indicates that no firm commitment to this effect was made. Instead, relaxation of press controls evolved according to the procedure outlined in the 'friendly settlement' proposals put to the Council of Europe. The convoluted process began in autumn 1969 with the abolition of prior censorship but retention of controls by administrative decision. On September 30, Papadopoulos, in his capacity as Prime Minister, ordered[28] Chief of the Armed Forces General Odysseus Anghelis to limit the application of the Law on the State of Siege. Anghelis issued a proclamation which curtailed Article 9 insofar as it entitled the military to ban news. Henceforth, his proclamation said, the publication of news and commentary was 'free' although post-publication confiscation would still be permitted in those instances where publications: '(1) aimed against public order, national security and national integrity, (2) [shook] public confidence in the national currency or aimed at damaging the national economy, (3) aimed at reviving political passions by referring to the past prior to the Revolution of April 21.'[29] Papadopoulos then issued detailed instructions to the Directorate General for Press and Information, spelling out extensive specific restrictions.[30] These covered all aspects of reporting on security, politics and economic matters (see Appendix C). Coincidentally, acting in his capacity as Minister of Defense, Papadopoulos issued orders to the Military Judicial Branch[31] which limited the jurisdiction of military tribunals to six offenses under the Penal Code,[32] three offenses under Emergency Legislation[33] and all offenses governed by Article 5 of the Law on the State of Siege. The Press Control Service was abolished[34] but newspapers were required to deposit three copies – 'immediately after the start of circulation' – [35] with the Directorate where the staff carefully scrutinized them to see whether they contained any breaches of Papadopoulos' strictures which might give cause for seizure and prosecution. The inclusion of the elastic Penal Code Article 191 among those which could be heard by military tribunals meant that the regime retained an ample stick with which to beat the press if it felt in any way threatened.

Although Papadopoulos' executive controls were replaced by the Press Law on January 1, 1970, this did not, as had been imagined, have the effect of bringing into force the three suspended paragraphs of Article 14 guaranteeing press freedom. Papadopoulos' instructions to the Military Judiciary remained.

These were modified on April 19, 1970 by further pronouncements which substantially reduced the scope of the application of the Law on the State of Siege. Anghelis revoked his reporting strictures and introduced in their stead prohibitions aimed specifically against 'the practice of propaganda.' These banned oral or written propaganda, the possession of radio transmission equipment without military authorization and the possession of presses, photocopiers or duplicators which had not been licenced by the police.[36] Papadopoulos, again in his capacity as Defense Minister, issued fresh orders[37] further curtailing the competence of the extraordinary military tribunals as regards press offenses. They were now limited to crimes under Article 52 of the Press Law which referred to the 'revival of political passions;' the emergency legislation outlawing communism, Law 509/47; and Article 5 of the martial law. This last still gave latitude for interference but, theoretically, the arrangement left the press legally free to publish anything except political, particularly communist, views. Papadopoulos, returning to his metaphor of Greece as a patient in plaster, described this legal construct as 'a light walking cast.' The Law on the State of Siege, he said, was 'striving for breath, dying, trying in vain to stand on its feet.'

The general scope of the martial law was further curtailed a year later so that it applied only to thirteen specific offences under the Penal Code.[38] As far as the press was concerned, this move was arguably retrograde, for it was affected by six of the thirteen articles[39] and the notorious Article 191 which had been removed from the aegis of the military tribunals a year earlier was restored. Papadopoulos nevertheless argued that this arrangement reduced martial law to 'a mere shadow' and Byron Stamatopoulos, the new Under-secretary, went on record saying that henceforth no press offense would be heard by a military tribunal. To give the regime its due, none were, but the martial law still cast a long shadow.

The process of dismantling the Law on the State of Siege began on January 1, 1972 when it was lifted through the country except for the prefectures of Salonika, Athens and Piraeus[40]; on December 18, 1972, it was lifted in the northern capital as well.[41] In Athens, the seat of the national daily newspapers, it remained in force until after the referendum on the republic which confirmed Papadopoulos as president. It wasn't until August 19, 1973 that the amended version of the 1968 constitution was implemented[42] and the Law on the State of Siege finally lifted.[43] The amendments allowed that in the event of internal unrest, martial law could be imposed and extraordinary tribunals established solely by presidential decree,[44] and this is exactly what Papadopoulos did three months later when he reapplied the Law on the State of Siege on November 17, 1973 in an effort to quell the Polytechnic rising.[45]

The law imposed on this occasion was a modernized version of the 1912 text. It had been published as an Institutional Law on January 1, 1971[46] but held in abeyance by a government decision as long as the original version remained in force. Where the new text concerned the press, it was similar to its predecessor. Article 7 allowed the military to 'forbid the issuing and publication of information in any way, even through the press, and [to] suspend newspapers for a definite period.' This corresponded to Article 9 of the former law, although an ancilliary provision required publishers of suspended publications to continue to pay their staff for up to two months instead of for only one month as previously had been the case. Article 10 of the new law provided that military courts had jurisdiction over offenses involving security, the regime, the social system and public order. Again, this was almost identical to Article 5 of the old law although it reinforced the anti-communist element by the inclusion of offenses against the social system. What was decidedly different was Article 12 which said that trials before military tribunals could be heard *in camera* if, in the opinion of the court, 'publicity would be harmful to national interests or to the social system, the armed forces or public order.' This provision could have been used to prevent the press from reporting resistance cases where allegations of torture were made against the military or where political figures sought to use the court room as a forum in which to make political statements.

Restoration of the Law on the State of Siege was followed rapidly by the requisite proclamations from Commander of the Armed Forces, General Dimitrios Zagorianakos. These prohibited publications likely 'to cause anxiety or fear ... or to disturb public order,'[47] banned the dissemination of information liable 'to cause uneasiness or fear to citizens ... or aiming in any way to project or spread the views of political organizations and parties,'[48] and permitted the re-establishment of prior censorship and confiscation before and after publication.[49] Special courts martial were re-established[50] and Undersecretary at the Ministry to the Prime Minister, Spyridon Zournatzis, issued instructions to Armed Forces headquarters asking them to have all local commanders set up military censorship services. These had scarcely begun to function when the Papadopoulos government was overthrown by Brigadier Ioannides.

He dispensed with the censors but gave publishers the threatening option of either co-operating or being closed. An example was made of *Vradyni* which was arbitrarily shut down, the legal justification being provided only six weeks later in the form of a backdated martial law decision. Application of the Law on the State of Siege was extended indefinitely.[51]

Rule of law was only restored following the military's handover of power to the Karamanlis government and even then for a period of months the situation remained anomalous. The National Unity Government declared all civil liberties to be guaranteed and introduced general measures of amnesty for all political prisoners but did not immediately lift the Law on the State of Siege because of the 'exceptional external conditions' caused by the Cyprus crisis. The press was unaffected except for *Apoyevmatini* which was confiscated on August 14, 1974. It had carried a front page headline reading 'War on all fronts' which, although it referred to the Turkish invasion of Cyprus, was deemed likely to cause domestic alarm.

On August 1, 1974,[52] the 1952 Constitution was reinstated; it was restored fully to force on October 10, 1974 when the Law on the State of Siege was finally lifted and elections were declared. On June 7, 1975, a new Constitution drafted by the elected Karamanlis government was adopted by 208 votes. All the opposition members in parliament abstained because of fundamental objections to provisions governing civil liberties which they deemed too restrictive. Among those about which they complained was Article 48 on the implementation of the Law on the State of Siege. It allows the President, in the event of internal dangers, to proclaim martial law solely on the recommendation of the Prime Minister and to rule by decree for thirty days without parliament's consent.

The colonels' manipulation of the Law on the State of Siege to make possible the prosecution of journalists before courts martial was one of the hallmarks of the dictatorship. That this 'shadow' of martial law was necessary for the preservation of the regime was amply demonstrated by what happened when it was lifted during the abortive attempt at creating a guided political regime. The press felt at liberty to speak again and, even if it did so tentatively, in the knowledge that Ioannides waited in the wings, its limited dissent helped create the climate which led to the incidents that precipitated the Polytechnic occupation and began the downfall of the colonels.

The maintenance of even limited controls was one of the features which denied the regime acceptability in the international community. Papadopoulos, who understood perhaps better than any of his colleagues the political value of appearing to function within the law, made two attempts to introduce press legislation which would have got around the need for coercion. This would have been accomplished by

purging the press community of those who did not support the
regime and, for those who remained, creating a legal
framework which would have required them to act as
'functionaries.' The measures were contained in a Draft Press
Code and in a bill on the profession of journalism produced in
1971. These proposals were thwarted by press and political
pressures but the regime's intention of extending the
administration to embrace the press was certainly demonstrated. Even the manner in which the bills were drafted was
typical of the way in which the regime went through the form of
consulting the citizenry ultimately producing legislation of its
own design.

The process was instigated in January 1968 with the
establishment of the two committees on the functioning of the
press and on the profession of journalism under Constantine
Roubanis, vice-president of the State Legal Council. Each
included a legal counsellor from the Ministry to the Prime
Minister, two specialists in press legislation and a spokesman of
the proprietors' and journalists' unions. The proprietors' representative on the press committee was Nassos Botsis of
Acropolis and on the committee for the profession, George
Athanassiades of *Vradyni*. The respective journalists' representatives were Costas Zafiropoulos and Panayotis Troumbounis
both of *Eleftheros Kosmos*. They were all noted conservatives
but equally they were working journalists with an interest in
practical legislation. They could not have fathomed what
Under-secretary Constantine Sideratos wanted when he
instructed them to establish 'the press' *social function* within
the limits which prevail in all civilized nations.'[53] It was quite
inconsistent with Roubanis' declared aim of 'safeguarding the
freedom of the press while at the same time protecting the
citizens from the abuse of that freedom.'[54]

There were confused accounts about the committees'
progress as witnessed by the conflicting timetables set out for
Max van der Stoel of the Council of Europe, but it seems no
actual drafting was undertaken until after ratification of the
Constitution in November 1968 for the simple reason that no
one could be certain until then what its precise provisions
would be. Then, work proceeded quickly and, by January

1969, the committee on the press had produced a 69 clause bill which codified many of the provisions of the Standing Legislation. Appended to it were a pair of memoranda, one from journalists and the other from the ministry in which each set out how it would like to see the agreed text modified. The journalists wanted to include expansive provisions such as a public right to know, guaranteed free access to information, and a Press Council for self-regulation of the profession. The ministry wanted to include restrictive measures such as deposits for prospective publishers, increased penalties for press offenses and tougher controls on the publication of confidential documents.

A similar procedure was followed with the law on the profession although this was delayed because of fundamental disagreements. The Ministry to the Prime Minister insisted on the establishment of a register of qualified journalists which it would keep. The journalists' union did not oppose the principle of a register because this would provide it with a legal means of controlling the numbers it would have to enroll but it wanted to be the agency which kept the register in order to ensure that only professional selection criteria were applied. The impasse was unresolved when the drafts and their accompanying documents went forward to the government in May 1969.

Only then was it learned that Constantine Georgopoulos, a professor of constitutional law who was one of the principal architects of the regime's Institutional Laws, had been working on a draft which combined both strands of the committees' work in a unitary Press Code. Roubanis rowed with the Alternative Minister to the Prime Minister, Ioannis Agathangelou, and retired early. How many of the committees' recommendations were finally incorporated into the bill is unclear. A committee member has insisted that their drafts were 'democratic.' The Draft Press Code that was eventually published was so repressive that Papadopoulos' proponents tried to imply that it had been imposed upon him by regime hardliners. By his own admission though, it had his full authorization. A month before publication, Papadopoulos told the journalists' union executive, 'I have the texts of the law. I have studied them and your memorandum and I have given instructions to the

Alternate Minister to the Prime Minister [Ioannis Agathangelou] and I shall have the final text.'[55]

The Draft Press Code gave the government powers to purge the profession of all those politically opposed to the regime and to exercise financial controls over newspaper enterprises such as might be applied to public corporations. The Journalistic Register was to be kept at the Directorate and it was to be an offense punishable by imprisonment for a publisher to employ an unregistered person or for a journalist to work without being inscribed. Persons practicing the profession at the time the Register was established were to be vetted by a five-man committee headed by the Secretary General of the Ministry (Papadopoulos' brother Constantine) and those not recognized for registration were to be mandatorily dismissed from employment. In addition, the committee was empowered to include contract government press officers. This was a prelude to the creation of Georgalas' proposed National Propaganda Service and would have dovetailed with the special courses to have been given at a proposed school of journalism.

The initial selection completed, a permanent body, the Committee for the Recognition of Journalistic Capacity, was to be established to scrutinize all future candidates. It was to have its seat at the Directorate and its permanent rapporteur was to be the Director General for Domestic Press (who was then Major Christos Vamvakas, a close associate of the junta). Before candidates could get a hearing by this committee, they had either to have a year's training as an apprentice or a diploma from the school of journalism. The Minister to the Prime Minister (George Papadopoulos) was to designate how many apprentices could apply each year and, as well, decree all the criteria for the journalism school such as its curriculum and hiring policies. The decisions of these committees constituted 'executable act[s] of the Administration' and were 'subject to contestation before the Council of State', as is the case with government decisions concerning civil servants.

Discipline was to be maintained through a restructured union hierarchy which was to be reorganized into five categories: owners and publishers of daily newspapers, owners and publishers of periodicals, journalists of daily newspapers, journalists of periodicals and press employees (clerical staff, translators, etc.). The Minister was to have the right to define the catchment area of a local as well as the power to order mergers and splits. The locals were to draft their own charters, adopt their own regulations, elect their own administrative and disciplinary councils and operate their own systems of registration and expulsions but the Directorate was to be advised of all relevant decisions was well as of all elections and assemblies. Generally the locals were 'under the supervision of the appropriate minister in charge of press matters.'

The locals were to be formed into five national Federations which in turn were to be formed into a General Confederation of the Greek Press headquarters in Athens. Its Council was to be a seven-man body composed of a member from each of the Federations plus two academicians, one of whom would be the chairman. The minister was to appoint the Council of the Confederation, ratify its charter and supervise its activities. The Council was to draft a Code of Ethics for the profession within a year of the law coming into force. Union membership was to be mandatory and any journalist seeking to resign would be removed from the Journalistic Register and thus lose his professional capacity. At the local level discipline was to be enforced by three-member councils elected from among union ranks; the Federations were to have five-member committees with three journalists named by the General Confederation plus a civil and a criminal judge named by the judiciary; and the Confederation was to have a Supreme Disciplinary Council composed of an academician, a legal expert, a representative each of publishers and journalists and a chairman who was to be a vice-president either of the Council of State or the Supreme Court. Appointment of the chairman was the prerogative of the Minister and a senior Directorate employee was to act as secretary. The quorum for this Council was three, meaning that a hearing could go head in the absence of journalistic representation.

Disciplinary action could be instituted by the Minister, the union, a union member or 'any third party having a legal interest.' The range of offenses was extensive and remarkably ill defined, including such charges as displaying 'lack of faith in and devotion to the motherland and the national ideals' and 'improper conduct outside the field of professional work adversely reflecting on the dignity of the corps of journalists and of press employees.' Breaches of the Code of Ethics would be considered particularly grave. Penalties ranged from reprimands through fines to deprivation of the right to exercise the profession. Each offense was to be written into the Journalistic Register and one of the criteria for being banned from the profession was three convictions within two years for the same infraction no matter how minor.

This government supervision of journalists was to be matched for proprietors by state scrutiny of their accounts. With the exception of *Vradyni,* all the major press enterprises were, at this stage, private companies which did not have to publish figures. The draft provided for the establishment at the Directorate of a Committee for the Financial Audit of Publications which was empowered to demand information from any individual, company or state office. It was to be composed of a chairman from the State Audit Council together with four members, one each from the Bank of Greece, the press Directorate, the Athens Chamber of Commerce and Industry, and the State Corps of Auditors. Newspapers were to be required to draw up balance sheets each January and submit them to the Committee together with supporting documentation. This done, the newspaper was to publish the accounts together with any remarks made by the Committee. A balance sheet found to be false or inaccurate would be referred to a prosecutor for criminal investigation and the owner, publisher and financial manager were liable to prosecution. Conviction carried a penalty of imprisonment of up to six months, a fine and the lifting of the right to duty free newsprint for up to one year. In a measure aimed specifically at communists, the law said that 'the concealment of income from abroad constitutes a particularly aggravating circumstance when the penalty is determined.'

To ensure that business concerns could not buy favorable press copy, the draft made it an offense punishable by imprisonment of up to two years for anyone to 'advertise any economic enterprise through news reports for personal gain, material or otherwise' and to prevent newspapers currying favor with industrial concerns by offering them discount advertising rates. The draft also required newspapers to set a price list twice a year and to place this on deposit with the Directorate. Only the Audit Committee would be authorized to allow changes within the half yearly period. Persons found guilty of doing special deals faced imprisonment of at least three months, plus a fine and the loss of duty free newsprint for up to a year.

Needless to say, publication of the draft infuriated journalists and publishers alike. The normally quiescent journalists' union denounced it as a humiliating document which aimed at 'subjugation of the journalistic function to a state agency.' It reiterated that there was no objection to the idea of a register but said that to put it under 'the complete and misguided control of the Directorate ... implies policing of the profession.' It claimed that the Code paid no attention to the committee drafts and complained, 'Whoever drew up the [present] law seems completely ignorant of the conditions of the functioning of the journalistic profession and gives evidence of hostility and malice towards it.'[56]

Thirteen press organizations united in a joint appeal to the Prime Minister calling for the establishment of another committee to draw up fresh legislation. The government refused but did say that it would consider all useful and reasonable suggestions to improve the existing draft. On September 24, the thirteen submitted a joint memorandum which Alternate Minister Agathangelou said would be taken into consideration in the final formulation. When the law was eventually published on November 15, he claimed that the cabinet had devoted more than thirty hours in three sessions to the amendment process. It is difficult to imagine why because essentially all that happened was that matters relating to the organization of the profession, such as the Journalistic Register and the new union structure, were hived off to be dealt with at a later date.

The majority of the offenses contained in the Press Law (L.D. 346/69) were also to be found in the Standing Legislation although in the regime's version the penalties were consistently stiffer.

Three new offenses had been added concerning
'journalistic accuracy' although they bore no relation to truth in
any objective sense of the word, instead defining inaccurate
news as anything which was critical of the regime. Article 57 for
example, made it incumbent on journalists, editors and
publishers to 'check ... with diligence' the authenticity of their
reports and the reliability of their sources. The offense,
however, lay not in publishing false news but rather in
publishing the wrong news – 'news ... of such a nature as may
cause the disturbance of public order or diminish the stature of
any persons. ...' The penalty was imprisonment of up to five
years and a fine. Similarly, Article 71 made it a crime to publish
'information or rumors that can shake public confidence in the
national currency or the economy.' Again, this was not a
prohibition against the publication of incorrect economic data
but a proscription of information which did not square with
regime pronouncements. It was, in fact, antithetical to the
accuracy which the law purported to pursue. This offense was
punishable by a minimum of six months imprisonment and a
fine. Finally, Article 70 made it an offense to publish headlines
which did not correspond precisely to their story. It was
intended to stop the use of trick headlines but the manner in
which it was used in a prosecution of Ioannis Horn of the
Athens News,[57] illustrated what an effective political weapon it
could be. The penalty for the offense was also a staggering
minimum six months imprisonment plus a fine.

There were also two new articles containing overt political
strictures. Article 52 made it an offense punishable by a
month's imprisonment to promote the former parliamentary
system or the politicians who participated in it and Article 49
made it a felony punishable by up to twenty years imprisonment to publish anything aiming at provoking rebellion or over-
throwing the established constitutional order, a form of words
meaning anything to promote communism.

The law retained the provision concerning the Committee
on the Financial Audit of Publications but, although its
members were appointed, they held only one meeting at which
they took notice of the provision of the law that 'details of the
operation of the Committee and of the remuneration of its

members ... are determined by a joint decision of the Minister competent for the press and the Minister of Finance. ...' As this was never forthcoming, the Committee never met again, although the threat of its activation remained. The law also had incorporated new provisions pro-rating newsprint duty relief to circulation. These economic accretions were clumsy additions to what was otherwise a tidy, albeit restrictive, piece of legislation. When the press complained that in many respects the Law was more severe than the condemned Draft, Deputy Premier Pattakos snapped back, 'Severity is the mother of justice and freedom. ... For those who do no wrong, no laws are necessary.' The Press Law entered into force on January 1, 1970.

Legislation on the profession was reworked and on July 12, 1971 a new 33 article Draft Law was unveiled by Georgalas and Minister without Portfolio Loukas Patras. It sought to introduce measures of control like in kind although different in form to those of the original Code. The idea of the Register was abandoned but a new vetting system was devised through membership of the journalists' union. Membership was to be compulsory but subject to a loyalty test. These tests of national mindedness (ethnikofrosini) had been introduced during the civil war to ensure the loyalty of persons applying for positions in the civil service and associated fields such as the law and education. They required the individual to provide a complete resumé of his political background, to abjure communism as subversive and treasonous, and to commit himself to 'national obligations and duties as they are determined by law.' Ordinarily the checks were administered by the police who, after confirming the facts, made their own evaluation of the individual's political orientation and, if they approved, issued the certificate. Under the draft legislation, the assessment for journalists was to be made by a three-member committee of union representatives to be established by order of the Minister. Successful applicants, once enrolled in the union, were to be issued with membership cards that had to be certified annually by the Minister. The union and the government were to be empowered to demand a new loyalty test each year and judgment as disloyal meant the witholding of certification. Non-certification meant removal from the union. Publishers employing disqualified persons were liable to a minimum of one month's imprisonment while journalists using an uncertified card faced imprisonment of up to six months.

Journalists were to practice their profession according to a Code of Ethics designed to ensure they performed their 'public function.'

He shall perform the task entrusted to him conscientiously and with diligence, endeavoring to uphold truth and justice. Nobody shall be obliged to write inaccurate reports or reports manifestly tending to impose views which are illegal or against the public interest.

He shall observe a proper decency and moderation of expression and show proper solidarity with his colleagues, always having in mind that his task is an educational one.

In performing his task he shall serve the interest of the people and the nation and shall be inspired by Greek Christian traditions.

He shall perform his task with complete freedom while realizing that individual rights and freedoms should not impede the enjoyment of the same rights and freedoms by other citizens or groups of citizens.

Insofar as he is performing a public task, he shall not serve illicit, private or other interests with malicious intent, nor shall he use his status to the detriment of third parties.

He shall not make use of information in his possession the publication of which may be detrimental to the public interest.

The publication of texts or use of his journalistic status for purposes other than the enlightenment of public opinion and exercise of the public mission of the press shall be incompatible with the journalistic profession.

To enforce this code and to monitor professional conduct generally, there were to be Councils of Honor comprised of judges sitting together with journalists handpicked by the Ministry to the Prime Minister. The Councils were to have civil service secretaries and to be financed by the government. The Councils were empowered to enforce a graduated series of punishments ranging from warnings, through fines to suspension and finally exclusion from the profession. Many of the offenses admitting of suspension were either politically coercive or so nebulous as to allow no objective judgment. They included, for example, 'exercise of journalism in a manner contrary to the public interest' or 'in a manner contrary to the Greek Christian tradition.' The conditions for exclusion were those of the constitution – sedition, revelation of military secrets, projection of communist views – with the addition of a tautological provision taking its force from the law which said that a journalist could be excluded 'if it is evident from a series of similar acts that the culprit habitually behaves or exercises the journalistic profession in a manner contrary to the rules of journalistic ethics.'

Georgalas cunningly argued that the Code would give a journalist the legal means by which to confront an employer who might require him to write against the public interest as defined by the regime. It would 'liberate him from the belief that he is a "porter" of his publisher's wishes. . . . The bill enables the journalist to react against any deliberate attempt to distort the truth when he is required to overlook objectivity for the sake of opportunistic aims.' It was at this time that Georgalas was developing his thesis that publishers opposed the regime out of self interest and that journalists should throw in their lot with the government.

While the draft was before the mini-parliament, *Vradyni* obtained a copy and published it. It caused a furore which, because of the more relaxed nature of press controls at the time, became public. The publishers' union described it as 'unconstitutional.' Christos Lambrakis signed a front page editorial in *Vima* claiming that the draft aimed at 'The elimination of freedom of expression for journalists and the reduction of their status to that of a government propaganda employee.' The Union of Journalists of Macedonia and Thrace described the law as 'unacceptable . . . striking directly at the freedom of the press' and the Foreign Press Association, the members of which were also to be subject to the Councils of Honor, described it as 'contrary to international practice.' The sole voice of approbation was that of the Athens journalists' union which, before the full text was published, put out a statement welcoming provisions regarding the reduction of working hours. Once the full version became known, however, the membership convoked a special general assembly and forced the executive to endorse a statement decrying the Code of Ethics, the Councils of Honor and the state supervision of journalists. The provisions, the statement said, were 'unacceptable' and 'useless' and their application would 'lead to the ruin of journalists and their professional organizations.'

Confronted with this reaction, the regime agreed to modify some of the more extreme measures. To begin with, the closed shop provision was abandoned. Unions were still bound to register anyone who applied but the compulsion to apply was now removed. The loyalty tests were eliminated and the right restored to a union's executive to consider 'the general ethical standard of the applicant and his adherence to the norms of the journalistic profession.' Unions would issue their own professional cards, although these still had to be endorsed by the Minister. The Councils of Honor were abolished and the right of meting out discipline restored to the unions although the government insisted that the disciplinary committees should contain judicial representatives. A first instance disciplinary committee was to be made up of two journalists elected by the union's general assembly, sitting together with a lower court judge, while an appeal committee was to be composed of four journalists together with an appeal court judge. The catalog of offenses was extensive and included such things as an 'undignified mode of life which would be conducive to an unfavorable impression regarding the journalistic profession' and 'negligence in the exercise of journalistic responsibilities. ...' The penalties were similar to those of the Draft, although expulsion was now to be from the union and not from the practice of the profession. The specification that the minister for press might initiate disciplinary proceedings was dropped though the law allowed for instigation 'upon the request of anyone having a lawful interest.'

The Code of Ethics was replaced by a version of the draft International Code of Ethics for Information Personnel drawn up in 1952 by the United Nations Subcommission on Freedom of Information and the Press.[58] The regime, when discussing its law in public, laid heavy stress on the fact that it had employed the U.N. draft code, implying that it was thus a model liberal document. What the regime failed to mention, however, was that the U.N. draft code had been modified to give its moral suasions the force of law. The ultimate article of the U.N. version reads:

> This Code is based on the principle that the responsibility for ensuring the faithful observance of professional ethics rests upon those who are engaged in the profession and not upon any government. Nothing herein may therefore be interpreted as implying any justification for intervention by a government in any manner whatsoever to enforce observance of the moral obligations set forth in this code.

The regime's ultimate article, however, ended with the words 'observance of professional ethics rests upon those who are engaged in the profession.' Thus the essential condition that there shall be no government intervention to enforce moral obligations was abolished. Also, the recommendations of the U.N. code were rephrased in such a way as to make them legally binding. For example, where the code says journalists 'should' check their information, the law said that journalists 'shall be under obligation' to check their information.

The Greek version tellingly omitted the preamble which says 'freedom of information is a fundamental human right and is the touchstone of all the freedoms. . . .' It also dropped Article III which enshrines journalistic privilege – 'professional secrecy should be observed in matters related to confidence and this privilege may always be invoked to the furthest limits of the law.' The Greek law said only that 'journalists shall maintain . . . the secrecy dictated by the nature of the journalistic profession' with no acknowledgment that privilege might be invoked before the courts. This modified law (L.D. 1004) entered into force on November 1, 1971.

The colonels were proud of their press legislation and pointed to it as one of the accomplishments of their administration. It was a mark of the merit of their style of government, they argued, that they had succeeded in accomplishing a task which had for so long eluded the former politicians. What they failed to acknowledge was that the last government to successfully produce comparably comprehensive legislation had been the Metaxas dictatorship.

NOTES

[1] Legislative Decree 2493, July 31/August 1, 1953.

[2] The crime, according to the legal interpretation, lay in the knowledge of the falseness of the reports.

[3] Faith has a fiducial connotation referring to the ability of the State to meet its monetary obligations.

[4] The metallic drachma, now abolished, was worth about half the value of the ordinary drachma.

[5] Compulsory Law 230, Government Gazette 235, December 27/28, 1967. The junta's economic performance in its first year was abysmal. The rate of growth in G.N.P. dropped from 11% in 1966 to virtually nil in 1967 and the balance of payments which was presented to the public as being in surplus was actually in deficit, having been put in the black only by means of an accounting sleight of hand and drawings from a special gold reserve.

[6] Legislative Decree 372, Government Gazette 264, December 11, 1969. The government had the previous month cancelled its much criticized contract with Litton Industries which had been signed in May 1967. Under that agreement Litton was to have found $840 million worth of investment capital over twelve years in return for a fee and commissions. When the deal was called off, Litton had turned up only $3.5 million at a cost of about $3.25 million. Instead, in December 1969, the junta began to make overtures towards Aristotle Onassis and Stavros Niarchos about deals which were later to be even more contested, but because of these strictures, never in the press.

[7] Legislative Decree 735, November 28, 1970.

[8] Compulsory Law 790, December 31, 1970.

[9] Law 774, April 20, 1978.

[10] See George Krippas, 'European Press Law', Committee of Experts on the Mass Media, Council of Europe, Strasbourg, October 29, 1979.

[11] Law 5060, June 30/30, 1931.

[12] Compulsory Law 1092, February 21/22, 1938.

[13] These were superseded by Law 1072, Government Gazette 209, September 12, 1980.

[14] Legislative Decree 346, November 15, 1969/January 1, 1970.

[15] Legislative Decree 1004, November 1, 1971.

[16] Law 10, March 3/6, 1975.

[17] Law 780, June 3/6, 1978.

[18] The colonels' Draft Code proposed an innovation calling for printing works and news vendors to be registered with the police. In the case of the print shops, the text was careful to stipulate that this did not constitute prior authorization as that would have been an unconstitutional intervention in freedom of expression. 'The establishment of printing shops is free,' it said, but added that 'he who sets up a printing shop must notify accordingly and without fail the police authority of the district where he establishes it.' (Article 14) Interestingly, in the light of the constitutional position, no penalties were set out for failure to do so, although presumably the police could have acted to close the premises. Vendors, who had traditionally been licenced by the Ministry to the Prime Minister now were to register their names, addresses

and other details with the police before being enrolled on a government list of vendors. Failure to register was to be punishable by imprisonment of up to six months. The law eventually promulgated retained the registration of printing works but not of vendors.

[19] The editors of *Vima, Nea, Athinaiki, Acropolis, Kathimerini* and *Kyriatiki Eleftherotypia* all ignored the ruling and on March 15, 1976 were sentenced to four months imprisonment. The sentences were quashed on appeal but the court upheld the right of the prosecutor to impose such bans.

[20] Law 4069 Delta Chi Theta/October 1912 as modified by Legislative Decree 4234/1962.

[21] Article 8, the individual shall be tried by the court constitutionally assigned; Article 95, there shall be trial by jury; and, Article 97, civilians shall not be tried by extraordinary tribunals such as courts martial.

[22] Royal Decree 280, April 21, 1967.

[23] Constituent Act Beta, May 5/6, 1967 and Constituent Act Kappa Omicron, September 10/13, 1968. A discussion of the legal mechanics is found in 'A juridical swindle,' *Greek Report*, no. 3, April 1969, p. 23.

[24] Ministerial Decision 19603/Gamma, April 29, 1967. A parallel decision, 19602/Gamma, instructed regional military governors, in conjunction with the gendarmerie and prefecture officials to establish committees to censor their local provincial press. It said 'particular attention is drawn to the selection of the persons who will be carrying out the censorship service. They should be devoted to the National Government and have the appropriate and indispensable knowledge of grammar.'

[25] This *de facto* argument was given the force of legal precedent on October 25, 1968 when the Supreme Court rejected appeals to nullify the results of the constitutional referendum on the grounds that a Revolution which has prevailed establishes the right to create its own laws.

[26] Ministerial Decision E.P. 579/Lambda, January 25, 1968.

[27] Article 12, 'no one shall be removed ... from the jurisdiction of the judge assigned to him by law;' Article 111, 'press offenses fall under the jurisdiction of the regular criminal courts;' and, Article 112, on the creation of special tribunals.

[28] Order No. 447, September 30, 1969.

[29] Martial Law Proclamation 46, October 2, 1969.

[30] Ministerial Decision E.P. 980, October 3, 1969.

[31] Order No. 7000//00/25/1334, October 3, 1969.

[32] Treason (Penal Code Articles 134–137), secession (138), sedition (183–185), disquieting the public (190), dissemination of false information (191) and incitement to discord (192).

[33] Attempting to overthrow the established social order (Law 509/47), spying (Compulsory Law 375/36) and disclosure of information concerning defense installations (Compulsory Law 376/36).

[34] Ministerial Decision E.P. 987, October 6, 1969.

[35] Instruction A.P. 42170/Kappa/3181, October 7, 1969.

[36] Martial Law Proclamation No. 47, April 10, 1970.

[37] Order No. 700/00/44/367, April 10, 1970.

[38] Order of the Minister of Defense No. Fi-610/E.M. 170054, April 17, 1971.

[39] Sedition (Penal Code Articles 183–185), incitement to sedition (186), dissemination of false information (191), incitement to discord (192).

[40] Royal Decree 787, *Government Gazette 280*, December 31, 1971.

[41] Royal Decree 781, *Government Gazette 229*, December 18, 1972.

[42] Presidential Decree 155, *Government Gazette 181*, August 19, 1973.

[43] Presidential Decree 167, *Government Gazette 186*, August 20, 1973. The Athens Special Court Martial was formally abolished by Presidential Decree 218 of September 8, 1973.

[44] Motion on the amendment of the Constitution of November 15, 1968. Article 13. Ministerial approval was required to extend it for more than thirty days and parliamentary approval to extend it beyond three months.

[45] Presidential Decree no. 411, November 17, 1973.

[46] Legislative Decree 798, *Government Gazette 1*, December 30, 1970/ January 1, 1971.

[47] Martial Law Proclamation No. 1, November 17, 1973.

[48] Martial Law Proclamation No. 3, November 17, 1973.

[49] Martial Law Proclamation No. 6, November 18, 1973.

[50] Decision of the Minister of National Defense Nikolaos Efesios, November 17, 1973.

[51] Constituent Act 1, *Government Gazette 326*, December 17, 1973.

[52] Constituent Act, *Government Gazette 213*, August 1, 1974.

[53] Speech, January 5, 1968, my italics.

[54] Roubanis, 'A report [on] the Progress of the Work of the Press Committees,' p. 2.

[55] Statement to the E.S.I.E.A. executive, July 21, 1969, *To Pistevo Mas*, vol. Epsilon, p. 193.

[56] Communique, August 23, 1969.

[57] In October 1971, the *Athens News* ran a story on the visit of U.S. vice president Spiro Agnew headlined 'Bombs, recruited schoolchildren greet Agnew.' The paragraphs referring to these facts were missing from the story when the paper appeared having been, it was claimed, 'accidentally' dropped on the stone. Horn was charged in a civilian court with violation of Article 70 and sentenced to seven months imprisonment. The appeal process was allowed to drag on for eighteen months in hopes that the threat of imprisonment would force him to moderate the paper's opposition line but he continued. In February 1973, he flouted the ban on reporting the students' demonstrations; in March, he founded the periodical *Politiki Themata* (Political Topics), an early issue of which included an article by four former chiefs of the General Staff who called for the military to withdraw from power; and, in April, he reprinted the Karamanlis call for the colonels to resign. Within days of this last challenge, Horn was imprisoned. While inside, he was interrogated for five hours by military investigators about possible court martial under Article 191 of the Penal Code, despite the government's promise that no journalist would be tried by military tribunals. Horn was given an early release on grounds of ill health but the point had been made that the regime had many means by which to enforce its authority.

[58] There are remarkable echoes of the colonel's efforts to control the membership and practice of the profession in U.N.E.S.C.O.'s proposals to licence journalists and to create a code of ethics to govern their activity.

VIII NEWSPAPER ECONOMICS

The years immediately prior to the *coup d'etat* had been fat years for publishers. A circulation of only 20,000–30,000 was all that was necessary to break even and thereafter profit margins were high. A number of factors contributed to this including indirect government subsidies through state advertising, direct government subsidies through the provision of duty free newsprint and a preferential tax rate for press concerns.

State advertising contributes up to a quarter of newspapers' advertising revenues. National and local governments provide mandatory advertising such as the publication of accounts, compulsory notifications of expropriation and legal adjudications and there is extensive promotion of state supervised activities. The Ministry to the Prime Minister, through its numerous directorates and secretariats of sports, culture, tourism and public exhibitions, is responsible for advertisements covering subjects as diverse as horse racing, the state opera, casinos and agricultural fairs. In addition to these, there are advertisements by public companies such as the Public Power Corporation and the National Telecommunications Organization, banks such as the Bank of Greece and the

Hellenic Industrial Development Bank, state agencies such as the Social Insurance Institute, and lotteries such as the National and Popular. This major contribution to press finances traditionally provided governments with a means to favor friendly newspapers or to punish opponents. Governments denied it, of course, but long before the coup, *Le Monde* correspondent Marc Marceau, asked to investigate such allegations for the I.P.I., wrote,

> 'in the fourteen years that I have been in Greece, I have regularly seen various governments support friendly newspapers. It is simply a question of discrimination, regrettable certainly but, when all is said and done, difficult to prevent.'[1]

Direct subsidy through the alleviation of duty on newsprint is more open but also potentially subject to political manipulation. Virtually all paper used in Greece is imported and, as a non-essential item, it is subject to a high rate of excise tax. The grant of duty free newsprint was first introduced in 1905, selectively by ministerial decision though in 1911 the law required that the privilege be extended generally. Following the abolition of a Newsprint Allocation Committee in 1964, newspapers and periodicals were said to have an automatic right to duty free newsprint. Despite its political origins, proprietors said it was 'not a favor conferred on the publisher but on the reader and the recognition of the press' vital role in a country under development. Its purpose was to keep the price of a daily so low that even the poorest section of the population could afford it.'[2] Nonetheless it represents a substantial concession to publishers and is an essential feature in their production cost equation. The relief amounts to about a quarter of the total cost of newsprint and represents a subsidy of millions of drachmas a year for large circulation dailies.

Successive governments have argued that in order that this concession not be abused and the state not suffer too great a loss of revenue, the Ministry to the Prime Minister should retain powers to stipulate certain matters affecting the consumption of newsprint. These have included the type of paper, the size of page, the number of pages,[3] the print run relative to the number of copies sold, the number of allowable extras per year, sale price and procedures for pulping unsold copies. Many of these measures were first introduced in the period immediately following the liberation from the Nazis when the import of a non-essential such as paper was a true luxury in a nation of starving people. In the ordinary run of things, these controls are not an impediment to newspapers, although obviously they are a potential device for government interference. In May 1965, for example, Helen Vlachou, then riding high with her two large-circulation dailies, *Kathimerini* and *Mesimvrini*, complained to the I.P.I. that the Papandreou administration which she opposed was restricting the number of allowable pages in order to protect smaller pro-government newspapers. A March 1964 decision had reduced the fortnightly allotment from one hundred and thirty-two pages to one hundred and twelve pages. Mrs. Vlachou claimed that, convoy fashion, this reduced all newspapers to the level of the lowest and interfered with market forces which guaranteed freedom of the press. The Institute observed that the rationing of newsprint and its accompanying regulations 'are a real obstacle to the commercial development of some papers [and] in a sense this may affect press freedom, as the financial bases of these papers are weakened while the position of their competitors is protected.'[4] Equally though, their rapporteur pointed out that 'a certain multiplicity in the Greek press is thus guaranteed which would be justified in view of the party system which depends upon rather small personality groups and is itself therefore diverse.'[5] Successive press laws have allowed the courts to temporarily suspend the right to duty free newsprint for ten days to a year as part of the sentence for press crimes and the cost of such a suspension is usually far in excess of any fine.

The third major government aid to newspapers prior to the coup was a preferential tax rate. Introduced by a Karamanlis government in 1957,[6] it provided a separate schedule for newspapers based on circulation rather than income. No tax was payable on circulation up to 15,000 copies and thereafter increments were smaller than corresponding rates of corporation tax. If a newspaper chose to be taxed according to this schedule, distribution agencies merely declared the circulation figures to the revenue office which then automatically assesssed the tax payable. Thus, as well as being cheaper than ordinary tax, the system saved newspapers a great deal on administrative costs. They did, however, have the option of choosing to declare according to the ordinary scale of corporation tax. The book keeping required for this was extensive and the inspection rigorous. If an inspector did not like what he found he was empowered to assess an amount of taxable income. The option meant, however, that a paper which showed limited profits or a loss, either through low circulation or high overheads, could escape tax altogether whereas under the circulation scheme tax was payable regardless. Ordinarily, papers chose the circulation assessment and the difference between the tax according to this schedule and that payable according to the corporation tax rate constituted a handsome subsidy. To take a hypothetical example, a newspaper with a circulation of 100,000 copies could expect to pay 3,052 drachmas per day or approximately 936,964 drachmas per annum in tax according to the circulation scale, whereas if it made only a modest profit of ten million drachmas it would have had to pay tax of 4,752,400 drachmas under the ordinary schedule.

Figure 1. Newsprint duty payable according to Article 20 of Legislative Decree 346/69.

Circulation	% duty and ancillary taxes payable
0– 25,000	Nil
25,001– 50,000	50
50,001– 75,000	75
75,001–100,000	90
100,001– and over	95

The colonels, in their effort to curb the influence of the press, set out to economically emasculate it by systematically stripping it of all these privileges. The 1969 Press Law abolished the right to duty free newsprint and said that henceforth duty would be payable according to a scale pro-rated to circulation (see Figure 1). It was intended to be punitive and was designed to hit hardest at the large circulation opposition newspapers, but, according to George Aidinis, counsel to the Union of

Publishers of Daily Newspapers of Athens, the government had been badly briefed and didn't realize that the tariff then in force for newsprint was only 4.2%. When they learned this, they were furious and announced that a new rate of duty would also be set. Publishers anticipated 17%, comprised of 7% excise duty and 10% supplementary taxes, the maximum then allowable under international trade agreements to which Greece was a signatory. When the new rate was announced at the beginning of February 1970, it was set at nearly 100% of list price. Publishers immediately launched an appeal with the Committee on Customs Disputes which, not unexpectedly, supported the government. Its ruling was based on a spurious technicality by which it was claimed that Greek newspapers were printed, not on white newsprint, but on a special tinted luxury paper which was not covered by the international agreements. Appeal bodies upheld this ruling. Publishers' hopes were raised when, on May 1, new customs duty regulations were published defining newsprint by its 'normal and natural classification according to existing Greek laws and international agreements'[7] but, on July 6, Finance Minister Adamantios Androutsopoulos issued *ad hoc* instructions by telegram specially amending the tariff scheme for newsprint to make it subject to a so-called 'contraband duty' of 90–95%. Ordinarily such a rate would only have been applied in the event of someone fraudulently importing newsprint duty free by claiming that it was to be used to publish a newspaper and then using it for some other purpose. Press concerns were assessed duty at this punitive rate retroactively to February 1, 1970. The effect on the large circulation popular publications was to double their total outlay for newsprint (see Figure 2).

In anticipation of the 17% duty increase, publishers had put up their prices on January 1, 1970 by 50 lepta, from 1.5 drachmas to two drachmas, the first price increase in sixteen years. With the application of the new duty rate on February 1, they imposed a further 50 lepta increase, making a total price increase of 67% in six weeks. Pro-regime newspapers were able to keep their price at two drachmas because their low circulation rates meant that they were either exempt from duty or paying at the lowest rates. Expecting

Figure 2. Comparison of newsprint costs for the Lambrakis newspaper
group before and after the application of Article 20 of Legislative Decree
346/69 as supplemented by Customs Code revisions.

	Daily circulation at March 1969	Cost of newsprint	Taxes	Daily circulation at March 1970	Cost of newsprint	Taxes
Vima	43,322	8,396,366	—	36,485	7,767,001	3,416,050
Nea	126,432	22,674,743	—	93,901	23,421,297	19,226,474

improved circulation, Savvas Constandopoulos, publisher of
Eleftheros Kosmos, launched an afternoon newspaper,
Simerina (Today's [News]), but even cheaper prices could not
bolster the flagging sales of the pro-regime publications at this
time when prior censorship had just been removed. Taken
together, the papers which supported the colonels achieved
only about 15% of total sales and they continued to decline.
Nea Politeia's circulation dropped to as low as 7,900 a day by
the time it finally collapsed on June 30, 1972. *Simerina* had
plummetted from an initial high of 58,959 to a low of 9,984
before it too folded on January 7, 1974.

In contrast to this 'contraband tariff' applied to the press, the
regime passed in 1968 a special act[8] which allowed duty free
paper to be issued for the 'publication of historical archives . . .
or books on national subjects. . . .' This was designed specifically
to allow the government to import cheap paper to print such
publications as Papadopoulos' collected speeches and the
Papaconstantinou civics book. Similarly, in 1969, a law[9] was
passed providing that publications which 'contribute to the
raising of people's spiritual and moral standards' would be
authorized to print more pages per fortnight than the number
designated by the Minister. This was in anticipation of
Georgalas' proposed regime-sponsored theoretical journal, but
it never materialized and the three member committee appointed to oversee the legisation was never convened.

Newspapers which did not print on duty free newsprint,
whether of volition or through some court ban, were supposed
to be free of all countervailing measures of government control.
Theoretically, therefore, a publication which had had its duty
free privileges suspended could have made up for the loss of
subsidy by printing more pages to take in more advertising. The

Press Law took care to prevent this, however, by limiting publications printed on duty paid paper to a surface area only 30% greater than that set by the Minister for comparable publications using paper on which there was excise relief.[10]

The provision governing the number of pages was regularly violated and political governments usually turned a blind eye. The colonels, however, repeatedly used it as a device to warn erring publishers of the greater difficulties they might face if they continued to step out of line. The most calculated instance of this was on April 2, 1970, the day that the court martial verdicts were handed down on the *Ethnos* editorial board. The editors of six newspapers, including the pro-regime *Eleftheros Kosmos* and *Nea Politeia*, were simultaneously charged with breaches of the regulations governing the limits on the number of pages. All were sentenced to four months' imprisonment. The term was translatable to a fine but the conviction provided a psychological rap across the knuckles which let the papers know that there were many ways they might be liable to prosecution. During the year following the lifting of prior censorship, there was such an accumulation of these administrative offenses in court lists that in December, the government passed a newsprint offenses amnesty.[11]

Publishers repeatedly lobbied the Papadopoulos government for revocation of the punitive tariff rate but to no avail. It was only with the advent of the Ioannides regime that it was finally relaxed, ironically by Prime Minister Adamantios Androutsopoulos, the man who, as Papadopoulos' Finance Minister, had initially imposed it. By December 1973, rampant inflation had pushed up the price of newsprint to then record levels of sixteen drachmas per kilo. Publishers told Androutsopoulos that if the government wouldn't reduce the duty, then they would have to have an increase in sale price. Otherwise some of them would go bankrupt. Ioannides' administration, for which the curbing of inflation was a priority, was unwilling to see price rises so Androutsopoulos allowed a reduction of duty by 50% for a three-month trial period[12] and at the end of it abolished the duty altogether for a further trial period of three months.[13] By the time this order ran out in July 1974, the Ioannides government was too pre-occupied with other issues to pay the matter any heed and the duty remained suspended. Publishers' counsel George Aidinis stresses that this was 'not an act of goodwill' but was motivated solely by the desire of the Ioannides administration to be seen to be curbing inflation.

In tandem with the Press law which incorporated the new duty rates, the Papadopoulos regime introduced legislation which eliminated newspapers' tax privileges.[14] A simple four-article act abolished the option to be taxed according to circulation and said that, as of January 1, 1970, 'revenues of any nature . . . will be subject . . . to provisions of income.' Returns would not be accepted on trust; newspapers would have to go through the rigmarole of a full tax inspection annually. It has proved impossible to obtain actual figures to illustrate the effect of this but Alternate Minister to the Prime Minister Ioannis Agathangelou, when he made the bill public, gave hypothetical figures which indicated that newspaper taxes would increase five and six fold (see Figure 3). Tax exemption for newspapers was not justified, Agathangelou said, because it created a double standard, while the constitution provided that all Greeks were equal before the law and should contribute to public expenses according to their financial capabilities. 'Previously', cackled Pattakos in a statement to journalists the day after the law was gazetted, 'there was a dictatorship of the press. It had special privileges. Now on the basis of tax redistribution we have a democracy of the press.'

While, theoretically, the measure was equitable, the junta's

Figure 3. The effect of Legislative Decree 345/69 on the taxation of newspaper profits.*

Circulation	Tax according to L.D. 3787/57	Taxable Income	Tax according to L.D. 345/69	Percentage
50,000	290,000	4,224,000	1,920,000	(562)
100,000	960,000	(8,897,959)	4,870,000	(407)

*Athens News Agency Weekly. No. 43, November 11–17, 1969.
The figures in parentheses are my interpolated estimates. To be pedantic, these figures are loose. The figure of 290,000 drachmas represents an annual sum of tax for 340 issues and the figure of 960,000 the annual tax for 315 issues, whereas the average number of issues in 1969, the year of the example, was 307. This would make the figures 261,564 and 936,964 respectively. The tax from 4,224,000 in income should be 1,922,160 drachmas or, conversely, the taxable income producing 1,920,000 worth of tax should be 4,219,592.

application of it involved severe harassment of newspapers. Squads of tax men backed by armed police would descend on newspaper premises in lightning checks of accounts. The tactic was used effectively to kill *Ethnos* even before it was so savagely kicked into its grave by the court martial. *Vradyni* was repeatedly the target of such raids and an eyewitness to one of them recalls at least three dozen men entering the building with large sacks and sweeping into them whole shelves full of files. Athanassiades managed to stall paying what he considered to be an over assessment of 240,000 drachmas until the restoration of the Karamanlis government when he was let off by the courts. Christos Papoutsakis was not so lucky. As well as his beatings by the military police following the launch of *anti*, his finances, both business and private, were subjected to minute tax scrutiny. His architectural practice was the beneficiary of a number of internal family loans which were illegal according to the letter of the law and he was personally assessed half a million drachmas in back taxes.

The combined measures of increased duty and taxation obviously meant a significant drop in profits, particularly for the large circulation newspapers of the Lambrakis and Botsis groups. Both have refused to provide balance sheets to illustrate the effect, but *Eleftheros Kosmos* published an account (see Figure 4) in which it claimed that its profits for 1970 were slashed to just over a third of what they'd been the previous year. If the paper most favoring the regime was hit in this way, then the profits of the opposition publications were, presumably, much more sharply curtailed. '. . . The solution at which [the new law] aims,' said Agathangelou at its launching, 'is the freedom of the press; of course, not that freedom which coincides with irresponsibility and emanates from an intention of high profits in ignorance of . . . public interest.'

As well as these structural measures to curb press profitability, the regime resorted to selective state advertising and illegal interference with circulation to punish papers which stepped out of line. This was done particularly in the period immediately following the lifting of prior censorship. For a matter of weeks, the placement of government advertisements in all opposition newspapers was interrupted, a tactic which

Figure 4. Statement of profit and loss for *Eleftheros Kosmos*.*

Outgoings	1969	1970
General expenses	9,813,820	9,813,820
Wages	12,283,430	12,283,430
paper (without duty)	12,017,081	
(with duty)		20,429,037
Amortization	481,000	481,000
Interest	—	200,000
	34,595,331	43,207,287
Income		
Sales (at 1.5 drachmas)	18,575,601	
(at 2 drachmas)		24,705,549
Subscriptions	214,839	214,839
Advertising	22,197,329	22,197,329
	40,987,769	47,117,717
Profit before tax	6,392,438	3,910,430
Tax (according to circulation)	419,404	
(on income)		1,768,510
Net Profit	5,973,034	2,141,920

* The figures appeared in an editorial published on February 15, 1970 in which Savvas Constandopoulos explained to readers how he would be able to hold the price of the newspaper to two drachmas while other publications were raising their price to 2.5 drachmas. The figures are at variance with those which he provided in April 1977 when, in response to my questionaire, he claimed profits of 3,262,000 drachmas for 1969 and 5,960,000 drachmas for 1979. Queried about the discrepancy, his office replied that the costs of an advertising campaign for the launching of *Simerina* had subsequently been deducted from 1969 profits. No explanation was offered for the discrepancy in the 1970 figure. Perhaps the larger sum incorporates earnings from *Simerina* for the year. Nonetheless, the sample account presented here does graphically illustrate the theoretical problems created by the tax and duty increases. Equally the unsuccessful attempt to get actual figures adequately illustrates the practical difficulties of trying to get accurate financial information about the Greek press.

caused some to moderate their tone. The ban for them was lifted. For *Vradyni*, its economic stablemate *Naftemboriki*, and the *Athens News*, however, the boycott continued until the downfall of the dictatorship. George Athanassiades calculates that it cost him twelve million drachmas a year for five years, nearly two million dollars all told. Ordinarily such a boycott would have broken the newspaper but *Vradyni* was able to offset the loss in advertising revenue by improved earnings from circulation which increased threefold because of the paper's opposition stance. The same was the case for the *Athens News*.

Interference with circulation was not an innovation of the colonels but never before had it been practised so systematically. Between September 1969 and January 1970, the provincial sales of some anti-regime newspapers dropped by as much as 56% with the consequence that those of the smaller circulation pro-regime papers rose by up to 75%. The government refused to acknowledge its interference, instead attributing the problem to reader resistance. 'Quite obviously,' said Pattakos, 'readers are disgusted with these provocative headlines and have stopped buying the papers.' There is evidence to suggest, however, that the disruption originated within the military hierarchy. In an open letter to Prime Minister Papadopoulos on November 20, 1969, former Foreign Minister Evangelos Averoff, a man noted for his excellent military contacts, alleged that the disruption was carried out 'in compliance with strict verbal instructions issued by the local security authorities.' In an inquiry for the I.P.I., Armand Gaspard found several techniques being practised. Sometimes the gendarmerie would order a local distribution agency not to release opposition papers to specified villages. On other occasions, when the papers had already been released, local distributors were 'advised' to return unopened the bundles of those newspapers which 'do not serve the national interest.' In other instances street vendors were summoned to the local gendarmerie headquarters where a senior officer would 'ask' them to adopt a 'civic attitude' and to stop selling papers that were described as 'anti-national.' Resistance to such a request was countered by 'threats of vexatious bureaucracy.' Gaspard visited several provincial towns, including Larissa, Volos, Corinth, and Kiato, a sub-departmental capital on the Corinth-Patras road. He found that in none of these towns could he purchase *Vima, Nea, Acropolis, Apoyevmatini or Ethnos* and very rarely could he find *Vradyni*, whereas the pro-government papers were always available. At one provincial distribution center he watched how 'parcels containing forbidden papers are returned unopened to the central distribution agency as unsold material. The operation is carried out under discreet surveillance.'[15]

The proprietors of the affected newspapers repeatedly

lobbied the government demanding an end to this disruption. Each time they were fobbed off with an assertion that the government had nothing to do with it: if it was happening, it must be the work of overzealous officials. Thus a group of publishers, led by Lambrakis, indicated that they intended to take legal action against distributors under the new Press Law, Article 43, which made it an offense punishable by three months' imprisonment to interfere with circulation. On January 29, 1970, Papadopoulos received the proprietors individually and advised them not to waste their time. They would only find, he said, that the martial law still superseded all other and under it military commanders could ban anything they deemed dangerous. The following day, the report arising out of Gaspard's investigation was published by the I.P.I. and received worldwide publicity. The government dismissed it as 'lies and slanders,' but the wholesale interference did stop – not however before a typical incident involving *Ethnos*. It dared to print the I.P.I. report, as a consequence of which the regime sought to stop circulation of the paper but without a formal confiscation order. Police were sent from kiosk to kiosk advising vendors not to sell the particular issue while, at the same time, the press ministry insisted that there was no official ban on the paper. *Ethnos* staff set up a special stand outside their building and sold directly to the public nearly 20,000 copies. Persons who had heard of the paper's contents by word of mouth came from all over Athens especially to buy a copy.

One of the most contentious aspects of press finances under the colonels was newspapers' loans. Whether they came from state institutions or from commercial banks, they required government authorization. This was the province of the Monetary Committee, a standing body of which the current Minister of Co-ordination was always the president. Used by the government to control the money supply, one of its functions was to determine the levels and terms at which industry could borrow. In most sectors this was a general decision and the committee required no detailed knowledge of the individual loans contracted. In the case of newspapers, however, this only applied to short term working capital where a framework decision governed the limit to which newspapers

could discount bills of credit. Long term loans for capital investment were authorized *ad hoc*. Under the dictatorship, this
became a political act and, every loan of every kind required
prior authorization from the Ministry to the Prime Minister. For
a time, for example, *Vradyni* couldn't even discount bills.

The regime was remarkably candid about the element of
reciprocity it saw as implicit in any state aid. 'Inasmuch as a
paper accepts or requests the government's help and support,
it voluntarily renounces its real independence,' wrote Director
General for Press and Information Dimitrios Zafiropoulos.
'Logically speaking a paper that claims to be free and non-
conformist should, of its own accord renounce the kind of
support which inevitably implies certain obligations.'
Zafiropoulos claimed that the newspapers *Vima* and *Acropolis*
both had received attractive and generous loans through which
they 'managed not just to survive but to secure the most up to
date technical equipment.'

Details of the borrowings of the Lambrakis and Botsis
groups only came to light in September 1975 – after the
dictatorship – when a pro-junta lawyer defending a group of
military policemen accused of torture, alleged in court that the
two publishing groups had received loans of 80 million
drachmas and 415 million drachmas respectively. He claimed
that these had been obtained as a consequence of secret
collaboration between the newspapers and the colonels'
regime. The lawyer made his allegations to score a political
point, arguing that the press was hypocritical, taking money
from the regime while it was in power then attacking its supporters once the dictatorship had fallen. He said he was making his
accusation about the loans in open court in the hope of being
sued by the publishers because they would then be required to
produce documents concerning their alleged secret financial
dealings. Both newspapers admitted receiving loans for the
purchase of new printing plant and for the construction of
premises to house it. Lambrakis said he had received 35
million drachmas and Botsis said he had 50 million drachmas.
These figures were confirmed by the then Under-secretary to
the Prime Minister Panayotis Lambrias, who, in a public statement designed to calm the speculation surrounding the allega-

tions, broke with precedent and revealed details of the records of the Monetary Committee. He said that as well as the 35 million drachmas capital loan, the Lambrakis group had received 13.5 million drachmas at 'various other times' and that in addition to their 50 million drachmas, the Botsis papers received a further 6 million drachmas. Lambrias added that other papers had also received loans but as their probity was not at issue he would not reveal details.

Nassos Botsis served notice on all Athenian newspapers the day the lawyer's allegations were made, saying that he intended to sue for slander. He apparently did not follow through with the suit and declined to answer all questions about the loans except to say that they had been received 'on the basis of bank criteria.'[17] Christos Lambrakis, in a statement at the time of the allegations, counterclaimed that his application for a loan had been perfectly in order and that it had been the government which had acted illegally in delaying it. He said that his request to the Mortgage Bank had gone forward in June 1971[18] backed by the offer of 'guarantees of several times as much as the loan' and that the administration refused to authorize it for three years. It was only granted in April 1974 following a successful appeal to the Council of State which ruled that the refusal to approve the loan was illegal. Lambrakis did not sue the lawyer over the allegations of collaboration. Instead, comments made about the lawyer in the group's newspapers caused him to file suit for libel against the publishers and editors of Vima and Nea. In this suit, the court found the allegation that the paper had received its loan through collaboration with the dictatorship to be 'baseless' and said that the lawyer's tactics in making the allegation had been unethical. The group considered this to be sufficient vindication not to proceed further.

The collective effect of the economic measures introduced by the colonels was to change the nature of Greek publishing. They marked the end of the era of the private concern and the beginning of a corporate phase leading to the creation of a press industry. To compensate for the drop in profits, newspapers had to give over a good deal of space to advertising, making them much more creatures of the market place.

Since there was no longer any tax advantage in being private and the government would anyway require publication of accounts through the special Audit Committee established under the Press Law, publishers formed limited companies. This was advantageous in the light of the new tax provisions and limited liability at a time of extreme economic uncertainty. In 1970, Lambrakis formed a company holding *Vima, Nea* and all the group's other publications; Constandopoulos did likewise for *Eleftheros Kosmos* and *Simerina*. The Botsis brothers followed suit in 1972, although initially they placed only *Apoyevmatini* under the aegis of the company. Virtually all the papers publishing today are owned by corporations or trusts. The major exceptions are *Kathimerini* and *Estia*.

NOTES

[1] Marc Marceau, Letter to the I.P.I., August 1, 1960.

[2] 'Pressure on the Uncowed Press, Report sent from Athens ... by Greek members of I.P.I.,' *Greek Report*, No. 20/23, Sept.-Dec. 1970, p. 19.

[3] Originally set in fortnightly allotments leaving the daily number of pages to the discretion of the newspapers, this was modified in 1980 to weekly allotments set by ministerial decisions valid for three months to one year.

[4] Per Monsen, director of the I.P.I., letter to members of the executive of I.P.I., January 19, 1966. The Institute did not, however, conduct an inquiry as demanded by Mrs. Vlachou for fear of 'getting mixed up in Greek politics.'

[5] Dr. Viktor Meier, memorandum to the I.P.I., January 15, 1966.

[6] Legislative Decree 3787, October 11/12, 1957.

[7] 'Pressure on the Uncowed Press. . . .' *Greek Report*, No. 20/23, p. 20.

[8] Compulsory Law 618, *Government Gazette 261*, November 11, 1968.

[9] Legislative Decree 217, June 18, 1969.

[10] Legislative Decree 346/69, Article 22.

[11] Legislative Decree 770, *Government Gazette 279*, December 17/19, 1970.

[12] Legislative Decree 253, December 31, 1973.

[13] Legislative Decree 374, April 5, 1974.

[14] Legislative Decree 345, November 15/15, 1969.

[15] Armand Gaspard, 'Greece, The Independent Press in Serious Danger,' Zurich, The International Press Institute, January 30, 1970.

[16] Open letter to the I.P.I., February 17, 1970.

[17] Memorandum, n.d. (c. end-May 1977).

[18] Zafiropoulos' initial remarks about loans to *Vima* had been made in February 1970.

IX TRADE UNIONS

Journalists prior to the coup were overworked and underpaid.
Wages rates were so low that most had several jobs to make
ends meet and the unions which might have been expected to
be the vehicles for improvement seemed to be more concerned
with internecine rivalry. Union activity was hampered by a legal
theory which said that journalists did not have the right to sign
binding wage agreements because this would constitute
unwarranted interference in the constitutionally guaranteed
right of freedom of expression. Instead, salaries were set according to verbal agreements between the journalists' and
proprietors' unions. This principle was contested in the courts
in the early sixties and, in January 1964, an arbitration tribunal
awarded journalists their first ever national minimum wage.
Even this was achieved via an oblique process. The arbitration
court decision had to be endorsed by the Minister of Labor
and, when he accepted it and published it in the *Government
Gazette,* this gave the award the force of law. Publishers
appealed the decision right up to the cabinet but failed to
convince the centrist government of the day to reverse it. The
award set a rate for reporters of 1,600 drachmas (then $53)

per month during their first three years of service, rising to 3,075 drachmas per month after 21 years of employment, with a scale for deskmen ranging between 1,800 and 3,800 drachmas. Both proprietors and the unions are quick to point out that few people were actually paid such low rates and even the arbitration court which set the figure noted that at least two-thirds of all journalists received more. Yet the figure was indicative of an attitude about what a journalist's work was worth. Most had at least two jobs, working for a morning and an afternoon newspaper, or for a newspaper and the radio, or as a part-time journalist and a part-time press officer. A further agreement, signed in 1966 to clarify problems arising as a consequence of the mandatory pay scale, acknowledged in law the gyrations that some journalists had to go through to make a decent living. The minimum applied, the agreement said, to journalists working on a maximum of two newspapers, one morning and one afternoon. It was not to apply to those working on two morning newspapers, or two afternoon newspapers, or on three or more daily newspapers.

The organization of journalists' unions is fragmented. There are three covering journalists working on provincial dailies,[1] one covering journalists working on periodicals,[2] plus several others for clerical and printing staff. In 1967 there were two covering journalists working on the Athenian daily newspapers, the Union of Journalists of Daily Newspapers of Athens (E.S.I.E.A.) and the Union of Journalists of the Athens Press (E.S.A.T.).[3]

E.S.I.E.A., founded in 1914, was the established journalists union, with 495 members, comprising the majority of senior national daily journalists. E.S.A.T., with 446 members,[4] was the haven for all those who could not get into E.S.I.E.A. Because of the restrictions on collective bargaining, the unions existed principally to provide welfare benefits for their members and inequalities in these led to divisions in journalists' ranks. Members of E.S.I.E.A. together with their colleagues on the large Salonika dailies, were covered by a pension fund known by its Greek initials as T.S.P.E.A.Th., an organization which also administered the unemployment benefit fund for all journalists regardless of which union they belonged to. T.S.P.E.A.Th.

provided pensions averaging 3,525 drachmas a month. Over and above this, E.S.I.E.A. members got full first class medical care and supplementary benefits (a lump sum of up to 240,000 drachmas on retirement and a regular increment of up to 2,500 drachmas per month on their pensions) financed by the proceeds of a special Journalists' Lottery. This concession, granted to the union by the Metaxas government in 1936, involved an annual drawing for apartments and houses. It was highly lucrative, netting 36.4 million drachmas in 1966, 75% of which went to E.S.I.E.A.

E.S.A.T., by comparison, was a poor cousin. It had started life in 1935 as a union for journalists of non-daily publications from across Greece but by 1945 had taken in so many Athenian daily journalists who could not gain entry to E.S.I.E.A. that the union changed its name and charter. Because of a technicality, however, this inclusion of daily journalists in a periodical union meant that E.S.A.T. no longer qualified for the special legal characterization as a journalists' union and there were repeated court actions during the Fifties and Sixties contesting its legitimacy. E.S.A.T. members got pensions more or less equal to those of their E.S.I.E.A. counterparts through a fund for the periodical press but, despite repeated lobbying, they were excluded from the proceeds of the lottery. They also tried to improve their health care by obtaining access to a surcharge on advertising known as the *angeliosimo* but this went instead to T.S.P.E.A.Th. and to other press employee insurance funds. E.S.A.T. was able to offer a medical scheme but it was nothing like as extensive as that provided by E.S.I.E.A. Shortly before the coup, E.S.A.T. did get a government grant[5] to found a supplementary benefits scheme.

Journalists who could not gain entry into E.S.I.E.A. and who had to settle for the penurious E.S.A.T. alleged that E.S.I.E.A. excluded candidates in order to protect its privileged level of benefits by not diluting its resources. E.S.I.E.A. maintained that it limited membership because of its high standards. This is something with which the union has always been concerned because recognition as a journalist in Greece carries with it a great many perquisites, including substantial tax concessions, as well as travel and communications allowances. E.S.I.E.A.

members got free transportation on buses, trains and ships, free entry to all public entertainments and tax free passports. E.S.A.T. members got some of these concessions but not others. For a time there were reductions for all journalists on import duties on cars but these were abolished by the colonels. The most substantial allowance was a 25% reduction in income tax up to a maximum of 50,000 drachmas annually. This was introduced by the Karamanlis government in 1955. On December 18, 1971, Papadopoulos announced that this was to be extended. 'For my friends the journalists, the tax free amount of salaried income, regardless of amount, will be exempted up to 50%. . . .' This was subsequently modified so that only 50% of taxable income up to 400,000 drachmas and only 75% of income up to 800,000 drachmas needed to be declared. Thus a journalist making 800,000 drachmas a year would declare only 500,000 drachmas and pay tax of 124,400 drachmas as opposed to 250,400 drachmas.

Above all, however, journalists have an access to bureaucrats and politicians which is denied to ordinary citizens and, in a society where so much business is conducted by personal petition and patronage, this was of inestimable worth and has traditionally made journalists highly influential even if not well-heeled. E.S.I.E.A. has been at pains over the years to exclude from membership those persons who seek the title of journalists solely for the perquisites and the influence. E.S.A.T., it is true, did attract many second-rank journalists and hangers-on such as public relations men. It had also acquired a leftish tinge because E.S.I.E.A. was particularly rigorous about admitting communists to its membership. Equally, however, E.S.A.T. included among its members senior conservative journalists such as *Mesimvrini* editor Panayotis Lambrias who simply could not penetrate E.S.I.E.A.'s exclusivity. Given the opportunity to join E.S.I.E.A., most journalists readily abandoned E.S.A.T. The 'big union,' as it was known, regularly used to raid E.S.A.T.'s ranks for its new recruits. E.S.A.T. thus came to be seen as a corridor into E.S.I.E.A., a fact particularly galling to E.S.A.T. executives who were trying to build up the union as a viable alternative to E.S.I.E.A.

The unions' singular concern with money matters created a mentality which precluded them from providing a focus of opposition to the regime. It was epitomized by an incident on the morning of April 22, 1967 during the session at which Farmakis outlined the rules of censorship to political reporters. When he finished, Farmakis asked the group's spokesman, Panayotis Troumbounis, who was also vice-president of E.S.I.E.A., if there were any questions. 'None,' Troumbounis is reported to have replied, 'but now that there is a dictatorship, will the government please prohibit publishers from requiring journalists to work after midnight.' Obviously this was an important concern for men doing two shifts, from six a.m. until noon on an afternoon paper and from six p.m. until midnight on a morning, and the union official who got guarantees against enforced overtime would be well regarded, but to pursue it at the expense of freedom of expression was typical of the way in which moral considerations repeatedly took a back seat to monetary concerns.

The E.S.I.E.A. leadership chose a policy of accommodation with the colonels. Shortly after the coup, the regime disbanded 280 unions and replaced the executives of many others with their own nominees. It was argued in E.S.I.E.A. councils that, rather than have this happen, it would be more practical to work with the junta to obtain what advantage could be had through compromise. The decision did not mean approval of the dictatorship; it just meant that they were being realistic in the face of it.

Similarly, the closure of so many newspapers which threw many journalists out of work meant that those remaining in jobs acquiesced in press controls more readily than they might otherwise have been expected to have done. That is not to say that they accepted them but, mindful of the need to eat, they did less to oppose them than many would have, had they had the security to be able to do so. Some journalists were notable for their outspoken opposition but, by and large, they were those with other means. One such was Chris Economou, a constant scourge of the E.S.I.E.A. leadership and its compromising stance. He was roundly applauded when he spoke out at a union General Assembly in 1969 saying, 'I would a thousand times rather sell shoes than serve the junta.' But then, his wife ran a profitable shoe store. This is not to denigrate his courageous stand but only to argue conversely that many of his colleagues who applauded his stance quite literally could not afford to emulate it. When the *Athens News* provided Economou with a regular column for his anti-regime views, for which he accepted nominal payment, he was refused authorization of his union card on the telling pretext that he was jeopardizing other journalists' standards by accepting a wage below the union minimum.[6]

The junta, recognizing this mentality in the journalistic community, threw E.S.I.E.A. into utter confusion by cancelling the Journalists' Lottery in July 1967. The move left the union suddenly lumbered with 17.6 million drachmas worth of debts relating to outstanding mortgages and left its pensioners with no source of income except their basic pension from T.S.P.E.A.Th. The unemployment fund which T.S.P.E.A.Th. administered was so overburdened by the sudden onslaught of 421 out of work journalists simultaneously claiming benefit that it had to have recourse to the state-run Organization of Occupation and Unemployment for a five million drachama loan. This abolition of the lottery, officially done for 'reasons of social equality,' had the effect of making E.S.I.E.A. directly dependent upon the regime both for the continuing benefit of its members and for its future solvency. The fact that pensioners could vote in E.S.I.E.A. assemblies also helped to account for the union's accommodation. In the early weeks after the cancellation of the lottery, union leaders could get no private access to junta members in order to discuss the decision and so they used public press conferences to pursue their problems. It was a situation which baffled foreign correspondents unfamiliar with the circumstances. While they demanded to know about freedom of the press, their Greek counterparts pressed for details about their pension scheme, a situation which caused much disdain among the uncomprehending foreigners.

It was against this backdrop that an acrimonious dispute between the union and Mrs. Vlachou was played out. When Panos Kokkas closed *Eleftheria,* he paid compensation to all his staff, but Mrs. Vlachou, who had taken a political stand, claimed *force majeure* and, when she terminated the contracts of her 251 employees on May 1, 1967, she offered no severance pay. The total cost of settlement would have been about 12.5 million drachmas. The staff, Mrs. Vlachou said, 'willingly accepted their dismissal without compensation as a gesture of solidarity with our stand. . . .'[7] But not all of them. Her 45 printers, members of the traditionally tough typographers' union, sued, claiming the *force majeure* was illegal and their contracts still valid. E.S.I.E.A., pressed by the government, endeavoured to act similarly on behalf of its members but, of the 150 journalists on the two papers, only 52 of them belonged to the union and of these only 28, most of them *Kathimerini* staff with long years of service and a great deal to lose, were prepared to authorize the union to sue on their behalf. (Independently of the union, three staff members sued for continuation of contract and four sued for severance pay.) Mrs. Vlachou accused E.S.I.E.A. of 'playing the government's game' by 'diverting attention from the only question of interest to the international family of journalists – the liberty of the press – towards the economic ... relationship between employers and employees.'[8] The courts found against Mrs. Vlachou in every instance and, in September 1967, she had to pay out 6.7 million drachmas to the 35 journalists and in December a further 3.8 million drachmas to the printers. Those staff members who did not sue did not get any settlement.

To further step up the economic pressure to get Mrs. Vlachou to re-open her papers, the regime used its new found influence with T.S.P.E.A.Th. to order the fund to cut off unemployment benefit to those 42 journalists still entitled to draw it who had refused to file suit. This was done by means of a new labor law[9] which said that a person was only legitimately out of work so long as he was prepared to 'seize any opportunity offered to be employed in his professional capacity.' This was broadly interpreted by the Ministry of Labor to mean that those persons who would not file suit were not taking advantage of 'any opportunity offered' and, on September 15, 1967, the fund agreed that benefit was to be discontinued to anyone who had refused to sue. After the downfall of the dictatorship,

T.S.P.E.A.Th. stressed how it was acting on orders in suspending benefit although at the time a statement spoke of how the failure of the journalists to sue 'burdened unjustifiably and, more importantly, illegally,' the special unemployment fund. Mrs. Vlachou, who described the T.S.P.E.A.Th. action as an 'illegal and inhuman decision . . . an act of vindictiveness . . . a harsh act of vengeance,' said she would make up the benefit to those who were denied. It was a gesture that cost her some 700,000 drachmas. The government twisted the knife by refusing to allow it to be offset against tax, classifying it instead as a donation. Following the restoration of political government, T.S.P.E.A.Th. paid back 453,000 drachmas to Mrs. Vlachou.

The issue of pension increments was finally settled at the end of 1967 with the passage of legislation[10] creating a new supplementary benefit fund called the United Journalistic Organization of Supplementary Insurance and Medical Care (E.D.O.E.A.P.) covering recognized union journalists and the clerical staff of the Athens and Salonika newspapers. E.S.A.T. members were excluded. This fund had an initial capital of just under 20 million drachmas put up by the four unions involved and thereafter it was to be financed by apportionments from the existing angeliosimo and through the creation of new ones.

This concept of a surcharge on advertising to provide benefit for press employees had first been conceived in 1941 following the widespread closure of newspapers by the German occupation forces. Then, it comprised a 15% levy on all commercial advertising in Athenian newspapers. A decade later a 12% surcharge was levied on the advertising in Salonika newspapers to provide pension benefits for their journalists, clerical staff and printers and in 1966 a 15% levy had been applied on all radio advertising to provide supplementary benefits for the employees of the National Broadcasting Institute and to increase the revenues of T.S.P.E.A.Th. and other funds.

The law establishing E.D.O.E.A.P. increased these levies to 20%, 16% and 20% respectively and added a surcharge of 20% on Armed Forces Radio advertising plus a levy of 3–20% on periodical advertising. The allotment to E.D.O.E.A.P. produced revenues of 33.2 million drachmas for the fund in its first year of operation, more than offsetting the loss of revenues from the lottery. E.D.O.E.A.P. also assumed E.S.I.E.A.'s debts relating to the lottery, although the union was to set aside 20% of its revenues annually towards repayment. 'The voting of the new law which foresees the replacement of the social means of the abolished lottery fills us with joy,' said E.S.I.E.A. president Leonidas Petromaniatis in his speech of thanks to the government as the scheme was announced. This was more than just rhetoric.

In the colonels' purge of the trade union movement, both E.S.I.E.A. and E.S.A.T. were ordered to expel from membership all political opponents of the regime. On June 5, 1967, Petromaniatis was presented by the Directorate General for Press and Information with a list of approximately 100 people accused of 'grave communist and anti-national activities.' It is believed that the list was compiled by the Greek Central Intelligence Service. The E.S.I.E.A. executive balked, arguing that to describe many of the names on the list as communist was patently absurd. Among those included were George Androulidakis who, as well as being the editor of *Eleftheria*, was the stringer for the *Daily Express* of London and for U.P.I.; George Anastassopoulos of *Vradyni*; and Leon Karapanayotis, editor-in-chief of *Vima*. On June 15, a second list was produced, this time reduced to some forty names. The union procrastinated and continued to try to find some way around the problem but finally was told that expulsion was 'imperative.' On July 12, the E.S.I.E.A. executive finally agreed to strike off thirty names. Of those, at least eight were communists who had already been interned on Yiaros and a number of others were persons who had gone underground to escape arrest. At least one man was abroad. Three members of the executive, Ioannis Katris, George Drossos and Christos Philippides, resigned in protest.

At E.S.A.T., president Costas Sismanis was summoned, also in June, to appear before Security Police Inspector Vassilios Lambrou who first indicated all those members thought to be communist and then demanded that union cards be revoked for all those who were unemployed. Those included all members, communist and non-communist alike, who were abroad, as well as those who were not full time journalists. It also included many individuals who were simply out of work because of the closure of their papers. Sismanis says the union executive was uncertain about how to react – 'everybody was panicked at the time' – but in the end it refused to sign any expulsion orders.

There followed a year of maneuvering, with the regime applying constant pressure for removals and the union repeatedly invoking its constitution and regulations to explain how this was impossible. Finally, in June 1968, there was an ultimatum to expel or to be shut down. Again the union refused and so, on August 28, 1968, the government filed suit to have E.S.A.T. dissolved. Legal counsel to the union, Theodore Papastathopoulos, says he is not sure the regime would have proceeded, even at this juncture, if it had not been for an incident in which unions were asked to send a telegram of congratulations to Papadopoulos on his escape from an assassination attempt on August 13. This E.S.A.T. refused to do.

Ultimately, according to Papastathopoulos, there were three meetings directly with Papadopoulos at which there were discussions about the conditions under which the union might continue to function. A list of persons to be expelled was negotiated, including people who were either not regularly practising journalists or who were out of the country. Sismanis says it included at least one journalist acting as a police agent within union ranks. It also included Manolis Glezos, the imprisoned former political director of *Avgi*, and Andonis Brillakis, the spokesman abroad of the resistance organization, the Patriotic Front. A list containing 97 names was attached to a memorandum Sismanis submitted to Prime Minister Papadopoulos on November 25, 1968. Apparently the case put in that document was insufficient for, three days later, the court ruled against E.S.A.T.[11] The decision was based on the legal technicality about the union's status which had plagued it during the pre-coup period. The court declared that the existence of E.S.A.T. was 'contrary to public order by creating confusion and irregularities in the granting of [journalistic] privileges called for by the law. . . .'

E.S.A.T. ceased to function immediately, although it wasn't until the following year, on November 6, 1969, that its offices were locked and barred and all its property given to the union of periodical journalists. E.S.A.T.'s funds, said by Sismanis to total a meagre 110,000 drachmas, were sequestrated. On May 11, 1973, Sismanis was arrested and remanded in custody for non-payment of social insurance premiums for secretarial staff but he was acquitted at his trial five days later.

In 1969, E.S.I.E.A. took in 95 full members and 27 probationers were absorbed from the ranks of E.S.A.T. Speaking before the International Federation of Journalists (I.F.J.) in May that year, E.S.I.E.A. president Panayotis Troumbounis cited as an example of the degree of trade union freedom allowed to his organization the fact that it had enrolled 122 new members. He gave no details about how they had been acquired. Apart from those, E.S.I.E.A. signed up only 62 new members during the course of the entire dictatorship, a rate of 12 a year.

As the *quid pro quo* for E.S.I.E.A.'s general attitude, the junta allowed the union to carry on a semblance of normal union activities. After expelling the thirty members, the executive was allowed to resign (July 20, 1967) and the union to hold its biannual elections (August 3, 1967) which should have been held in June. These were the first elections in any union or professional organization since the coup and the last for some time to come. The membership returned the incumbents and filled two of the three vacant places with pensioners' representatives. President Leonidas Petromaniatis, although a conservative, was not a supporter of the colonels, nor did he have their confidence.[12] When E.S.I.E.A. sent a delegation to the conference of the I.F.J. in the summer of 1967, the government demanded a list of some forty possible representatives. It shortlisted seven from which the union was to choose three. Neither Petromaniatis nor the secretary general of the union were included on the government's short list, although vice-president Panayotis Troumbounis was. 'We had serious doubts whether he had a free hand,' commented I.F.J. president H. J. Bradley.[13] Quite to the contrary, Troumbounis was not under pressure to act on behalf of the junta but actively supported them of his own volition.

When Petromaniatis died suddenly of a heart attack in May 1969, Troumbounis automatically acceded to the presidency. Later he was elected by the membership. Partly this was a question of journalists voting for the man most likely to catch the ear of the regime and thus most able to further their interests. They also elected to the General Council Elias Malatos, Papadopoulos' personal press secretary. It has been alleged, however, that there was manipulation of the voting. Troumbounis prematurely adjourned an assembly at which a bid was made to unseat him as interim president and it is claimed that all those persons who stood out against him were then called in and questioned by the security police. 'The other members of the union took the warning and, to protect their right to have elections, accepted the candidates approved of by the government.'[14] On June 27, 1969, Troumbounis was confirmed by an overwhelming majority and his presidency was renewed at regular intervals until the downfall of the dictatorship.[15]

Prior to the coup, Troumbounis had been political correspondent of *Athinaiki* and the Salonika newspaper *Makedonia*, both centrist publications, but with the collapse of *Athinaiki*, he moved over to work for the pro-regime *Eleftheros Kosmos*. It is difficult to fathom what motivated his support for the dictatorship, whether it was reaction to the regime's opponents (he had been among a party of Greeks attacked by a mob of anti-junta demonstrators in Stockholm in May 1967 when he was jeered, jostled and spat on) or some more positive identification. In any event, he appeared abroad as a witness for the regime before the Council of Europe's Subcommission on Human Rights and he repeatedly pleaded the regime's case before the I.F.J. until he finally pulled E.S.I.E.A. out of that organization in September 1972, complaining of the 'unfriendly spirit shown by certain delegates.' The Federation had debated at length whether to expel E.S.I.E.A., ultimately concluding that to do so would have only a fleeting effect while to maintain contact would provide a continuing channel for pressure. In the course of their deliberations they despatched a special investigator to Athens and his confidential report to the secretariat succinctly summed up both Troumbounis and the situation which sustained him in office:

> We were completely wrong when we thought that the union's delegation at I.F.J. meetings always included a spy of the junta. Troumbounis does not need any spy. He is unquestionably on terms of confidence with the regime. The doors of all governmental offices are open to him. Troumbounis has a refined sense of estimating to what extent he can intervene in favor of a colleague involved in difficulties without running any risk for his own position. Seen from outside, it looks as if the union is in favor of the regime and does not do anything for the colleagues, except for the material help. Despite all this, Troumbounis will be re-elected to the presidency of the union ... because the members see no advantage in putting at the top of the union a man who would give the regime an opportunity of dissolving the organisation.[16]

Troumbounis was almost unseated for his endorsement of the provisions of the draft 1971 law on the profession of journalism which called for annual state loyalty checks. At an extraordinary General Assembly, he avoided a motion of censure only by procedural maneuvering and even so a three-man committee was appointed to assist him in his dealings with the government over union demands for amendments. He remained in office just six weeks after the downfall of the colonels.

As the dictatorship relaxed, so E.S.I.E.A.'s attitudes became more openly hostile. For example, in March 1973, after the regime's clamp down on coverage of the student demonstrations, a hundred journalists endorsed an internal union resolution demanding that the executive publicly explain why coverage had ceased. Nothing came of this. In the June 1973 union elections, Troumbounis was returned with only 69% of the vote compared to 93% on the previous occasion and Papadopoulos' press secretary was voted off the Council. Two weeks later, the union executive published a resolution calling for the government to implement 'measures to establish and secure the free and unimpeded exercise of the journalistic profession.'[17] The union even staged a strike from July 18 to

20, 1973, in support of a wage demand although this, rather than being an action against the regime, had attributes of having been manipulated by them. The union's grievance was real enough. Inflation was soaring and journalists' salaries had fallen well behind. Publishers had just been granted sale price increases and the union sought a 35% wage rise to bring their members up to par. The strike ballot, however, was taken among only 45% of the membership and the July 18 walkout came right at the height of the run up to the referendum on the republic. *Estia, Eleftheros Kosmos* and *Simerina* agreed to pay the increase pending the outcome of the dispute which meant that only *Vima, Nea, Vradyni, Acropolis,* and *Apoyevmatini* were shut down. The union claims the action was not politically motivated. It did, however, have political ramifications. The five newspapers had been playing up the communiques of the Committee for the Restoration of Democratic Legality and during their closure statements from former parliamentary speaker Dimitrios Papaspyrou and deposed Prime Minister Panayotis Kanellopoulos went unpublished. The pro-regime papers meanwhile were carrying attacks on Constantine Karamanlis for his critical comments about the referendum. Journalists ultimately called off their strike because of their 'duty to the public.' The pay claim could not be taken up again until after the demise of the dictatorship.

Under the Ioannides regime, not even the toadying Troumbounis was immune from difficulties. Following the closure of *Vradyni* and *Christianiki,* a special general assembly was convened at which a resolution of protest was approved. It said union members 'firmly adhere to the internationally accepted principles of freedom and unimpeded functioning of the press and journalistic profession' and decried the fact that in Greece these had been 'shaken for nearly seven years.' The resolution was sent to the government and the I.P.I. but not disseminated publicly within the country. Troumbounis was detained for questioning on January 24, 1974 and warned off future such actions.

Not all the dictatorship's dealings with journalists involved only the stick. There were occasional measures presented as carrots too. One such was the proposed creation of a school of journalism. The fact that there is none in Greece is a perennial political football. So, in the law settling the supplementary benefits question, the colonels incorporated measures designed to remedy the lack. As he presented the legislation in a ceremony on January 5, 1968, Under-secretary Michael Sideratos showed remarkable modesty, implying that the idea had originated with the publishers' union, E.I.I.E.A.[18] The proprietors, he said, 'had created a special fund which, at their suggestion, is to be used for the establishment of a school of journalism. . . . The capital provided by the publishers' association is pledged for the purpose of funding this school and we give them the honor and pleasure of founding the school themselves.'

The fact of the matter was that the law expropriated the reserves of E.I.I.E.A. and ordered their use for establishment of the school. While the publishers had the 'honor and pleasure' of founding it, the regime reserved the right to run it. Details 'regarding organization and operation of the school' were to be settled by a joint decision of the Prime Minister and the Minister of Education.

Matters relating to entry examination and to lessons in which candidates will be examined, to the numbers of students to be taught, to the rights and obligations of students, to the engagement of teachers and other personnel, to the latter's position and salaries, to the administration of the school as well as to any other details concerning its organization and operation, are determined by Royal Decrees issued on the proposal of the appropriate Minister in charge of press matters.

Moreover, this minister – Papadopoulos himself, as Minister to the Prime Minister – could send fifty journalists a year to the school for 'supplementary training' plus a hundred 'leading members in the field of media concerned with the enlightenment of public opinion.' They were to undertake 'a special course of lessons determined by the appropriate Minister in charge of press matters.'[19] This latter group would have provided the core for Georgalas' proposed National Propaganda Service.

The sum sequestrated amounted to 22 million drachmas and the proprietors were given five years in which to establish the school. They procrastinated and in the back-room bargaining that went into the elaboration of the final version of the law on the profession of journalism in 1971, the provisions which had been included in the draft law were shelved. As the five year deadline approached, the proprietors secured a four-year extension of the time limit. When the regime collapsed, the idea was abandoned altogether and, in January 1977, the year by which the school should have been established, the Karamanlis government passed legislation which restored the frozen funds to the proprietors with interest. Asked why the proprietors did not of their own volition put up the money towards a school of journalism once political government had been restored, their spokesman, George Aidinis, said that the proprietors' view was that a journalism school should not be a separate entity but integrated with a university and, in any event, 22 million drachmas was 'nothing these days.' Any school eventually founded should be 'properly funded so as not to be a failure.' The school of journalism remains a political football.

NOTES

¹ The Union of Journalists of Daily Newspapers of Macedonia and Thrace, *Enosis Syntakton Imerision Efimeridon Makedonias-Thrakis;* the Union of Journalists of Daily Newspapers of the Peloponnesus, Epirus and the Islands, *Enosis Syntakton Imerision Efimeridon Peloponesou, Ipeirou kai Nison;* and the Union of Journalists of Daily Newspapers of Thessaly, Sterea-Hellas and Euboea, *Enosis Syntakton Imerision Efimeridon Thessalias, Stereas-Ellados kai Euboias.*

² The Union of Journalists of the Periodical Press, *Enosis Syntakton Periodikou Typou.*

³ E.S.I.E.A. stands for *Enosis Syntakton Imerision Efimeridon Athinon* and E.S.A.T. for *Enosis Syntakton Athinaikou Typou. Syntakton* actually translates as editor, *dimosiografos* being the correct word for journalist. The use of *syntakton* is the legacy of the era when newspapers tended to be small operations and editors were at one and the same time journalists, as is currently the case on many provincial newspapers. The title of editor is also used generically to distinguish editorial from clerical or manual staff who go under

the respective titles of personnel and press workers. Equally, the Greek press does not make the management-staff distinctions common in North America and Europe. There are proprietors and publishers and everyone else is an 'editor,' eligible for membership of the union and theoretically subject to a common pay scale, although in recent years union contracts have included increments for actual editors acknowledging the extra responsibilities implicit in their duties. In practice editors have always negotiated individual agreements with proprietors which give them over-scale rates.

[4] These figures are for April 1967.

[5] The budget of the Ministry to the Prime Minister contained a special fund with tens of millions of drachmas for assistance to journalists which could be dispensed at the discretion of the Under-secretary.

[6] Panayotis Troumbounis, letter to the International Federation of Journalists, April 28, 1972, cited in *The I.F.J. and the Situation in Greece*, a background paper for the eleventh World Congress of the I.F.J., September 11–16, 1972.

[7] Helen Vlachou, *House Arrest*, p. 43.

[8] Helen Vlachou, letter to the editor, September 19, 1967, *I.P.I. Report*, October 1967, p. 6.

[9] Royal Decree 456, *Government Gazette* 143, August 7/22, 1967.

[10] Compulsory Law 248, December 30/30, 1967.

[11] Decision number 24375 of the Athens First Instance Court, November 28, 1968.

[12] Petromaniatis did, however, try to be all things to all men. In a letter to Theo Bogaerts, secretary general of the International Federation of Journalists on August 11, 1967, he portrayed the resignations which, although belated, had been scheduled, as a 'strong protest to the government for the censorship which has not yet been lifted in Greece and for the loss of our resources through which we were able to grant medical care to all our members and to the members of all [sic] journalists' families throughout Greece as well as a monthly allowance to supplement low pensions.' The emphasis on financial matters is typical.

[13] Internal I.F.J. memorandum, July 1967.

[14] David Tonge, 'Democracy: a Greek journalist's viewpoint,' *The Guardian*, London, September 1, 1971.

[15] June 27, 1969: Troumbounis elected by 410 votes in a ballot of 472. June 25, 1971: Troumbounis elected by 424 votes in a ballot of 454. June 6, 1973: Troumbounis elected by 379 votes in a ballot of 548.

[16] Dr. Sepp Raminger, 'Report on Mission to Greece,' International Federation of Journalists, Brussels, May 1971, p. 1.

[17] *Nea*, June 22, 1973.

[18] *Enosis Idiotikon Imerision Efimeridon Athinon*, the Union of Publishers of Daily Newspapers of Athens.

[19] *Draft Press Law*, Book C, Chapter VI, Article 154, Para. 2.

X THE MEDIA

In Greece, the radio always was,
and is 'His Master's Voice'.[1]

Dictators have an unerring sense of how best to project their views in order to maximize their influence and thus it was that radio was introduced into Greece by the Metaxas regime and television by the colonels. The Radio Broadcasting Service was founded in 1936[2] and first went on the air two years later. It was replaced during the occupation by a collaborationist corporation which did, however, substantially extend broadcast facilities and these were incorporated into the new National Broadcasting Institute (E.I.R.) when it was established on June 15, 1945. The Constitution made no provision for a broadcast network, so E.I.R. was created by means of a Constituent Act[3] and a law[4] which gave it a monopoly of all broadcast rights in Greece for both sound and pictures. E.I.R. was a government agency responsible to the Ministry to the Prime Minister. Its program structure was modelled on the British Broadcasting Corporation with National, Second and Third programs broadcasting news, general information, entertainment and cultural material from Athens over a countrywide grid. Local stations at Salonika, Patras, Volos, Komotini and certain islands served as relay centers and could insert local material but the system was controlled from headquarters in the Zappeion building, a nineteenth century exhibition hall, situated in a park adjacent to the National Gardens in the heart of the capital.

While the service took its structure from the B.B.C., it failed to embrace its spirit in which broadcasters and not their political masters are responsible for the news. Partly this was the result of the fact that there was no opportunity for the evolution of an independent tradition. First there was the Metaxas dictatorship, then the occupation, and finally the civil war in which the radio network became a vital weapon in the hands of the central government. Indeed, at times it was Athens' only link with communities isolated behind communist insurgent lines. Preventive censorship on all programing of political content was introduced in 1946[5] and not abolished until seven years later.[6]Government interference need not have continued in the reconstruction years but it is not in the nature of a Greek politician to release his grasp on any political mechanism once he has laid hands on it. Consequently, E.I.R. became the voice of the incumbent government. Its director was a civil servant who could be hired and fired by the Ministerial Council and, between 1945 and 1965, there were 27 of them.[7]

Two examples will serve to illustrate the degree and style of government intervention. On July 15, 1965, following the resignation of George Papandreou, an official order was issued by the incoming government of George Athanassiades-Novas that no statement made by Papandreou was to be broadcast over E.I.R. Papandreou's appointee as director, Anastassios Peponis, was about to disregard the order as the station prepared for its extended midnight news bulletin. The magazine *Eleftherotypia* takes up the story:

> At five minutes to midnight Miss Xenitou from the Palace Press Bureau brought to the broadcasting studios the royal letters that were sent to George Papandreou in the course of the last two weeks. Meanwhile, there also arrived a representative from the [two hour old] Novas government to supervise the news broadcast...Mr. Peponis ordered that the news broadcast be delayed. From that point on, a

dramatic struggle began between the news department and the representatives of the new government.... The news finally came out at 12.50 a.m. and lasted fifty minutes. The Papandreou statements were read while various threats were heard in the background.... [8]

Peponis, needless to say, was replaced as director by the incoming government.

The second example involves cultural censorship with political connotations. It is not generally realized that, even before the coup,[9] the songs of Mikis Theodorakis were banned from E.I.R. because he was an MP for the United Democratic Left party and his music was thus deemed political propaganda. The ban became an issue in the run-up to the 1967 elections but it was upheld by the caretaker Under-secretary at the Ministry to the Prime Minister, Professor Dimitrios Nanias.

Mr. Theodorakis must not mix politics with art; it is this which constitutes our objection especially as elections are coming on. The intellectual production of political persons broadcast by the State Radio is a weapon of political struggle against their adversaries and is forbidden in democratic regimes because pleasure may be transformed into guidance and art may become militarized under various political or ideological flags. Nobody is naive enough to help put forward art by instruments belonging to the nation [i.e., E.I.R.] when it is known that these will, without doubt, influence persons and help convert them from one party allegiance to another.[10]

Until 1981, there were committees at the radio and television centres to vet song lyrics, usually for salacity although occasionally for political content.

In parallel with its civilian system, Greece has had a nationwide Armed Forces network which also broadcasts to the general public. It was initiated as a pirate radio station during the civil war by soldiers of a communications company using military channels to beam pop songs to their buddies in the field, but its potential was quickly recognized by the General

Staff who in 1949[11] took steps to establish the Central Radio Station of the Greek Armed Forces at a site near army headquarters in the Athens suburb of Holargos. The station operated under the Army Geographical Service, providing entertainment for the troops together with nationalistic programs including royal and ministerial addresses, progovernment battle news, interminable religious services and cultural items laced with liberal doses of patriotism. With the end of the war, questions were raised about the station's legality in the light of E.I.R.'s broadcasting monopoly but a government act of 1951[12] authorized its continued existence. In the reconstruction years and during the Cold War its programming was accepted as a counterweight to the vast volume of communist propaganda beamed into Greece via the Greek language programs of eight eastern European radio stations but in the more liberal Sixties its arch-conservative tone became an irritant in domestic political life and there were repeated calls for it to be closed down. It nonetheless survived and succeeded in expanding into television.

The junta, astutely, gave top priority to the control of the media. Included in its inner circle was Lieutenant Colonel Ioannis Anastassopoulos, head of communications at ASDEN, the Higher Military Command of the Interior and the Islands, and on the night of the *coup d'etat* he was assigned both tanks and crack raiding forces to secure the Athens control rooms of the civilian and military broadcast networks. The two could be linked into a unitary national grid and for the first six days after the coup, Armed Forces radio was the sole domestic source of broadcast news and commentary about the takeover. On the seventh day, E.I.R. went back on the air but only after Farmakis had conducted a rigorous review of all material already scheduled and issued instructions for complete censorship of everything that was to appear in future. The result was programming which ranged from the blatantly propagandistic to the insipidly banal.

Lieutenant Colonel Anastassopoulos became the Director General of E.I.R. and proceeded to insinuate junta supporters into all key positions in the operation[13] thus securing the network's future loyalty. The colonels attached such importance to the actual physical control of the broadcast facilities that the Zappeion headquarters was permanently occupied by a military unit.[14] There was triple security on the entrance – military, police and civilian – and for the longest time there was a sandbagged mortar emplacement carefully hidden on the roof.

The regime was entirely justified in showing such concern, for, when Constantine staged his abortive counter-coup on December 13, 1967, it was the colonels' control of the radio networks which caused the king's defeat. Constantine decamped from Athens for Kavalla, site of the army's Eleventh Division Headquarters and of an Armed Forces radio local station. There he recorded an address to the nation saying he was acting to end 'anomaly and violence.' It was broadcast on the low power local transmitter and a copy was despatched by air to First Army Headquarters in Larissa for broadcast on the more powerful station there. These measures were intended to be his back-up; his real objective was to seize control of the broadcast facilities in Salonika from where his message could be beamed across the whole of northern Greece. By this means, he hoped to secure enough pledges of loyalty from military commanders to allow him to negotiate with the colonels for the return of constitutional authority; he was, by his own admission, unprepared to fight. 'If we had taken Salonika . . . everything would have been finished. I would have spoken on the Salonika radio . . . and all the generals who were hesitating would have stuck.'[15]

Instead, the junta swiftly reinforced its Zappeion defenses and routed the Minister of Northern Greece, Brigadier General Dimitrios Patilis, out of his sickbed to secure the Salonika military facilities. More than two hours before Constantine's message was first heard from Larissa, orders from Patilis were broadcast from Salonika all across Macedonia and Thrace demanding that troops 'obey my commands . . . and [those] of the Revolution of the 21st of April.' Patilis called upon the populace to 'listen to Salonika and Athens radios. They are broadcasting the true facts.' Apart from being late, Larissa was barely audible outside the central plain and at a press conference the following day, Papadopoulos gloated about how the king had only been able to find 'a heretofore dead radio station . . . which was not heard well.'[16]

With his master-plan collapsing about him, Constantine flew to Komotini, near the Turkish border, to link up with his remaining loyal generals. Athens radio, meanwhile, was broadcasting how the king and his co-conspirators were 'trying to escape, running from village to village for a place to hide.' By the time large numbers of Greeks heard the text of the king's rallying call on the evening Greek language transmissions of foreign radio stations, the colonels were already on the air with a six-minute recording of the ceremony swearing in a Regent and a new Revolutionary Government under the premiership of Papadopoulos. There was nothing left for Constantine to do but to slink off to exile in Rome. Armed Forces Radio crowed:

> The unity of the nation has been saved. Greece has won. The anti-national conspiracy has been crushed. Within a few hours the conspirators, the ambitious fools and remnants of corruption and all their sins met their just fate. They became outlaws just like the anarchists and the enemies of the nation. . . . They sought the glory of power only to become themselves humble fugitives worthy of pity. No one moved against them; they crashed down by themselves. The National Revolutionary Government did not even for one moment lose its self-confidence, cool headedness and strength; it dissolved the gangsters without even having to confront them. The state of law which has been tempered in the ideals of the national uprising of the 21st of April prevailed simply by its presence. With the withdrawal of the cowardly and the flight of the conspirators, the National Revolutionary Government has now become all powerful, like steel. . . .[17]

This crude propaganda was typical of much that passed for political commentary on the media under the dictatorship.

Greece was unique among western European countries in not having television until the middle Sixties and it has been claimed that this lack of counter balance to the frenetic press did much to contribute to the climate which led to the takeover. This argument fails to take into account the fact that the radio networks were under political control and television could hardly have failed to be any less an instrument of the incumbent party. Thus it would have been just another strident voice in the already heady mix. Indeed, political machination was the reason that there was no network in the first place. E.I.R. had obtained approval in the mid-Fifties to operate a television system and over the next decade there were three international tenders for preliminary installations. Each was interrupted or annulled for political reasons or because of business irregularities. Finally, in 1963, the Public Power Corporation established an experimental station in Athens but the government, invoking E.I.R.'s monopoly, intervened yet again and the transmitter was removed to the Zappeion. This location was totally unsuitable and the transmitter was later moved to the building of the National Telecommunications Organization on the other side of Athens. The first experimental broadcast, one and a half hours long, was finally transmitted on September 21, 1965 and a limited schedule of regular broadcasting began five months later.

Early in 1964, the Armed Forces Broadcasting Service sought permission from George Papandreou to expand into television but was refused. The King was said to be anxious to establish an Armed Forces network as a countervailing force to the centrist controlled E.I.R. In the confusion which followed Papandreou's downfall, the Army acted without further government consultations to install near Athens transmission equipment left over from a television demonstration project at the Salonika trade fair. Thus, in April 1966, the Armed Forces Broadcasting Service also began airing to the public general interest programs on three nights a week. Their transmissions began at nine p.m., about the time that E.I.R. was closing down. Consequently, from the outset, a following for it was firmly established.

Initial programming consisted of ancient American serials, French and German travelogues and British and American information service documentaries. An early domestic feature on E.I.R. was The Greek Newsreel, a round-up of the week's events using film clips prepared for cinema distribution by the Ministry to the Prime Minister. These films, in the style of the old Pathé newsreels, were of general interest, however such political content as there was projected, not unexpectedly, the government of the day. This eventually gave way to a daily bulletin which consisted of a studio announcer reading a script to camera interspersed with occasional extracts of footage from the Newsreels or of film from freelance sources. The scripts, as with those at the radio, were rewrites of press directorate handouts. There was no tradition, even before the coup, of independent television reporting.

In 1966, the government laid plans to refurbish E.I.R.'s radio and television network with seventeen new transmitters for each medium. These were to be installed over the next decade and were intended to provide coverage for 80% of the population. The colonels took over the scheme in its entirety and placed it within the framework of their Five Year Plan 1968–72, allocating $47 million for capital investment and moving forward the completion date to April 1972, the fifth anniversary of the *coup d'etat.* They also proposed to construct new headquarters for E.I.R. in the Athens suburb of Aghia Paraskevi at a cost of some 500 million drachmas.

About the time that these measures were made public in February 1968, details surfaced of a proposed bill which would have made E.I.R. more independent of government. Instead of being directly responsible to the Ministry to the Prime Minister, it would have become a public company, Greek Radio-Television, S.A., in which the shareholders would be the Greek state, Greek banks, the Public Power Corporation and the National Telecommunications Organization. The shareholders were to form an administrative council which would appoint a governor and a director general to run operations. The Ministry was to have only a supervisory role. Presumably this was something which had been under consideration either prior to the coup or during the period of the king's association with the colonels. It did not correspond to the regime's views about the need for close control of the media and, after a passing reference to the concept in the press, it dropped from view.

The re-equipment program vigorously forged ahead, although as in the pre-coup period, the bidding was not without complications. There were ten offers from both western and eastern bloc countries, and, according to the adjudication announced in July 1968, the successful bid was $16,366,325, submitted by Page Europa, S.P.A. (an Italian subsidiary of the giant American conglomerate Northrop) in conjunction with Marconi, U.K. The underbidders were Thomson-Houston C.S.F. of France at $16,748,631. Despite the strict censorship of the time, *Estia* twice called on Premier Papadopoulos to investigate the 'iniquitous' contract. It was, nevertheless ratified by E.I.R. in November and by Papadopoulos in December. Then, suddenly, on January 15, 1969, Minister of Communications Spyridon Lizardos resigned and, on the same day, his temporary replacement, retired Brigadier Patilis, together with Prime Minister Papadopoulos, signed a joint decision rescinding Page Europa's deal. Thomson-Houston launched an appeal, challenging the accuracy of the figures which showed the Page-Europa bid to have been the most competitive, and the whole matter was turned over to a commission for reconsideration. The official version of events was that there had been an administrative error in the way in which the contract was ratified which meant that the necessary investment capital could not be imported for the project. Thus, the agreement had to be revoked so that this could be rectified and it was only when Thomson-Houston seized this opportunity to contest the original close decision that the auditors were brought in to check the calculations. 'I am responsible,' Papadopoulos told a group of foreign financial journalists on February 6, 1969, 'and after me the legal counsellors of the Minister and of the Broadcasting Institute,' In the event, Page was awarded the contract.[18] The censorship of the time prevented adequate investigation of the incident.

About the same time, but quite separately, there were reports that one of Papadopoulos' relatives was involved in an effort to secure a monopoly of television set production for a foreign company. For a time there was a ban on the import of foreign models but again the censorship precluded examination of the allegations. The Aghia Paraskevi headquarters were completed six months behind schedule at a final cost nearly 100 million drachmas over the original estimate. Subsequently there have been allegations of embezzlement and fraud although these have not been proven.

Nightly television programming began on the Armed Forces channel on November 1, 1968 and on E.I.R. in April 1969. Set ownership soared from 10% of the population in 1970 to 83% in 1977, partly because of the novelty value and partly for reasons of social prestige. The innovation wrought a dramatic change in Greek lifestyle. A once gregarious society, living in cafes, restaurants and cardrooms, became introverted, focussing on the domestic environment. This dovetailed with the colonels' emphasis on home and family. It also meant that the military men had a sedentary audience for their program of political re-education. News involved constant coverage of government activities. So many ribbons were cut, sods turned and cornerstones laid that Deputy Premier Pattakos became known to the public as Mr. Trowel. This putative news was interspersed with periodic hymns of praise of the regime in the style of the editorials which had been dictated to the press in the early days. Many journalists who were able to cope with projecting the government of the day could not accept these encomiums as news and either quit or were fired. They were replaced by pro-regime people, many of whom were not even professional newsmen.

There was a weekly compilation of news highlights presented by Chris Bitsides, the regime-appointed head of the Athens News Agency. Georgalas, who perhaps better than any other member of the regime appreciated the potency of the medium, took a regular slot each Friday evening for a program called 'Briefing the People.' In it he talked about everything from the price of bread to the preconditions for elections. No matter what his topic, he always arrived at the same conclusion, namely that the military takeover had not been a *coup d'etat* but a popular Revolution–social, economic and political – and that only once the Greek people had 'socialized' their anarchic individualism in the Aims of the Revolution could political life be restored. With his insidious professional's skill, he was able to present this propaganda as a positive contribution to civic education which he said had been denied to the public by the old party system.

It was during Georgalas' ministry that both the Armed Forces Broadcasting Service and E.I.R. underwent a basic re-organization to improve their effectiveness. An Armed Forces Information Service (Y.E.N.E.D.) was created[19] as a super-agency to embrace all armed forces publicity operations. It reported to the Psychological Warfare Directorate of the Armed Forces General Staff and its first director general was Brigadier General Triphon Apostolopoulos, a classmate and personal friend of Papadopoulos. Y.E.N.E.D.'s primary function was to provide information and entertainment although its mission was also defined as being to provide indoctrination–'national, moral and social education'–for both the conscript army and the public at large. The law provided that the military should produce, either on its own or in con-junction with independent producers, films 'fit to be projected to the general public.' In a separate decree, guidelines were laid down for the content of broadcasts and the General Staff appointed three-man committees to vet all output at the radio and television networks. Their terms of reference were that material should not offend public decency, contain political messages, be pessimistic or show a negative attitude to life. The control that these committees exercised extended to the most minute details such as the lyrics of individual songs.[20]

On the civilian side, the Directorate General of Press and Information was upgraded to a Secretariat General[21] and the media made directly accountable to it. E.I.R. was transformed into E.I.R.T., the National Radio and Television Institute[22] to be administered by a five-man board whose members were to be appointed directly by the Prime Minister. The chairman was always to be the Secretary General for Press and Information and the members were to be a senior state official of the Ministry of Communications and two persons of 'recognized ability, experience and specialized knowledge.' Anastas-sopoulos, now retired from the Army, was named the first secretary general and when the board was finally appointed some nine months later, three of the four council seats were taken by former junta cohorts, Brigadier Lycourgos Paravantis, an electronics specialist, who was also director general of the National Telecommunications Organization, Brigadier Vassilios Frangos, a former tank commander, who also held the post of director general of the National Theatre, and Major General George Raptis. The fifth post was filled by a state legal counsellor. Day by day operations were to be the the province of a director general acting under the supervision of the Secretary General and the first man appointed to this post was yet another former officer, retired Major General Ioannis Ploumbis of the Signals Corps. He was replaced nine months later by a former head of the Psychological Warfare Directorate of the General Staff, retired Major General Constantine Mitrelis.

Mitrelis' appointment was part of the larger shakeup in August 1971 in which Georgalas and Anastassopoulos were despatched as regional governors respectively of Crete and Western Macedonia[23] making way for Byron Stamatopoulos as Under-secretary and Loukas Papangelis as Secretary General. The new Secretary General was a lawyer who'd played a prominent role in the press debates in the mini-parliament. Outnumbered as he was on the E.I.R.T. council by military men, he would have been powerless to effect radical changes had he wished to. In fact, Papangelis was the consummate example of the sort of regime supporter Papadopoulos was trying to cultivate. Papangelis had no difficulty whatsoever in embracing the concept of using the media as means of proselytizing for the New Democracy.

A new revolutionary wind sweeps over state public information.... The radio and television will present new educational programs and thus contribute to forming democratic citizens within the framework of the overall effort to build the new state of the Constitution of 1968. New educational broadcasts based on the triptych of new institutions, continuous education and the Eternal Values of Hellenism will fulfill their aim within the framework of our ever developing modern society.... Greek film serials based on the nation's struggles [cf Y.E.N.E.D.'s new production mandate] will be shown for the first time on television. Concurrently with entertainment programs, the radio and television will...attempt to make a constructive effort in the course of their mission...to create democratic citizens of whom the new democracy under creation is in such great need.[24]

Such blatant propaganda did not produce many converts. It was insulting for viewers, who could buy daily newspapers containing photos of police dragging protesting students through the streets by their hair, to watch a television commentator blandly assuring them that the government was respecting university sanctuary. The average viewer tended to psychologically tune out the politics and to concentrate instead on the otherwise remorseless diet of pop culture and sport. This had its own subtle social effects and consequent political impact. The media became a sort of political pacifier. Men who might otherwise have gathered in coffee shops to complain of the effects of the dictatorship instead stayed at home to watch the World Cup and cabaret artists whom they could never afford to go out to see. Furthermore, television promoted a material outlook. Its imported programs revealed standards of living for North Americans and Europeans undreamed of by most ordinary Greeks and not unnaturally prompted a desire for emulation. The colonels played on these aspirations, suggesting that it was only the stability afforded by their continuation in office which would allow such standards to be achieved. The acquisitive attitudes engendered contributed to the rampant inflation which wracked Greece in the latter months of the dictatorship.

The advent of Ioannides produced little change. A retired Lieutenant Colonel Haralambos Karaiosifoglou, replaced Mitrelis as director general of E.I.R.T., another case of jobs for the boys, but at Ioannides' junior level of the military hierarchy. Costas Sismanis, a conservative journalist with many military contacts, and the last president of E.S.A.T., was named news director at Y.E.N.E.D. under inauspicious circumstances.

I was picked up by car and taken to the Pentagon where I began talking to an officer whom I did not know. I said I didn't know much about it, who was going to be in the government for example. The officer said that the Prime

Minister was to be Androutsopoulos.... [Sismanis spoke slightingly of him on personal grounds.] He got very upset and said 'he must be the man,' then stormed off. An officer friend turned up and asked what I'd done to make Ioannides so mad. 'Was that Ioannides?' I asked, convinced that I'd be arrested. I was hired nonetheless.[25]

The networks were treated with the same high-handed arbitrariness that characterized the new regime's approach to the press generally. Archbishop Ieronymos, primate of the Greek Orthodox Church who had been closely associated with the Papadopoulos regime, sought to resign after the Ioannides takeover and made an impromptu speech to this effect during a live relay of Sunday service from Athens Cathedral. He was cut off in mid flow and the announcer coolly evoked technical difficulties to explain the interruption.

The media's inheritance from the dictatorship was debt, ineptitude and confusion. Equipment had been bought at exorbitant costs because no one sufficiently expert was employed to assess the proper price. In some instances it was not even compatible with the broadcast systems. Y.E.N.E.D. showed a small profit because some of its personnel and communications costs were absorbed within the military budget but E.I.R.T. ran a perpetual deficit and had an accumulated debt in 1974 of 1.5 billion drachmas. It had some 2,000 employees of whom 770 were civil servants and only a handful professional production people. A B.B.C. report on E.I.R.T.-T.V. News commissioned by the Karamanlis government painted a picture of total chaos.

... It is extremely difficult to know where to begin a report on E.I.R.T.-T.V. News.... It has no permanent staff ... no staff reporters, no staff writers, no staff film cameramen, no staff film recordists, no permanent studio director, no librarian, no staff artists for graphics work: it has no effective news intake service, the minimum of technical services, no delegated budget, and is beset by the slowness of a large bureaucratic machine.

... News film is, in terms of technical quality and professional expertise, quite abysmal. It is considerably below the level of performance demonstrated by a great many home-movie enthusiasts. . . . E.I.R.T.-T.V. News runs, at the moment, on the enthusiasm and economic need of a number of part-time journalists who are also committed to work elsewhere.[26]

But worse than this confusion, the dictatorship left the media with a lack of credibility. They'd had little enough independence before the coup. Now, after seven years as an active tool of government propaganda, the networks' pronouncements simply had no authority. It is a legacy which has not been dispelled because of continued interference by successive political governments.

NOTES

[1] George Alexiadis, former Director General of the National Broadcasting Institute, in 'To radiofono syskotizei, ta gegonota; den exypiretei pleon ton lao,' *Eleftherotypia*, Athens, September 1965, p. 20.

[2] Compulsory Law 95, *Government Gazette 391*, September 3/7, 1936.

[3] Constituent Act No. 54, June 14/15, 1945.

[4] Compulsory Law 1775, June 15, 1945.

[5] Compulsory Law 818, *Government Gazette 3*, January 8, 1946.

[6] Law 2312, *Government Gazette 57*, March 10/11, 1953.

[7] 'To radiofono syskotizei . . .', *Eleftherotypia*, September 1965 p. 24.

[8] 'Dramatikes stigmes sto E.I.R.,' *Eleftherotypia*, Athens, July 1965.

[9] On June 1, 1967, Chief of the Army General Staff Lieutenant General Odysseus Anghelis outlawed all performances of Theodorakis compositions by a Martial Law Proclamation which declared that the music was capable of 'reviving political passions and causing discord among citizens.'

[10] Press ministry bulletin, February 15, 1967. In the post-dictatorship Karamanlis government, Professor Nanias was named Minister of Culture.

[11] Compulsory Law 968, 1949.

[12] Compulsory Law 1663, *Government Gazette 32*, January 24/27, 1951.

[13] The three senior civilian directors at E.I.R. were at first placed *en disponibilité* and finally in February 1968 were sacked.

[14] Initially the occupying force was billeted on the sound stage, sleeping on the orchestra risers. A curtained-off section of this room, fitted with an antique boom mike, was the 'studio' from which foreign correspondents were expected to circuit their despatches. I recollect the amazement of an editor in London who remarked, 'You sound like you've got a whole army of people in there with you.' I replied, 'I have,' and explained that all the dull thuds he could hear in the background were a squad coming off watch and dropping their heavy boots on the hollow risers.

[15] C. L. Sulzberger, 'An Interview with King Constantine,' *International Herald Tribune,* Paris, January 15, 1968.

[16] I clearly remember the Reuters correspondent frantically twirling the tuner of a large mains receiver looking for Larissa while from a small transistor nearby, Athens blared out how 'common adventurers . . . had misled the king . . . and forced him to turn against the national Revolution. . . .'

[17] Central Radio Station of the Greek Armed Forces, 2347, December 13, 1967.

[18] *Government Gazette,* vol. Beta, March 1969, p. 1421. The text of the contract is not included.

[19] Legislative Decree 722, *Government Gazette 252,* November 14, 1970.

[20] *Nea,* September 29, 1979.

[21] Legislative Decree 744, December 11, 1970.

[22] Legislative Decree 745, December 11, 1970.

[23] Anastassopoulos only took up his post in July 1972 having been out of government for more than nine months.

[24] Speech at a press conference to present the E.I.R.T. annual report, December 10, 1971.

[25] Mr. Sismanis remained as news director of Y.E.N.E.D. for several years after the restoration of political government.

[26] Alan Protheroe, 'E.I.R.T.-T.V. News & Current Affairs Broadcasting: Final Report & Recommendations,' April 1975.

PART THREE

XI THE AFTERMATH

Since the downfall of the dictatorship, the press has been going through a process of transition. The tradition of the small circulation, partisan publication has gradually been giving way to an industrial mentality and with the emphasis on the economic aspects of publishing has come, if not greater objectivity, then at least a degree of what might be termed neutrality. Newspapers have become more of a product than a passion. Their close association with particular parties or individuals has been superseded by a tendency to identify more with a political camp; right, left or center. Partly this has arisen out of a need to attract a broader spectrum of readers to increase circulation in a time of economic difficulties and partly it has reflected a drift within the political community itself towards larger bloc parties. The phenomenon of the political grouping based solely on the personality of its leader is increasingly a thing of the past. The major parties – the conservative New Democracy Party (N.D.), the Panhellenic Socialist Movement (P.A.S.O.K.) and the Communist Party of Greece (K.K.E.) – all have greater ideological foundations than their predecessors and will likely outlive their present leadership.

When the dictatorship collapsed on July 24, 1974 only six papers were still appearing: *Estia, Eleftheros Kosmos,* the Lambrakis papers *Vima* and *Nea* and the Botsis publications *Acropolis* and *Apoyevmatini.* The depleted ranks were quickly replenished and the first papers back were the pugnacious, old-style political publications, *Athinaiki,* and *Vradyni.* Ioannis Papageorgiou, owner of *Athinaiki,* had made a living publishing comic books during the dictatorship and had managed to hoard enough newsprint to be able to reappear on the first day. The paper's visceral style briefly caught public attention and circulation soared but its hectoring tone was out of tune with the new political climate and it soon fell from favor. Circulation was down to a quarter of its maximum levels when the paper was closed by a strike in September 1976. It did not re-open.

Vradyni followed a similar course. In the beginning its gleaming credentials of opposition to the dictatorship pushed circulation to record levels but it became virtually a house organ for the New Democracy Party and Prime Minister Karamanlis, and readership fell to less than 20% of peak levels before it stabilized. The paper suffered heavy losses but survived, supported by other successful business publications in the Athanassiades group. Athanassiades briefly resurrected *Imera* (Morning), a paper which he had published for a time before the coup. It was edited by the redoubtable Vassos Vassileiou but closed after only a matter of days. Officially he put the closure down to problems with staffing and plant.

Mrs. Vlachou was slow to re-enter the fray. She returned to Athens almost immediately the dictatorship ended but didn't recommence publication of *Kathimerini* until nearly two months later on September 15, the 55th anniversary of the paper. Advisers counselled her to bring out *Messimvrini* first as it had always been the more popular and profitable paper but she was intent on returning with her political flagship and felt that as all the other conservative morning papers were tainted with varying degrees of association with the dictatorship, there should be a significant market share for her. She modelled *Kathimerini* on the London *Times* and attempted to offer an independent editorial policy but it had limited appeal and circulation stuck at around 20,000 copies a day. Despite this, the paper developed a reputation as the most credible publication in Greece and thus was able to charge premium advertising rates which helped it to stay afloat. Mrs. Vlachou's financial straits meant that she was unable to republish *Mesimvrini* and in 1979 the title was finally sold to Christos Siamantas, a book publisher. He hired the paper's former editor, Panayotis Lambrias, away from his job as head of the National Tourist Organization and under him the paper has had a moderate success.

With the legalization of the Communist Party in September 1974, *Rizospastis* emerged from the underground, where it had come out as a monthly during the dictatorship, to appear as a legal daily for the first time in 27 years. It has been a doctrinaire paper which, according to editor Gregory Farakos, 'follows the exact policy of the KKE.' Facts are frequently exaggerated or misrepresented in order to make stories conform to party line which is justified, the editors feel, because ' . . . all material published in *Rizospastis* has the task of serving the interests of the party and, as a consequence, the interests of the working class.' As a consequence, it has been repeatedly prosecuted under various Penal Code provisions. *Rizospastis* was a strident critic of the New Democracy governments and particularly of the decisions to take Greece back into N.A.T.O. and to integrate the country into the European Community. Its circulation has fallen far short of the party's voting strength, reflecting the fact that there are still social pressures, particularly in the provinces, against open profession of communist views. There has also been police interference with circulation in areas outside the capital and volunteers who illegally try to sell the paper directly to the public, thus bypassing kiosk vendors who are often ex-servicemen, have been regularly harassed by the authorities.

Immediately the dictatorship fell, *Avgi* attempted to reappear as the paper of the legal United Democratic Left party but the National Unity government asked it to delay its appearance so that it did not provoke the military during the delicate days of the handover of power. The paper complied and did not reappear until August 4, 1974. It was unsuccessful in an appeal for compensation for the property confiscated by the colonels, although a state-backed loan was arranged. With the legalization of communism, *Avgi* declared its true colors as the organ of the Communist Party of the Interior (K.K.E.–E.s), a Eurocommunist splinter group. According to former director Andonis Brillakis, the paper has tried to cover all the news. 'There is no question of publishing only what is in the party interest.' There has, however, been a political coloration to copy and editorials have promoted the party line, although *Avgi* has been less doctrinaire than *Rizospastis* because it has sought to appeal to the whole range of readers on the highly fragmented marxist left. The paper has perpetually teetered on the brink of bankruptcy and has only been kept going through more government backed loans, subscriber donations and party subsidies.

With two communist papers already publishing, *Dimokratiki Allagi* did not reappear. Neither did the centrist publication *Eleftheria*. The publisher, Panos Kokkas, returned to Greece during the brief hiatus in the martial law in 1973 with the intention of re-opening but quickly shelved the idea following Ioannides' takeover. Kokkas developed cancer and died the following June. Former chief editor George Androulidakis died of a heart attack only two days before the dictatorship collapsed. The Kokkas family retained the title and at one time it appeared they might re-open in conjunction with the journalist, Paul Bakoyannis. The paper would have endorsed a group of centrists in the New Democracy party grouped around Constantine Mitsotakis but the possibility did not materialize.

Estia has continued in its idiosyncratic mode but has been much subdued following the death of Kyros Kyrou and the accession of his son, Adonis, as editor. The paper was sharply critical of Karamanlis for his arm's length approach to Cyprus but the days of Greek irredentism, like those of the paper, are past. *Estia* represents the last vestige of the pre-World War II type of partisan publication and, as such, is more of a museum piece than a newspaper. It has nevertheless continued to appeal to a residual readership and has staggered on, plagued by financial difficulties.

Eleftheros Kosmos, which suffered as much as the rest of the press under the Ioannides regime, briefly backed Karamanlis on his return but publisher Savvas Constandopoulos soon fell out with him over such policies as the legalization of the Communist Party and the paper drifted into nostalgia for Papadopoulos. From that position, it played a spoiler's role, promoting restoration of the monarchy and amnesty for the junta and campaigning for minority parties on the extreme right. In the 1974 elections it backed the Democratic Union under Petros Garoufalias and in 1977 the National Front under Stefanos Stefanopoulos. Despite its close association with the dictators, *Eleftheros Kosmos* was never subjected to any political purge. The idea was discussed in parliament where it was proposed that those found guilty of collaboration should lose the right to publish for five years but it became apparent as the debate progressed that the criteria by which Constandopoulos' offenses might be defined were also applicable in some measure to all the papers that had continued to publish under the dictatorship and so the idea was allowed to die. Constandopoulos faced repeated prosecutions under Penal Code Articles 181 and 191 and was several times condemned to terms of imprisonment, although on appeal these were reduced to a level at which they could be bought off. In 1981, it looked as if he might finally be incarcerated when he was sentenced to three years imprisonment for incitement to treason following a series of articles calling for the restoration of the monarchy. Once again he eluded his prosecutors. He died in a Stockholm clinic a week after the failure of his appeal. *Eleftheros Kosmos* ceased publication on June 27, 1982.

The Lambrakis and Botsis publications carried the stigma of having continued to appear under the dictatorship. *Nea* and *Vima* had clearly played an opposition role but had been more politic than *Vradyni*. Lambrakis blamed the constant pressure on him and his staff. 'Given the psychological situation and the harassment, I think it would have been difficult to do more. Even if we had done less, it would have been understandable in the light of what went on here.' *Acropolis* and *Apoyevmatini* carried much more opprobrium for having actually supported the Papadopoulos evolutionary policy in the 1973 referendum. Nassos Botsis[1] always denied that this meant endorsement of the dictatorship. 'Because at the time it appeared that the government's tendency was to gradually normalize political life, we reinforced that trend.' The papers of both groups held their circulation but won little of the new readership that was flocking to the restored publications.

A year after the downfall, both groups faced a severe challenge from *Eleftherotypia* (Free Press), an afternoon popular which ruthlessly used sensational tactics to claw its way to number three in circulation. Subsequently, a Sunday edition, *Kyriakatiki Eleftherotypia*, and a morning stablemate, *Proini* (Early), were published, although the second daily never shared the success of the original and eventually folded. *Eleftherotypia* arose out of a curious conjunction of interests. Its proprietor, Christos Tegopoulos, a wealthy book publisher of anarchic bent, bought the title from Alecos Philippopoulos of *Apoyevmatini*. Philippopoulos was a man with a chequered past. He was the first journalist to win one of Georgalas' awards for nationally-minded reporting. A writer of great facility, he also had a penchant for sensationalism. He brought with him from the Botsis paper several like-minded colleagues. Coincidentally, a group of veteran left-of-center journalists were trying to establish a P.A.S.O.K. paper but could not find the capital, so threw in their lot with this venture. The remainder of the staff were lured away from other papers with offers of salaries up to three times more than the going rate. Details of the sale of the title are disputed but apparently a nominal price was agreed on the understanding that journalists would form a collective, share in the editorial decision making and eventually participate in the profits.

Tegopoulos was scorned by many in the Athens press community as a frivolous man interested only in making money. He took himself very seriously. He described his personal philosophy as *situationist* after one of the groups in the 1968 Paris rising and said the role of the paper was 'to check and criticize the government of the day and the establishment.' The paper, he said, was open to all opinions except those of juntists and royalists because 'to find the truth you have to give all the opinions.' Tegopoulos was sufficiently calculating to acknowledge that the only way to have political clout was to have high circulation and realized that the way to achieve this in the Greek market was to be provocative. He opened the columns of the paper to the entire spectrum of opposition opinion and even had one regular commentator who wrote sympathetically about revolutionary groups such as the Baader-Meinhoff gang. The initial reaction of political commentators was that the paper lacked a line and, because of its inconsistency, could be disregarded. The tactic coincided, however, with a realignment on the center-left in which the extreme left was fragmenting, the Center Union dissolving and P.A.S.O.K. emerging as the dominant party. *Eleftherotypia* attracted readers of all stripes and other papers were forced to follow suit. The Lambrakis group which before the dictatorship, had intimately identified with the Center Union now sought 'to cover the camp, not just a party.'

The government presented an easy target for attack because of its policy of reconciliation. The military had handed back power to Karamanlis on the tacit understanding that punishment would be limited to those who had committed crimes such as treason, torture and corruption and that there would be no purge of collaborators. Karamanlis concurred because he believed such leniency would alienate the least number of people and limit the breeding ground for future revolt. The *quid pro quo* was the legalization of the Communist Party and free access to public life for left-wing citizens.

The press truculently demanded wholesale retribution and filled its columns with terrible tales of torture and the atrocities of the Polytechnic. The most delicate issue was Cyprus. The government tried to play it down in order not to provoke war with Turkey while the press hammered a wildly chauvinistic line. The government refused to reveal details of Greek involvement in the coup against Makarios and the press clamored for disclosures, claiming a cover-up designed to mask

American involvement.

Only weeks after taking office, Karamanlis, who at times is as blindly imperious as he ordinarily is astute, ordered Panayotis Lambrias, who was then Press Under-secretary, to spell out for the press just what the government considered to be the limits of responsible journalism. This was done in a series of meetings with publishers and when this had no effect, Lambrias made a public statement charging the Greek press with being 'the most yellow' in the western world. He said their antics threatened the very existence of the fledgling democracy.[2] This merely made the press even more belligerent and caused it to accuse the government of attempting to stifle press freedom.

As the circulation war heated up, the three big populars vied with one another as to who could be the most outrageous. *Apoyevmatini* for a time became a soft-porn sheet serializing books such as Xaviera Hollander's *Happy Hooker* and the sado-masochistic *Story of O. Nea* front-paged for weeks a quack cure for cancer. There were near riots throughout the capital as the supposed miracle water was dispensed while cancer deaths increased as sufferers abandoned conventional therapies. Such depths were plumbed that the journalists' union complained that 'basic principles of correct and responsible journalism [were being] violated'[3] and threatened to expel offending members.

The frenzy culminated in the coverage of the death of the Member of Parliament, Alexandros Panagoulis, who had become a folk hero after his attempt in 1968 to assassinate Papadopoulos. Panagoulis' death in a car accident in which the driver of the second vehicle temporarily disappeared was indeed suspicious but, instead of serious investigative reporting, the papers conducted a smear campaign of insinuation and innuendo directed against witnesses, the security forces and the government. In a supreme flight of fancy, *Nea* concluded that Panagoulis had been assassinated by intelligence agents using curare tipped darts which penetrated his car windshield without shattering the glass. Lambrias again castigated the press in an open letter in which he accused it of 'abuse of democratic freedom' and charged that 'freedom of the press itself is in danger of self-destruction.'[4] The papers consigned his

complaints to the back page while headlining opposition statements alleging a government cover up. But the incident did
seem to have a sobering effect. Subsequently, papers have
been a deal more sedate, although far from staid.

Two new populars have since tried to thrust their way into
the afternoon market. In March 1980, the brothers George and
Gerasimos Kouris founded *Avriani* (Tomorrow), a scurrilous
publication which produced a daily diet of mud-slinging allegations about figures in public life. For example, it alleged that
Karamanlis, now elevated to President, misappropriated a five
million dollar donation to the Navy from Christina Onassis and
that the wife of the new Prime Minister, George Rallis, had
obtained special import concessions for her clothing store. The
paper, which claimed it made its allegations in the name of
freedom of information, climbed to fifth place in circulation.
The tactic was to make the allegation and then leave it to the
accused to disprove it in court. At one point, the brothers were
concurrently fighting sixteen libel charges. In the end, both
were sentenced to terms of imprisonment. George managed to
flee abroad but Gerasimos served more than a year of his
sentence. These difficulties did not prevent the paper from continuing to appear and to attract the gullible.

In 1981, *Ethnos* was resurrected by George Bobolas, a
businessman with extensive trading connections with the Soviet
Union and who also published a Soviet encyclopedia. His chief
editor was Alecos Philippopoulos who left *Eleftherotypia* not
long after its launch, amid bitter recriminations about the failure
of the collective. *Ethnos* is Athens' only tabloid. It looks good
but the combination of left-wing politics and sensationalism has
meant that it has tended to do things like report football rioters
as mobs of fascist demonstrators. It has been alleged that
Moscow money was used to launch the publication, and to sub-
sidize its operations. Bobolas has denied this.

There were, in the early months after the restoration of
political government, a number of worrying physical assaults on
journalists. In March 1975, two newspapermen covering
demonstrations in connection with the trial of a student
accused of insulting a policeman, were beaten up by the police.
In January 1976, when right-wingers staged pro-junta demonstrations in a court where Savvas Constandopoulos was on

trial, it was three journalists, and not demonstrators, who were mauled as the police waded in to clear the court. Serious incidents took place at the funeral, on December 16, 1976, of Evangelos Mallios, a security police officer with a reputation as a torturer who had been assassinated by the same unidentified group which killed C.I.A. station chief Richard Welch. At Athens First Cemetery, former leading members of the colonels' regime, including George Georgalas, made incendiary speeches calling for revenge and off-duty policemen fired a hand-gun salute over the dead man's grave. Six journalists who entered the cemetery to report the incidents were set upon by neo-fascist thugs and savagely assaulted. Three were hospitalized with broken limbs and concussion while the others were badly beaten and bruised. Chris Economou, sent by the government as an observer, was one of those hospitalized. He says that as his assailants set upon him, policemen accompanying him screamed, 'Not this one, not this one.' On January 30, 1977, court reporter Nikos Kakaounakis, who had been threatened with assassination under the dictatorship and who had recently published a book on the colonels called *2,650 Days and Nights of Conspiracy*, was attacked in the street near his home in central Athens by three men, who beat him senseless then dumped his unconscious body in a lime pit on the outskirts of the city. He escaped more severe injury only because the lime was dry. There were fire bomb attacks on the advertising offices of the Lambrakis group and on the editorial offices of *Avgi* and an undisclosed number of parcel bombs were sent to newspaper offices.[5] The attacks were generally taken to be the handiwork of juntist remnants and they lent fuel to the press' demands for a fuller purge. The government insisted on treating them as purely criminal attacks and went out of its way to play down political overtones. This was consistent with its general policy of limiting retribution but futher undermined relations with the press.

Despite its disputes with the government, the press has been completely unfettered since the dictatorship. Its most serious constraints have been financial. Production costs have soared and, at one point, *Nea* was the only newspaper declaring a profit. (*Vima* suspended publication August 21, 1982.) All the papers contracted heavy loans to cover operating costs.

(These totalled 1.7 billion drachmas in 1982.) The sale price inched up from four drachmas in 1974 to seven drachmas in 1977, then leapt in inflationary bounds to stand at 20 drachmas in 1982. The rapid growth of television meant a loss of advertising revenues. Publishers claimed it absorbed up to 75% but advertising industry figures showed that it took only 50% and that it hit hardest at magazines, radio and the cinema. The daily press' proportion dropped off slightly but still accounted for over a quarter of the total market. In fact, the high prices for television time pushed up the rates that newspapers could charge. That said, while the monetary value of advertising rose dramatically, its worth in real terms declined slightly compared to the years before the dictatorship.

Increased wages were the most critical factor. Printers who operated a closed shop succeeded in getting their rates indexed to the cost of living and adjusted monthly. Their salaries cost half as much again as those of editorial staff. Between 1977 and 1980, journalists' basic rates multiplied between four and seven times depending upon seniority. Partly this was a consequence of the high rates Tegopoulos had been prepared to pay and partly it reflected competition from television where salaries ran ahead of those in newspapers. Also, there was a new mood of militance within the union which publishers learned to finesse by keeping settlements high. They took the lesson from a bitter strike in the spring of 1975. Troumbounis had been voted out of office on October 1, 1974 and replaced by Spyros Yannatos, a moderate leftist who had spent the dictatorship in exile in London. He immediately began negotiations for substantial pay rises. The demand, which had caused the strike in the summer of 1973 but had then been postponed because of the referendum, had been suppressed by the Ioannides government as part of its efforts to control the rate of inflation. Private arrangements had been made between publishers and many employees but the official base rate remained unchanged. E.S.I.E.A. negotiates the minimum wage for the profession as a whole and then an increment for its members. In December 1974, Yannatos won a 75% increase in the minimum rate and immediately put in for a 40% increase for the union. The demand meant union scale would apply to upper echelon salaries which proprietors had hitherto considered to be their prerogative to negotiate with the individual. After weeks of deadlock, the proprietors declared unilaterally that they would pay increases according to their terms. It is the last time that they attempted to act in such a high handed manner.

For procedural reasons, the union had to have fresh elections in March. The ballot returned Yannatos again, but with a council in which four of the nine members were even further to the left than he was. This executive was determined to confront the proprietors. On April 29, journalists went out on strike and stayed out until May 13. It was an acrimonious dispute because it was fueled by psychological factors that had nothing to do with the wage demands. A publishers' spokesman has described it as 'a delayed explosion of heroism' on the part of journalists who had gone in fear and kept their peace for seven years and were now striking as much about the right to strike as about anything else. Some journalists saw it as a punishment of publishers whom they felt had profited from the dictatorship at the expense of the dignity of the profession. Printers and vendors sided with the journalists so that the strike could not be broken and the proprietors were finally forced to concede. Subsequently they stopped short of pushing negotiations to the point of strike action.

The co-operation of the printers and the vendors in the strike led to proposals for a joint Syndicate of all press workers. A draft charter of 50 articles was drawn up and circulated among members of the three unions. Some journalists balked at too close an association because of the printers' reputation for militance. Instead of a formal constitutional link, E.S.I.E.A. agreed on January 10, 1976 to a statement of intent in which the three unions undertook 'to make joint and agreed moves appropriate for any matter that is of interest to the working press. . . .' The statement made it clear that this was not a legally binding arrangement.

It nonetheless had repercussions. On May 24-25, the trade union movement at large declared a 48 hour work stoppage to protest against new government legislation banning political strikes. It erupted in violence in which one person was killed, three were shot and about a hundred injured. The offices of

Vradyni were attacked by rioters and several tons of newsprint burned. Press workers had not participated in the general stoppage in order that the campaign might receive coverage but after the incidents the Syndicate pressed for a sympathy strike. Yannatos resisted but was ultimately overruled and on May 27 all Athens papers shut for a day. Within the week, Yannatos had quit. His letter of resignation spoke of 'threats and blackmail' and scuffles between left and right wing members of the executive.

The left-wingers were unable to consolidate their push, however, for the elections returned conservative vice-president George Anastassopoulos as the new chief executive. He was general manager of the semi-official Athens News Agency and later went on to be caretaker press Under-secretary during the 1977 elections. The left-wing saw him as a government man and even some moderate members viewed him as a representative of management who did not speak for working journalists. That said, there was no doubting the substantial improvements in journalists' welfare during his presidency. He also presided over the dismantling of the junta's law on the profession. The government was asked not to abolish this immediately because it contained a number of provisions about such things as late night and weekend working which were beneficial to journalists. The union negotiated the inclusion of these in wage contracts and then moved to amend its own statutes and regulations in such a way as to eliminate the need for the legislation. The law was finally abolished in August 1978.

The next major confrontation between publishers and the unions was in 1980 when the printers rebelled over the use of photo-composition for offset printing. A strike which turned into a lockout closed all but the communist papers and *Avriani* for four weeks. The owners declared that the typographers had broken undertakings given as long ago as 1974 to operate new technology and claimed that they were standing in the way of essential plant modernization. The printers countered that the agreements had been signed under the duress of the Ioannides dictatorship, that they had been set aside by the proprietors when it suited their purposes, and that the owners weren't realistically in a position to consider replacing their equipment in any event. A program of change to be implemented over a decade was finally agreed.

There have been two attempts at general Press Law reform. The first by Under-secretary Lambrias was a radical essay which would have ended government intervention and stressed the play of market forces. Lambrias convened a committee to work on the project in April 1975 which, to ensure political impartiality, included both the Secretary General from the previous National Unity Government and the New Democracy nominee, Ioannis Lampsas. An effort was made to include publishers' and journalists' representatives as well but while the proprietors agreed, the union declined on the grounds that it is 'in principle against specific legislation covering the press.' The union believes that journalists should be governed solely by those laws which apply to the community at large and that if special regulation is necessary, then it should be accomplished by a professional code of practice. Lambrias felt he could not invite proprietors to sit on the committee without employee representation and so the work was carried out in the absence of both parties. The draft went through several phases until, in December 1975, both publishers and journalists were again canvassed for their views. This time it was done by means of a circular which asked for comments on proposed areas of innovation. The proprietors replied that they couldn't answer without knowing the context from which the changes arose. The journalists' union, after taking legal advice about its position, again declined to contribute.

It had been planned to table the bill in parliament early in 1976. Parliamentary time had been set aside in government business schedules and it had been agreed with the speaker that Helen Vlachou, then a co-opted New Democracy deputy, would introduce the bill in the assembly. With the refusal of the profession to co-operate, however, the impetus was lost.

No official text was ever published but an incomplete version from the latter stages of the drafting process was made available for the purposes of this study.[6] It was a rambling, 102-

article bill, badly organized, but full of good intentions. The crux of its changes were contained in a single paragraph, Article 90:

As of the enforcement of this law, all restrictions concerning the press, its companies and related professions (especially special permissions or approvals) or all privileges of any nature (especially all exemptions from taxes, duties or fees) are abolished, unless they are provided for explicitly by this law.

For publishers, it would have meant the end of the provision of duty free newsprint and all the corresponding government restraints on page size, print run, maximum number of pages and minimum selling prices. For journalists, it would have meant an end to tax concessions. It would also have ended the existing distribution monopoly of the agencies and vendors. The scheme would have favored large press groups and further reinforced the tendency towards the creation of a press industry. It did, however, stipulate that multiplicity should be protected by the provisions of monopolies legislation and that state aid could be granted to publications which could not stand up to the competition. The draft was anxious to point out that such intervention would not mean state direction. 'Such assistance should not restrict but, on the contrary, safeguard the freedom and multitude of the press.'

The draft proposed measures to ensure that a publication's sources of income would be free of any covert influence. It required newspapers to rigorously distinguish between advertisements and copy and to label as an advertisement all texts for which any remuneration had been received. It also made it an offense for a state employee to place an advertisement except according to strict business criteria. Newspapers were to be required to publicly disclose the names of their benefactors. This was to take the form of a quarterly statement naming all persons with more than a 10% holding in the publication, listing all large donations or loans and their source, and noting all state aid. The provision would have meant that privately owned newspapers would have had to reveal their sources of funding and that public companies could not just bury unexplained sums in their accounts under headings such as 'other revenues.' The object was to ensure that the public knew just who was publishing what on whose account. If there were doubts about details such as to raise a question about a publication's probity, the State Audit Office could examine its books and publish the findings. This echoed the colonels' Committee for the Financial Audit of Publications but there were notable differences. Intervention was not mandatory – it was only to occur at the request of a professional, self-regulatory Press Council – and the punishments to be meted out if irregularities were discovered were fines rather than imprisonment.

Apart from these financial concerns, the bill embraced several measures which had been under examination by the press law committees prior to the coup. First, freedom of information: the draft said the press had 'a lawful claim' to information from government, the judiciary and public corporations. It made it incumbent on these bodies to provide the press with 'accurate and complete information within the quickest possible time.' All publications were to be treated equally; there was to be no favoritism for pro-government papers or prejudice against opposition publications, particularly the communists. This was a measure of the highest potential importance, for probably the greatest single problem in Greek journalism has been the lack of access to accurate official information. Statistics have been either late, limited or non-existent and the high degree of patronage in public life has meant that bureaucrats have been unwilling to take the responsibility for providing even basic facts for fear of revealing something which might displease their political masters. Politicians have tended to look on their privileged access to information as something to be bartered for influence. The press as a consequence has turned to speculative reporting. Sometimes it has hit the mark; more often not. Governments, therefore, have tended to deny anything which has not been officially disclosed, whether accurate or not. Occasionally, what is denied one week has been confirmed the next, all in the government's own good time.

Full freedom of information provisions, if accompanied by

the growth of a mentality of frankness, could have a fundamental impact on Greek public life, but even the draft law
hedged round the principle with general exceptions so vague
as to virtually nullify its worth. Officials could refuse to give
information, it said, if this would 'delay, cancel or jeopardize'
the work of government, the civil service or the courts, or if it
would 'impair an important public interest or a private interest
worthy of protection.'

Similarly, while the draft went out of its way to enshrine in
law the concept of a journalistic right of privilege, it then subor-
dinated it to the interests both of the state and of justice. It said
that journalists and print workers had 'the right to refuse,
before any public authority, to testify regarding the person who
has in any way provided information or documents, as well as
about the information provided.' When such privilege was
invoked, the authorities would have no right to confiscate any
documents or other evidence connected with the incident.
Then the draft virtually eliminated the right by saying that
courts or parliamentary committees of inquiry could require
revelation of sources if they were of the opinion that 'the public
interest in revealing the sources or in the way in which the information, document or other data has been obtained, is stronger,
in the specific case, than the public interest in protecting the
process of informing the press and in publishing the information. . . .' In any case, the right of privilege was not to apply to
cases involving military sources.

As a counter-weight to these rights, the draft proposed a
code of practice detailing journalists' obligations. The principles
which it set out are so fundamental to the practice of the
profession that one is surprised to see them itemized in law.
Journalists and editors must, it said:

> Exclude from a publication material of a punishable
> nature.
> Check with the diligence each case warrants, the
> accuracy, completeness and origin of the news and reports
> to be published.
> Weigh the interest in publishing with legitimate interests
> running counter to publication.

Prevent the distortion of news and reports by the way in which they are presented.

Avoid describing a suspect or accused person as culpable before he is convicted and give the same publicity in the event of his acquittal.

Inform the reader by means of the headline if a publication, report or news has not been sufficiently verified or is not complete.

State before every news [item] or report whether it comes from a news agency and which one, from a correspondent and who, or from other sources.

Mention the writer or the news agency for every item in the news section of the paper or periodical excepting the leading articles and comments.

Mention the printed [source] and the [date] of the original publication of every text reprinted in the news section of a newspaper or periodical. [Articles are frequently lifted from other publications in their entirety without regard to copyright.]

Publish together with the results of a public opinion poll, the name of the person who conducted it, the time and the place it was conducted, as well as the numbers of persons interviewed.

The fact that it was felt necessary to spell out such basics in law said a great deal about many press practices.

Finally, the draft made provision for a Press Council closely copied from the British model. This would have been a remarkable departure from form, in that it was to be a representative, self-regulatory body rather than an establishment bureaucratic structure. There were to be twenty-four members, including eighteen press representatives, each to be elected by his respective professional body; five representatives of the public to be appointed on the recommendation of the Under-secretary at the Ministry to the Prime Minister; and a lay chairman to be appointed by the Prime Minister after consultations with the leaders of the other opposition parties. The Council had the twofold duty of guaranteeing press freedoms and ensuring compliance with the law. For example, the

Council was to provide the forum for appeal by journalists who felt thwarted in their efforts to obtain information from officials; at the same time, it was to hear complaints by the public about how the press comported itself while carrying out its business. Council rulings were to be compulsorily published by the press and failure to comply was punishable by a fine of up to 100,000 drachmas. The Council was also expected to monitor the health of the industry and to report to government about such matters as the formation of closed shops or monopolies.

The area of the draft which was incomplete was that regarding civil liability. Lambrias wanted to make it easier for individuals who felt they'd been maligned by the press to sue without the civil action necessarily triggering a criminal prosecution under the Press Law or the Penal Code. There was a marked reluctance, particularly in the wake of the dictatorship, to bring newsmen to trial and he hoped that by hitting publishers in the wallet he could make them exercise stricter self-control over their publications. 'There is,' Lambrias said, 'a hidden blackmail in press matters in that a paper can write something against a person knowing that it is false because it also knows that the victim will be reluctant to bring the paper to court. Twenty thousand readers may see the original. If there is a trial, the controversy will reach the whole of the press. The victim feels more damaged morally by trying to substantiate his allegations. Shifting from a criminal to a civil procedure ensures a more cold and routine procedure, a less spectacular trial.'

Although Lambrias repeatedly said that his bill would be completed and put before parliament, it still hadn't appeared when he lost his seat in the November 1977 elections. A draft produced by his successor as Under-secretary, Athanassios Tsaldaris, codified much of the shambling original in a tidy 50 article bill but eliminated virtually all the innovations. The government economic concessions and concomittant controls were restored. Instead of expanding civil liability, the fines for press crimes were increased five fold. The freedom of information provisions were turned on their head. This draft said it was the responsibility of public authorities, 'as far as is possible and reasonable,' to inform public opinion. The provision amounted to a sanction for official turbidity. The expansive Press Council with journalists and the public looking over one another's shoulder, reverted to a typically crabbed bureaucratic institution. Renamed the Council of Journalistic Deontology, it was to be composed of a Supreme Court Judge, a member of the Council of State, a member of the Academy, two university professors, one newspaper proprietor, one journalists' union representative, and two private individuals, one each to be named by the Prime Minister and the leader of the opposition; that is to say, two journalists to five members of the establishment, with two political nominees. The tendency in such bodies is for the political nominees to engage in sterile partisan debate while the establishment figures keep their heads down until forced to make some decision, when they side with the government of the day.

In January 1979, Tsaldaris sought the opinions of both publishers and journalists about his draft. The proprietors said they accepted the broad outlines of the bill but with some specific objections. The journalists' union reiterated its policy that it wanted no special press laws. The Under-secretary said that the government had no intention of introducing contested legislation and the bill was shelved.

The government's control over matters such as sales price and number of pages as a consequence of its provision of duty free newsprint was reaffirmed by special legislation passed in 1980.[7] It arose out of a legally complex incident involving *Avriani*. The printers' strike bit heavily into all newspaper sales and to compensate publishers upped their price to 15 drachmas. *Avriani* which used non-union labour and published at inexpensive premises outside Athens attempted to sell at five. The proprietors' union appealed to the government to enforce a minimum selling price in order to prevent what they claimed was unfair competition. The Kouris brothers charged that the other publishers were effectively operating a trust and appealed to the Council of State. The court said that the government could intervene constitutionally but not within the terms of existing legislation. In response a three-article act was pushed through the truncated summer committee of parliament which allowed the government to set, in consultation with publishers, a floor price which, if breached, would mean deprivation of the right to duty free newsprint. The convoluted first article said this did not contravene the constitutional guaranteee of press freedom but rather secured it because a 'multiplicity and variety of information, opinions and ideas' were thus ensured. The consultations were to cover printing and publishing costs and 'other conditions' pertinent to securing this multiplicity. Shortly after passage of the law, the Monetary Committee authorized substantial loans to press concerns to help them recover from the effects of the strike.

Lambrias' intention that newspapers should be made to pay for their tendency to cast aspersions freely was finally realized in an *ad hoc* law 'On the Civil Liability of the Press' passed on July 2, 1981. It provided for compensation of up to 300,000 drachmas for persons who could demonstrate defamation in civil proceedings. The law distinguished this civil liability from any eventual criminal liability and made publishers and media executives liable even if the author was unknown to them or if the offense was committed unintentionally. The opposition unsuccessfully tried to have cabinet members excluded for fear that fair comment and disclosure of matters of public interest might be impeded.

The media, unlike the press, were not freed from government control. They have not been the active tools of propaganda that they were under the dictatorship but the news has projected government views almost exclusively and Y.E.N.E.D. remained a military station until a bill was introduced in August 1982 to declare it unconstitutional and to amalgamate it with the civilian network.

At Y.E.N.E.D., there was a limited purge of the senior military staff but its civilian personnel went largely unchanged. The station continued to receive military subsidy in the form of technical staff and transport and communications equipment but otherwise it was forced to be self-supporting. Consequently it became decidedly popular with a program schedule heavy in sport, variety and American serials. Y.E.N.E.D. was effectively disarmed by the race for ratings. It frequently topped these and because of high advertising revenues, operated in the black.

One of the principal arguments made for the retention of Y.E.N.E.D. as a military operation was its reputation for 'good housekeeping'. This was challenged, however, by staff unions in a memorandum published in 1979[8] which claimed that there was substantial waste caused by the incompetence of senior staff, too many of whom were unqualified pensioned officers.

Lambrias repeatedly promised to amalgamate Y.E.N.E.D. with the state network as soon as that organization was economically sound enough to sustain the merger, but Defense Minister Evangelos Averoff successfully fought a rearguard action by arguing that it would be an unnecessary affront to the military to deprive it of the operation. To dismantle Y.E.N.E.D., he said, would be like demolishing a socially useful hospital complex because there were some irregularities in the building process.

E.I.R.T. tottered on the verge of collapse when the dictatorship fell, all but paralyzed by massive debts and overmanning. 'It should have been called inE.R.T.,' insisted one of the executives who took over. 'The place was full of women sitting about in the corridors knitting.' About thirty junta-appointed executives were sacked and another thirty people connected with the news removed. They were replaced by nominees whose appointment reflected a mixture of professionalism and politics. The first director general was Dimitrios Horn, an actor who was a personal friend of Karamanlis; his deputy, Paul Bakoyannis, was a professional media man of liberal persuasion who had worked in West Germany during the dictatorship. By all accounts, the partnership worked well. Horn's artistic and administrative skills, together with his access to the Prime Minister, complemented Bakoyannis' technical knowledge and program sense. Their coverage of the first election on November 17, 1974 was generally accepted to have been even-handed. This obviously did not sit well with some elements of New Democracy for only hours after the first elected Karamanlis government was sworn in, the pair were asked to resign. As he stood down, Bakoyannis alleged in an open letter that certain New Democracy members 'believed the network to be the property of their party and the personal organ of their leader.' It was thought that Horn would be reappointed but he stuck by his deputy and the new secretary general was Angelos Vlachos, the civil servant who had been temporary Under-secretary at the Ministry to the Prime Minister in 1967. It marked the return to the sort of situation which had prevailed in the pre-coup period with directors general holding the post at the whim of the government.

Lambrias requested the assistance of former B.B.C. director general Sir Hugh Greene in drawing up plans to re-organize E.I.R.T. Sir Hugh's principal recommendation was that the network should cease to be part of the Ministry. He suggested instead a corporation functioning under private law with the state as sole shareholder. He recommended that the 770 civil servants either be transferred to other government departments, retrained, or pensioned off. The new broadcasting service, he insisted, should be free to hire and fire and to set its own salaries without reference to civil service regulations or government interference. 'The civil service mentality and the creative outlook on which good broadcasting depends are like oil and water. Promising men and women will never be attracted to a broadcast system which strangles initiative with civil service regulations.'9

Sir Hugh proposed a structure modelled on that of the B.B.C. First there was to be an Administrative Council, appointed following all-party consultations, the members of which would regard themselves as 'the trustees of Parliament and of the nation in the maintenance of political objectivity, fairness and impartiality. . . .'10 Day by day running of affairs would be left in the hands of a virtually autonomous director general who would be appointed by the Council. Both the Administrative Council and the director general would be accountable to an Advisory Council, representative of the nation politically, socially and geographically, a sort of media parliament. Sir Hugh recommended 50 members of whom only 17 were to be representatives of political parties and regional administrations. The remainder were to represent interest groups such as the church, the trade union movement, chambers of commerce, farmers' co-operatives, journalists, actors, authors and composers. To shore up the functioning of this structure he recommended that the constitution guarantee the independence of broadcasting.

The legislation eventually produced nodded in the direction of Sir Hugh's scheme, incorporating the broad outlines of its structure but completely ignoring its spirit. On the one hand E.I.R.T. was transferred into a limited company, the Hellenic Broadcasting Corporation (E.R.T.)[11] with one share held by the state which theoretically gave the network administrative and financial autonomy. On the other, both the Corporation and its operation were placed under the direct supervision of the Minister to the Prime Minister. This had been foreshadowed in the July 1975 constitution which, rather than guaranteeing the independence of broadcasting, included a special Article 15 placing it 'under the immediate supervision of the state.'

The hierarchy provided by the law comprised a seven-member Board of Directors, an executive director general with two assistants – one for programs and another for administration – and a General Assembly. The Board was to be appointed at the sole discretion of the government and its brief was purely administrative. The director general, too, was to be a government nominee, both his contract and those of his deputies being subject to approval by the Minister to the Prime Minister. The Assembly, instead of being a broadly based sounding board, was to be a traditional, pinched clique of officialdom, dominated by civil servants with six party political nominees who are not M.P.s. Its deliberations have been dominated by squabbles among the political members while its decisions, not surprisingly, have coincided with government policy.

Instead of providing that the government arrange to absorb E.R.T.'s civil service dead wood elsewhere in the state machinery – the one responsibility it might reasonably have been expected to assume – the law saddled the new corporation with the obligation to provide them with jobs. Staff for whom regular posts weren't immediately available were to be designated supernumerary and to be used as a reserve to fill any future vacancies. When, after prolonged delays, conditions of service were finally published, they established 1,178 staff and listed 940 contract posts.

Ioannis Lampsas, formerly secretary general at the Ministry

to the Prime Minister, was named as the first director general of E.R.T. He was faced with an almost impossible task. At one and the same time he had to try to balance a budget running an annual deficit of hundreds of millions of drachmas, oversee the negotiation of the loans for and the administration of a 1.5 billion drachma capital investment program, soothe the perpetually ruffled egos of creative program makers and ward off government efforts at intervention. The magnitude of the practical difficulties may better be appreciated when it is realized that the network did not produce a majority of its own programing. In the beginning, it was 45% E.R.T. output, 19% from outside contributors and a massive 36% from foreign sources. The first priority, therefore, was to increase in-house production. The Board of Directors sought to dictate programing and staff appointments from above while production staff demanded creative autonomy free of editorial and budgetary constraints. Major talents resigned following public rows. Noted filmmaker Robert Manthoulis quit as Assistant Director General for Programs, alleging government interference from without and apathy and resistance to change from within. He was replaced by Marios Vallindras, an ex-veterinary colonel and former program director at Y.E.N.E.D. Lampsas welcomed him. He had television experience and a reputation as a good administrator and he provided a bridge for an eventual merger with Y.E.N.E.D. Program makers, however, saw his appointment as yet another bureaucratic dead hand on creativity while opposition politicians believed his background made him too likely to be amenable to government persuasion. The press which was hostile to television in any event played up every such internal wrangle as though it were a scandal.

In the main, production criteria were purely professional, although this did not apply in the case of contemporary political issues. On the civil war, only nationalist views got an airing and the dictatorship, in keeping with the government's policy of reconciliation, was virtually a closed book. Lampsas pleaded special circumstances.

The civil war of 1947-50 left behind a lot of hatred within Greek society and the dictatorship of 1967-74 did nothing but add to the discord. Although the transition from dictatorship to democracy took place peacefully, great care was needed to avoid a revival of dangerous controversies. The top management of E.R.T. tried to avoid extremism from whatever direction it came.[12]

This policy meant that serious attempts to analyze the roots of these upheavals were barred from the air. This proved particularly galling to intelligent Greeks who were regularly confronted with insipid programs broadcast solely because they reiterated received nationalist views.

The censorship committees continued to function vetting material for salacious and inflammatory content. They banned at least one song by Mikis Theodorakis because of its lyrics by the Lenin Peace Prize winning poet Ioannis Ritsos. It seems a singular achievement to have been censored before, during and after the dictatorship.

Eventually Lampsas himself could no longer stomach the interference. He rowed with Tsaldaris and was sacked. In an acerbic press statement he charged that there had been intervention 'not only from the Ministry to the Prime Minister but from all the ministries without exception and from all the public authorities.' He accused Tsaldaris and others of trying to assert not only government but also party control over the network. He said 'intransigent elements' sought 'radical changes in personnel with political alignment as the sole criterion.' Lampsas was replaced by Constantine Chondros, a director of the nationalized Olympic Airways. When Chondros fell mortally ill shortly before the 1981 election, he was replaced by the Secretary General at the Ministry to the Prime Minister who held the two posts concurrently throughout the campaign. In 1979, Vallindras had been replaced as Assistant Director General for programs by a former opposition party candidate who had just joined New Democracy.

Nowhere was the pro-government bias more pronounced than in the presentation of television news which was a nightly cavalcade of the activities of the cabinet to the almost total exclusion of any mention of the opposition. The Greeks are not alone in this. In many otherwise democratic countries, the state-controlled media are seen as having a positive duty to reflect official policies in order to strengthen national stability rather than undermine it by the promotion of dissent. Former News Director Evangelos Bistikas spelled out the Greek attitude saying, 'Every day the government acts on national matters and the people must be informed about their activity. The opposition reacts on political grounds. The press exaggerates things. Before waiting to see what happens it jumps to conclusions. There must be a kind of equilibrium. When the newspapers are exaggerated, I don't say television must distort the truth, but it must restore the balance.'

As well as having to contend with this general bias, television news has labored under specific guidelines from the Ministry to the Prime Minister. Although constitutionally responsible for supervision of the networks, it had no legislated mandate for this. Thus, the rules were unwritten and entirely unofficial. Viewed in the abstract, they were not unreasonable. In practice, they meant that the news dealt with little that did not have the government's tacit sanction. Broadly, the criteria were that there was to be no reporting of unconfirmed rumors, no reporting liable to create propaganda from events, and no reporting of political remarks of a personal nature.

No reporting of unconfirmed rumours was taken to mean no reporting of political stories unless they emanated from a government source or had been confirmed by the government spokesman. Thus, if officials were unprepared to comment on an issue, it simply was not covered. This happened frequently on stories involving security, defense and foreign affairs. For example, Washington advanced Turkey $175 million towards the purchase of 40 Phantom jets. Television news reported the story at length concluding that the Greek government was 'doing all that was necessary to safeguard the national interest.' Translated, that meant that several days earlier, Greece had paid $161 million for eighteen F4-E Phantoms, a story which had been all over the front page of every newspaper. Television, however, had been unable to touch it because it had no authorized version.

The prohibition against making propaganda out of events has meant that there was minimal coverage of such things as strikes and protest demonstrations. The guideline permitted reports that workers had come out on strike but prevented interviews with strike leaders elaborating their grievances or reaction from politicians or the public because that was considered to constitute propaganda arising from the event. By definition this has excluded coverage of protest marches and rallies, unless they were officially sanctioned; then they became events in themselves and not propaganda. This led to absurdities such as film being shown of an authorized protest march but not of clashes between police and demonstrators which occurred on the same occasion. Prolonged strikes by teachers and civil servants went unreported save for occasional ministerial comments because it was considered that to allow the strikers access to the media to put their case would allow them a forum for propaganda contrary to the public interest.

The prohibition against the reporting of personal attacks might in some respects have been deemed to be reasonable, given that Greek pride requires that every criticism have a redoubled answer and that a sensible critique can quickly degenerate into vituperation. It prevented political slanging matches on the air, but also excluded opposition comment which criticized the policies or performance of individual ministers. It precluded, for example, statements such as, 'the Under-secretary's guidelines on news have produced politically biased coverage.'

This is not to say that the news was dictated. The men in the newsroom presented the pro-government line of their own volition. The principals at the networks were government nominees who in turn appointed sympathetic news directors. Bistikas, for example, went on to become President Karamanlis' personal press secretary. Journalists who for years had to tailor their copy to suit the requirements of several outlets had no difficulties working within the guidelines. Indeed they took a certain professional pride in having the skill to comply.

Seen in this light, it is perhaps remarkable that television news has demonstrated any independence at all. Certainly it has not churned out the sort of pernicious propaganda that was produced under the dictatorship and alternative controls proposed by some of the opposition parties would lead to even greater political interference. One suggestion has been that there should be an all-party committee to allocate time for political coverage. This has been done on occasion with recording of major policy debates in parliament. Blocs of anything up to four hours are divided according to the party strength in the House. It is boring bad television. What is needed is a change in mentality which will allow educated journalists to exercise legitimate news judgements free from all prior constraints.

The passage of years has expunged all traces of the dictatorship from the Greek press world except for the great white marble mausoleum which is E.R.T.'s headquarters. The colonels' laws have all been repealed and their collaborators consigned to a limbo more punishing than any short, sharp sentence might have been. The principal legacy has been psychological. By tackling the press on economic grounds and laying such stress on the financial aspects of newspaper operations, the colonels hastened the drift towards the industrial mentality which has increasingly seized the profession. A new paper today is much more likely to be the work of a businessman with an eye on the balance sheet than of an opposition hothead seeking to justify himself with a broadsheet.

The election of the Panhellenic Socialist Movement government on October 1, 1981 has provided a suitable watershed at which to conclude this study. The change of government has meant a wholesale change in state press personnel[13] though, on early observation, little alteration in practice. E.R.T., for example, is more open to left-wing views – indeed, conservatives accuse it of trying to rewrite 'national' history – but the news still projects the government. Like so many of its predecessors, the new administration is trying to revise press legislation. Newspapers continue to delight in their role as the scourge of authority. As one conservative editor rationalized after his party went down to defeat, 'Well it's much more profitable in opposition.'

NOTES

[1] Nassos Botsis, his brother Dionyssios who was a co-owner of the papers and Christos Philippidis, chief editor of *Acropolis,* all died within the space of a few weeks at the end of 1980. Beneficial ownership passed to the heirs of the Botsis brothers' sister through a complex of trust arrangements.

[2] Speech to the Foreign Press Association, September 11, 1974.

[3] Statement of the E.S.I.E.A. Executive Council, March 27, 1976.

[4] Open Letter, May 14, 1976.

[5] The Ministry of Public Order refused to reply to questions about these incidents.

[6] See also Robert McDonald, 'A New Press Law for Greece,' *Index,* Vol. 6, No. 6, November 1977, pp. 31-38.

[7] Law 1072, *Government Gazette 209,* September 6/12, 1980 on 'Protection of the Freedom of the Press.'

[8] Reporter, 'Y.E.N.E.D.: O mythos tis "noikokyras" oi alogistes dapanes kai ta troktika!' *anti,* no. 116, January 6, 1979, pp. 18-22.

[9] Sir Hugh Greene, 'Report to the Under-secretary Mr. P. Lambrias on Greek Radio and Television,' January 22, 1975, p. 2.

[10] *Ibid,* p. 5.

[11] Law 230, December 3, 1975. This is the network's offical translation of its title Elleniki Radiofonia-Teleorasis which literally translates as Greek Radio-Television.

[12] Ioannis Lampsas, 'Structure and Targets of Greek Broadcasting,' *EBU Review,* vol. 28, No. 2, Geneva, March 1977, p. 8.

[13] See Robert McDonald, 'Greek media since the elections,' *Index,* vol. 2, No. 2, April 1982, pp. 21–22.

APPENDICES
Censorship Regulations

April 29, 1967, MANDATORY REGULATIONS

Ministry to the Prime Minister
General Press Directorate
Serial No. 19603/Gamma
MINISTERIAL DECISION
Having regard to Article 9 para. 6 of Law Delta Chi Theta/ 1912 'On a state of siege,' as validated by the Royal Decree of 21/4/67
WE RESOLVE
the following:
1. A Press Control Service is to be formed at the General Press Directorate of our Ministry, which will take instructions from and be responsible to us for every oversight or omission in the preventitive control of every sort of published printed matter.
2. The Service functioning in this way has as its aim the prevention of publication in the newspapers (daily, weekly, etc.), in periodicals of every kind and in all forms of printed matter, of all general information or any comment or illustration or cartoon intended in any way to defame the general policy of the National Government or con-

stitutional institutions, or to harm the internal or external security of the country.

3. The Press Control Service will function through its subordinate agencies throughout practically the entire 24 hours in such a way as to exercise in good time its preventitive control of the newspapers and every other form of publication without delaying them in their usual hour of publication.

4. The Press Control Service will start to function at 7 a.m. for the control of the afternoon papers and will continue till 1 p.m. when the first shift of censors will end. The second shift will start work at 8 p.m. and will end when the last proofs have been submitted. During the interval, from 1 p.m. to 8 p.m., there will be a third shift consisting of a head of department and different employees who will deal with general control of the periodical press. Other, specially selected, controllers will deal exclusively with the control of books, theses, research studies, etc. Likewise, further shifts for press control may be created in accordance with the needs of the service.

5. Specifically, in regard to the control of books, theses, research studies, etc., the following control procedure will be strictly adhered to. The parties concerned will have to supply two sets of proofs before going to press. In general, no book will be published if presented already printed for control. Publishers must have all the copies of books or other publications in their hands stamped with the seal of the Publications Control Service.

6. The publication of newspaper supplements or special editions is expressly forbidden. In cases when, exceptionally, it is considered essential that the publication of a supplement be permitted, the publishers responsible must inform the Press Control Service in time and simultaneously present the contents of the special edition for approval.

7. The newspapers in general and all other printed matter for circulation will be presented to the Service for control in the form of two sets of proofs. The controller responsible, after reading the proofs and if he approves the content,

must initial both sets and stamp them with the Service stamp, giving one set to the newspaper which must conform completely with any excisions made in the text. The second set will then be initialled by the head of the shift or by another person charged with this function.

It is understood that the newspapers must expunge any cuts made and replace the material cut with other material approved by the Service.

It is expressly forbidden to leave blanks where information, comment or illustrations of any kind have been cut.

The Press Control Service must, in so far as this is possible, indicate to those responsible for the newspapers and other publications existing prohibitions regarding information, news, comment, illustrations, etc. in such a way as to facilitate the task of the press and thus prevent any delay.

8. After the final preventitive control of the newspapers and other publications, the newspapers and publications are obliged to send two copies to the Press Control Service so that the employee responsible can easily control whether they have conformed with the Service's instructions as regards any cuts and any other modifications suggested as necessary. Then the two copies will be stamped and one will be retained for the Service archives and the other will be given to the newspaper to show the Distributing Agency. Only after this has been submitted to the Agency will the circulation of the newspapers and other publications be permitted. For any transgression of this prohibition, the Distributing Agency will share responsibility with the publishers of the newspapers. Special attention must be paid to the regular and careful upkeep of the Press Control Service's archives in which the proofs and the copies of the newspapers, periodicals and other publications will be kept. One employee of the Service will be appointed as responsible archivist.

9. It is expressly forbidden for any controller to undertake the control of a newspaper or other publication on which he works for pay. Any violation of this, which may be denounced, will be severely punished.

10. The local offices of the Press Control Service, which will

function in accordance with local conditions of newspaper and periodical publication will be informed in time of all instructions and prohibitions issued and will be obliged to conform strictly to these. On this subject, that is to say the formation and functioning of provincial offices of the Press Control Service, a joint ministerial decision of the Under-secretary for National Defense and our own Ministry will have been previously issued, determining exactly all details and their functioning.

11. All communications and instructions transmitted to the Press Control Service in Athens and the Provinces will be entered on receipt in a special book with special reference to the hour they were received. If these are in the form of public service documents, they will subsequently be kept in the archives. Their contents will be entered in the special book.

12. In general, the objective aims of the Press Control Service offices are:

a) the quick and accurate control of printed matter in complete conformity with general instructions for the preservation of national interests.

b) the control must take thought to facilitate the newspapers, as far as is legally possible, in their speedy circulation. No public service is permitted to intervene in the extremely delicate work of the Press Control Service which is subject only to our own Ministry. In a case where intervention is considered necessary on the part of another public service, this must be done through us.

13. The head of the Press Control Service is charged by the present decision to take speedy steps for the staffing of the Service's offices with suitable personnel, strictly selected, both as regards the heads of shifts and the other employees, so that the Press Control Service may function as a model of efficiency and not give rise to complaints by the publishers concerned.

14. A text of instructions is attached herewith on the basis of which press control will function in general outline and which employees of the Press Control Service must bear in mind in their daily difficult task.

Athens, 29th April 1967
G. Papadopoulos
Minister to the Prime Minister

To be communicated:
to the following Military, Police and Civil Authorities for their direct communication to the locally formed and functioning Press Control Committees.
Military Commands
Royal Greek Gendarmerie Command and Police Directorate of Royal Greek Gendarmerie
Town Police Command and Police Directorates of Athens, Piraeus, Patras and Kerkyra (Corfu)
to all newspapers for their information
Attached: General Instructions (3 pages)

GENERAL INSTRUCTIONS FOR THE OPERATION OF THE PRESS CONTROL SERVICE

General instructions to facilitate the work of the Press Control Service employees are furnished below for the information of the responsible publishers of newspapers and other printed matter.

A.   In general it is prohibited to publish:

1. any article, commentary or news item which is disrespectful, directly or indirectly or in any manner whatsoever, of the person of His Majesty the King, Her Majesty the Queen, the members of the Royal Family and of the Royal Court in general or the institution [of monarchy]; similarly forbidden is any reproduction from a foreign newspaper or periodical.

2. any article, commentary or news item and any reproduction from any source whatsoever, whether from within the country or abroad, which criticizes, directly or indirectly or by any means, the Prime Minister and members of the government or their actions in the carrying out of their duties, or which injures their honor.

3. criticism or abuse of foreign Heads of State in any manner whatsoever.

4. historical accounts which by reference to the past can reawaken passions and sow discord.

5. translations of historical accounts or even of news items which refer to changes of regime, rebellions or revolutions and which tend in any manner whatsoever to defame or denigrate other regimes or Heads of State.

6. transcriptions of broadcasts by foreign radio stations of left-wing content, more especially of communiques, news items or commentaries from the radio of the K.K.E. (Greek Communist Party).

7. communiques from any organization of the Left, including the E.D.A. party and its associated organizations.

8. caricatures or photographs which would insult in any manner whatsoever the Sovereigns and members of the Royal Family or of the Court, the Government, the armed forces or the operation of the machinery of government in general.

9. features, humorous columns, titles of theatrical works, films or books which would insult the above mentioned persons.

10. anything which, in the opinion of the Press Control Service, is harmful to the work of the Government.

B. The language of the newspapers must be the current (Kathomiloumeni); it is forbidden to use the vulgar (Demotiki), formerly used by certain newspapers and periodicals. Texts written in this language will be completely deleted.

C. In general it is obligatory to publish (with a headline drawn from the text and in a form corresponding to the importance of the subject):

1. the speeches of His Majesty the King and court communiques.

2. the speeches, declarations or communiques of the Prime Minister and members of the Government, and news concerning the work of the Government and the activities of Ministers, without omitting anything.

3. the communiques of the Directorate General for Press and Information, without omitting anything.

4. cables transmitted by the Athens [News] Agency from

abroad which refer to the situation in Greece, without omitting anything.

5. photographs distributed by the [Press Control] Service (or by photographers approved by the Service) referring to the work of the Government, on page one or on the back page.

6. at least one commentary per day referring to the Government and its work.

D. New instructions concerning possible prohibitions will be issued in time for those concerned to be aware of, and conform to them.

E. Finally, the hours at which the page proofs must be submitted to the Press Control Service for a definite authority to proceed to sale are fixed as follows:

1. for morning papers in Athens and Salonika, 1 a.m.

2. for provincial morning papers, midnight.

3. for evening papers throughout Greece, 11 a.m.

Any change in the above timetable concerning publication and offering for sale of the newspapers will be notified in time.

JANUARY 25, 1968, GENERAL EXCLUSIONS

URGENT
Circular Order
Athens 25.1.1968
Kingdom of Greece
Prime Minister's Office
General Directorate of Press
Office of the Under-secretary
Serial No. E.P. 579/Lambda
Under-secretary
To:
a) The Prefects and regional Military Commanders
b) The Directorate of the 7th Staff Bureau of the General Staff
c) The General Director of the Radio Service
d) Our Press Surveillance Service[1]
e) The Gendarmerie Command and Sub-commands and the Police Directorates
f) All newspaper and periodical publishers, to be circulated to them by the prefects and regional military commands.

Subject: Press Surveillance
Having regard to:
a) Article, para. 6 of Statutory Decree Delta Chi Theta/1912
b) The Penal Law Code
c) Prime Ministerial Decision No. 299/Alpha/11.1.1968
d) Decision by the Minister to the Prime Minister No. 19603/
   Gamma/29.4.67
e) Circular Order of the Ministry to the Prime Minister
   (General Press Directorate) No. E.P. 1787/Zita/11.7.67 and
f) in view of experience acquired on the subject of Government decisions and the intended definite suspension of
   press surveillance.

WE RESOLVE
On reception of the present order:
1. newspapers and all other periodical publications have
   complete freedom to decide on questions pertaining to
   page setting and the emphasis to be placed on certain
   matters, according to their judgment.
2. all daily and periodical publications are free to exert by
   their articles responsible, bona fide and constructive
   criticism. The exact meaning of this statement is rendered
   by the following point in the Prime Minister's address to
   journalists: 'Certain errors are committed which are not
   known to the Revolutionary authorities and which are not
   desirable for the Revolution. I am saying then that everybody should regain a sense of his responsibilities to
   develop the courage necessary in order to denounce the
   sinners, those who act illegally, and it is for this reason that
   the press is granted the right of such bona fide criticism.'

   Further what is understood to be the proper way for
   newspapers to carry out their criticism is completely
   clarified in the following explanatory sentence from the
   same speech of the Prime Minister. He said: 'You should
   begin your criticism at this very moment and such criticism
   must be inspired by a sense of responsibility. As long as
   you have a sense of your responsibilities, please try to
   break the monotonous aspect of the newspapers. As no
   two things are identical in real life, let there be no two

identical newspapers in Greek life today.'

3. the publishers and editors of newspapers and periodicals are fully responsible for the sources of information on which such criticism is based.

4. judgments and news items relating to foreign policy questions are under the complete control of the Government.

5. publicity for social questions which contributes to the success of the Government's endeavours to solve them must be treated according to the editors' judgment and under the newspapers' responsibilities. The same is true of any criticism of decisions or acts of Public or Private law institutions. The publication of correspondence by the readers is absolutely unrestricted, as long as the responsibility for its contents is assumed by the signatory and the management of the newspaper.

6. the decision that reference to publications of any kind relating to the former political parties or their leaders, either in a critical or complimentary manner, or even in connection with their participation in 'society life', is to be avoided remains in force as a general principle.

On this particular subject, it goes without saying that an exception is made of criticisms addressed to the anti-national, illegal and anarchist actions of the communist organizations (Communist Party of Greece, E.D.A.)

7. more specifically, we draw your attention to the problem of Cyprus because of the great importance of this national question. On this subject the policy followed to this day will be continued. This means that no news item may be published unless it has its source in the Athens News Agency or the Directorate General for the Press and no commentary, article, etc. opposed to the Government line may be published.

8. the Government reserves its absolute right to require, without any limitations, the publication of news items and announcements coming from the Directorate General for Press.

9. In cases where declarations, speeches, etc. by members of the Government are published simultaneously, their presentation must be absolutely 'equal' unless the subject

matter makes it necessary to decide otherwise. More specifically, the following have been decided on this matter: a) Government communiques, either with an indication of their sources of from 'authorized sources', may not be modified in any way whatsoever. b) the full texts of speeches made by the Ministers on any occasion will be sent to the newspapers by the Directorate General for Press. These speeches may be published freely, according to the judgment of the newspapers (either in full or in summary or in excerpt form).

The same discretionary permission is granted as concerns the publication of descriptions of receptions of members of the Government as well as of all other Government events.

10. articles from the foreign press as well as news dispatches from abroad may be published under the provisions of the present order. News items from foreign agencies may be used freely, provided they do not refer to events related to national, foreign and international politics to which paragraphs 4, 6 and 7 of the present order apply.

11. no interference concerning the language used by the publications is allowed, provided that the use of a given linguistic form does not represent a provocation.

12. the news dispatches from abroad of the Athens News Agency bearing the notice 'Urgent' are to be published on a priority basis.

13. the newspapers assume full responsibility for the publication of texts and photographs relating to 'sexual' matters, as well as to all matters falling under the provisions of the laws concerning the press and in particular Articles 29 and 30 of Law No. 5060/31. This means that on these matters the provisions pertaining to the repression of the violation of the laws must be applied mercilessly.

14. *General Principles:* a) Under the conditions specified in the present order, the page setting, news reporting, editorializing commentaries and the choice of subjects are left to the discretion of the newspapers. b) The obligation to publish certain texts is abolished with the exception of government communiques and the news items

distributed by the Directorate General for the Press labelled 'compulsory.' Refusal to publish such 'compulsory' texts will immediately have as a consequence the application of the provisions of the Martial Law. c) Athens News Agency cables from abroad bearing the indication *'Urgent'* must always have top priority. Their publication is compulsory.

15. the text of laws and decrees published in the 'Official Gazette' may be reproduced.

16. the newspapers are free to present the news items coming from the Directorate General for Press but under no circumstances will they be allowed to modify them as to their substance and the respect of the original text.

17. the General Instructions, sub-titles A, B, and C under the heading 'It is forbidden to publish,' attached to the Prime Minister's decision No. 19603/Gamma 1967, are no longer in force and are replaced by the provisions of the present order.

18. it is generally forbidden to publish all texts contravening the prohibitions foreseen by the provisions of the laws in force: a) Article 181 of the Penal Code modified by Article 4 of decree 2493/53; b) Article 191 of the Penal Code modified by Article 2 of Compulsory Law 250/67; c) Article 168 of the Penal Code; d) Article 153, paragraph 1, subparagraph (b) of the Penal Code; e) Article 5 of Compulsory Law 509/47; f) Article 107 of the Constitution; and in general all provisions of the laws in force.

19. All earlier decisions and orders which contradict the above are no longer in force.

20. the scrupulous application of the present order is intimately connected with the success of the Government's action and it reflects the decisions taken by the Prime Minister and the National Government.

21. all agencies concerned with press surveillance under your orders must be checked and subjected to severe penalties in cases where the present order is not applied.

22. the present order shall be communicated to interested parties in our region as a confidential document.

23. in cases of doubt or when any problems arise related to

the scrupulous application of the present order, these agencies should address their inquiries to the Directorate General for Press (Division for Press Control or National Press Division).

Michael Sideratos

Under-secretary

Attached:

1) 19603/Gamma Our decision
2) 1787/Zita Our instructions
3) Relevant articles from laws referred to in para. 18 of the present

Circulation:

1. Internal Press Directorate
2. Foreign Press Directorate
3. Office of National Orientation   (All of the Ministry)
4. Directorate of Studies

NOTES

[1] This text changes the name of the censorship office from the Press Control Service to the Press Surveillance Service.

OCTOBER 3, 1969, EXECUTIVE DECISIONS[1]

Athens, 3/10/69

The Prime Minister
to the Directorate
General of Press
Subject Freedom of Press

1. In view of our order No. 447/30-9-69 addressed to the Chief of Armed Forces regarding the way of application of Article 5 and 9 of Law Delta Chi Theta/1912 concerning the state of siege and the relevant proclamation to all Military Commanders, we order the following:

2. Upon receipt of this order, the publication of information, news and comments by the press is now free. Henceforth is hereby permitted the commenting in good faith of the actions of the Authorities, in order to inform public opinion and to serve the public interests.

3. Restriction of the above freedom of press is permitted in publications, newspapers and magazines, in the following cases only:

A) *On publications regarding national security matters, the territorial integrity, or the public security.*
    i) the disclosure of classified or confidential information regarding the organization, composition, armament of the armed forces or the defenses of the country.
    ii) Matters pertaining to mobilization plans.
    iii) The slogans and leaflets distributed by clandestine organizations or parties, aiming at the overthrow by force of the existing legal order.
    iv) Publications tending to reduce the confidence of the citizens to the armed forces and the weakening of the sense of security.
    v) Publications offending the idea of the nation and all national symbols.
    vi) Publications tending to endanger the peace of the country.
    vii) Publications inciting the crime of high treason.
    viii) Publications insulting the King, the Queen, the Crown Prince and him who enacts Royal authority.

B) *Publications concerning statistical information in general.* In this instance the following are also classified in the same category.
    i) Publications rousing the citizens to disobedience towards the laws, regulations or any other legal orders of the Authorities.
    ii) Publications inciting violence against the people, the armed forces or the security troops.
    iii) Publications rousing those serving in the army, the security troops, public services and organizations, to contravene their service obligations.
    iv) Publications inciting to the resistance against the established authorities, rising in revolt and forming guerrilla units.
    v) Publications inciting people to join in forbidden

gatherings, mob demonstrations or strikes.

C) *Regarding publications attacking the national currency or aiming at the causing of damage to the National Economy.*

In this instance are included untrue informations or rumors, liable to cause worrying to the citizens regarding the evolution of the national economy, or to shake the faith of the people in the value of the national currency or to disrupt the smooth development of the national economy or to serve the speculative interests and aims of individuals or groups at the expense of the economy of the state. Is also included the publication of classified state information of economic nature.

D) *All publications concerning the reshuffling of the period prior to the 21st April Revolution and the rekindling of political passions.*

In this instance, are also included in particular, publications which would provoke mutual distrust between the citizens, and raise hatred, diffidence or violence.

The Prime Minister George PAPADOPOULOS

URGENT
Ministry of National Defense
Armed Forces Command
Judicial Department
TO: The prosecution officers
      before Courts Martial
      regular or special,
      and the Presiding
      officers and Crown
      Prosecutors of Courts
      Martial, regular or
      special.
SUBJECT: Judicial Matters
1) In view of:
   a) The provisions of Law Delta Chi Theta/1912 'On the State of Siege'.
   b) The provisions of Royal Decree 280/21-4-67, putting

into effect the aforementioned law, and in particular para. 2 therefore by virtue of which 'Existing Courts Martial exercise their competence under Law Delta Chi Theta/1912, in accordance with special instructions of the Minister of National Defense.'

c) Constituent Act Beta/1967, endorsing Royal Decree 280/21-4-67

d) Para. 2 of Article 136 of the Constitution

We order that

2. Crimes falling under the common Penal Code brought under the jurisdiction of Courts-Martial (regular – special) after April 21 by order of the Prime Minister, will, henceforth, come under the jurisdiction of ordinary criminal courts, with the exception of Crimes under Articles 134–137 'On High Treason', 138 and those which follow on 'Betraying the Nation', 183–185 'Sedition', 190 'Breach of Public Peace', 191 'The Spreading of False information' and 192 'Provocation of Discord'.

3. All cases pending in judicial offices and before Courts Martial falling under para. 2 of the present, are transferred to ordinary criminal courts.

4. Cases falling henceforth under the jurisdiction of Courts Martial are:

a) Crimes under Article 5 of Law Delta Chi Theta/1912, i.e. those aimed against state security, the regime under the Constitution, and public peace and order, regardless of the capacity of the perpetrators.

b) Those under Compulsory Laws 509/47 'On Security Measures' etc., 375/36 'Espionage', 376/36 'Security Measures for Defense Positions, etc.'

5. Our order No Fi 454/10/338629/ 10-5-67 and any other issued after 21-4-67 determining the competence of Courts Martial are abolished.

G. PAPADOPOULOS
Prime Minister and Minister of National Defense.

NOTES

[1] This is the official translation.

BIBLIOGRAPHY

Books and Pamphlets

Anastassopoulos, G. N. et al. *Provlimata Typou kai Dimosiografias*. Athens, Enosis Syntakton Imerision Efimeridon Athinon, 1977.

Athenian [Rodis Roufos]. *Inside the Colonels' Greece*. Trans. Richard Clogg. London, Chatto and Windus, 1972.

Campbell, John and Sherrard, Philip. *Modern Greece*. London, Ernest Benn Limited, 1968.

Carmocolias, Demetrios. *Political Communication in Greece, 1965–1967*. Athens, National Centre of Social Research, 1974.

Clogg, Richard and Yannopoulos, George, eds. *Greece Under Military Rule*. London, Secker and Warburg, 1972.

Council of Europe. *The Greek Case*. Strasbourg European Commission of Human Rights, [1970], 4 vols.

Georgalas, George. *To Elliniko Provlima kai i lysis tou*. Athens, 1975. See particularly pp. 166–169 and 241–243.

– *I Ideologia tis Epanastaseos*. Athens, Directorate General for Press and Information, 1970.

– *Greece, the Foreign Press and the Truth*. Athens, Press and Information Department, Foreign Press Division, 1970.

– *The Greek Case Before the Commission of Human Rights of the Council of Europe*. Athens, Ministry of Foreign Affairs, 1970.

– *The Greek Penal Code*. Trans. Nicholas Lolis. London, Sweet and Maxwell, 1973.

K.K.E. – Esoterikou. *Archeio Paranomou Antistasiakou Entypou 1967–1974*. Athens, 1974.

Krippas, George. *Nomoi Typou Dimosiografias Kinimatografou-Theatrou*. Athens, A. N. Sakkoula, 1977.

Legg, Keith R. *Politics in Modern Greece*. Stanford, California, Stanford University Press, 1969.

Meynaud, Jean. *Les Forces Politiques en Grèce*. Lausanne, Études de Science Politique, 1965.

– *Rapport sur l'abolition de la démocratie en Grèce*. 2nd ed., Montreal, May 1970.

Papaconstantinou, Theofyllaktos. *Politiki Agogi*. Athens, Kavanas-Hellas, 1970.

Papadopoulos, George. *To Pistevo Mas*. Athens, Directorate General of Press [and Information], April 1968–April 1972, 7 vols. See particularly Volume Alpha, pp. 54–64 and Volume Gamma pp. 168–173.

– *'Press Freedom in Greece.'* [Athens, Ministry to the Prime Minister, 1970.]

Stathatos, Nikolaos. *To Dikaion Tou Typou*. Athens, G. Rodi Bros. 1966.

Theodorakis, Mikis. *Journals of Resistance*. Trans. Graham Webb. London, Hart-Davis MacGibbon, 1973.

Vlachos, Helen. *House Arrest*. London, Andre Deutsch Ltd., 1970.

Young, Kenneth. *The Greek Passion*. London, J. M. Dent and Sons, 1969.

Zigdis, Ioannis. *Protimisa ti Fylaki*. Athens, Kedros, 1977.

Zilemenos, Constantin. *Droit de la Presse Helénique*. Paris, Librairie Genérale de Droit et de Jurisprudence, 1970.

Articles and Documents

Anastassopoulos, Nikos. 'Chroniko tis elliniyis tileorasis.' *Optikoakoustiki*, August 1976, pp. 65–69 and September 1976, pp. 55–59.

'The Colonels' choice to discipline the Greek Press.' *IPI Report*, vol. 19, no. 6, October 1970, p. 5.

Dankert [Peter]. 'Report on the situation in Greece.' Strasbourg, Council of Europe, April 24, 1972. Doc. 3114.

'The Death of a Newspaper.' *Greek Report*, no. 14–15, March-April 1970, pp. 14–15.

'Dramatikes stigmes sto E.I.R.' *Eleftherotypia*, July 1965, p. 10.

'Ethnos falls in glory.' *The Greek Observer*, no. 13–14, April-May 1970, pp. 13–14.

'Freedom by Order – the official text.' *IPI Report*, vol. 16, no. 11, March 1968, pp. 2–3.

Gaspard, Armand. 'Christ, the King and the morality of youth,' *IPI Report*, vol. 18, no. 6, October 1969, p. 8.

– 'A free press vanishes.' *IPI Report*, vol. 16, no. 8, December 1967, pp. 4–10.

— 'Greece, The Independent Press in Serious Danger.' Zurich, The International Press Institute, January 30, 1970.

– 'Make-up can vary but not the news.' *IPI Report*, vol. 18, no. 1–2, May-June 1969, pp. 20–22.

Granitsas, Spyridon. 'Greek junta's "code" is mockery of press.' *Editor & Publisher*, September 13, 1969, p. 64.

Greene, Sir Hugh. 'Law does provide opportunities.' *New Greece*, February 1976, pp. 10–15. [Interview, accompanied by text of 1975 law on broadcasting.]

– 'The IFJ and the Situation in Greece.' Brussels, International Federation of Journalists, September 1972. [Background paper for the XIth World Congress.]

– 'A judicial swindle.' *Greek Report*, no. 3, April 1969, p. 23.

Koumantos, Georgios. 'Les media constituent-ils un contre-pouvoir democratique?' *To Syntagma*, vol. Beta, 1976, pp. 430–445.

Krippas, George. 'Brief History of the Greek Press.' *Yearbook of the Greek Press*, Athens, Ministry to the Prime Minister, 1969, pp. 9–19; 1970, pp. 11–25; 1976, pp. 7–20.

– 'The "Epanorthosis anakrivon dimosievmaton" in Greece.' *The Right of Reply in Europe, possibilities of harmonization*, ed. Martin Loffler, et al, Munich, 1974, pp. 194–195.

Lambrakis, Christos. 'The Big Lie Crumbles.' Observer Foreign News Service, London, no. 24367, October 13, 1967.

– 'Greek press prints all main currents of political opinion.' *IPI Report*, vol. 24, no. 2–3, February-March 1975, pp. 2–3.

Lampsas, Ioannis. 'Structure and Targets of Greek Broadcasting.' *EBU Review*, Geneva, European Broadcasting Union. vol. 28, no. 2 March 1977, pp. 6–9.

Leonidas, N. 'I Logokrisia kai ta troktika pou tin yperetisan kata tin 7 etia.' *anti*, no. 1, September 7, 1974, pp. 38–40.

Marceau, Marc. 'With full freedom, the Greek Press is making steady progress.' *IPI Report*, vol. 13, no. 8, December 1964, pp. 4–5.

Massavetas, Georgis. 'O Neos Nomos peri Typou.' *anti*, no. 47, June 12, 1976, pp. 8–10.

McDonald, Robert. 'Greece: April 21, 1967.' *The Massachusetts Review*, Winter 1968, pp. 59–78.

– 'Greek media since the elections?' *Index*, vol. 2, no. 2, April 1982, pp. 21–22.

– 'The Greek Press under the Colonels.' *Index*, vol 3, no. 4, winter 1974, pp. 27–41.

– 'A New Press Law for Greece.' *Index*, vol. 6, no. 6, November 1977, pp. 31–38.

'Mockery of the Press: the full text – 101 Articles of the Monstrous Law Replacing Censorship by Even More Repressive Measures.' *Greek Report*, no. 12, January 1970, pp. 8–20.

'La nouvelle loi sur la presse.' *Problèmes politiques et sociaux*, Paris, La Documentation Française, no. 26, June 26, 1970, pp. 13–14.

'The Press and Broadcasting in Greece.' Athens, Foreign Press Division, Ministry to the Prime Minister, Reference Paper 191, June 1966.

'The Press in Greece Today.' *Hellenic Review*, vol. 1, no. 5, October 1968, pp. 6–7.

'Press, Pressmen and Pressure.' *Greek Report*, no. 5, June 1969, pp. 20–21.

'Pressure on the Uncowed Press, Report sent from Athens. . . by Greek members of IPI.' *Greek Report*, no. 20–23, September-December 1970, pp. 19–20.

'To radiofono syskotizei ta gegonota; den exypiretti pleon ton lao.' *Elefetherotypia*, September 1965, pp. 20–24.

Reporter. 'Y.E.N.E.D.: O mythos tis "noikokyras" oi alogistes dapanes kai ta troktika!' *anti*, no. 116, January 6. 1979, pp. 18–22.

Siegmann, [W. A.] 'Report on the Situation in Greece.' Strasbourg, Council of Europe, January 22, 1968, Doc. 2322.

'The Slow Squeeze on the Greek Press.' *IPI Report*, vol. 18, no. 11, March 1970, p. 1ff.

Stathatos, Nikolaos. 'O Nomos peri typou tis diktatorias den tropopiitai, mono katargitai.' *anti*, no. 4, October 19, 1974, pp. 13–14.

– 'O Typos kai to Schedio Syntagmatos.' *anti*, no. 10, January 11, 1975, pp. 14–15.

Tonge, David. 'Memorial to freedom in blue china.' *The Guardian*, London. June 3, 1974.

– 'Onward Christian Democrat.' *The Guardian*, London, December 4, 1973.

– 'Profession in search of a future.' *The Guardian*, London, May 12, 1975.

van der Stoel, Max. 'Introductory Report on the situation in Greece.' Strasbourg, Council of Europe, September 22, 1969. Doc. 2637.

– 'Introductory Report on the situation in Greece.' Strasbourg, Council of Europe, January 18, 1971. Doc. 2892.

– 'Report on the Situation in Greece.' Strasbourg, Council of Europe, May 4, 1968.

– 'Report on the Situation in Greece.' Strasbourg, Council of Europe, January 28, 1969. Doc. 2525.

– 'Report on the Situation in Greece.' Strasbourg, Council of Europe, January 23, 1970. Doc. 2719.

– 'Report to the Consultative Assembly.' Strasbourg, Council of Europe, September 25, 1968. Doc. 2467.

Vlachou, Helen. 'Today more than ever, papers must be free to have a reason to exist.' *I.P.I. Report*, vol. 16, no. 11, March 1968, pp. 1 and 11.

– 'Statement.' *Congressional Record – House,* Washington, September 15, 1971, pp. H8507 – H8510.

'What is the new press law about?' *Greek Observer*, no. 10, January 1970, pp. 29–30.

'When Censorship is Preferable.' *Greek Report*, no. 7–8, August-September 1969, pp. 12–13.

Zilemenos, Constantin. 'Le régime juridique de la presse hellénique.' *Revue internationale de droit comparé*, no. 2, 1966, pp. 423–438.

Unpublished material

Gaspard, Armand. 'Grèce: La presse 4 mois après le putsch.' (Confidential report to the director of the I.P.I.), September 20, 1967.

– 'Mission à Athènes (16 October-24 October, 1967).' (Confidential report to the director of the I.P.I.), November 1, 1967.

– 'Situation actuelle de la presse grecque, Rapport à l'Institut International de la Presse.' June, 1967.

Gazeau, Dominique. 'La Presse sous la dictature des Colonels, 1967–1974.' Doctoral thesis for the Université de droit, d'Economie et de Sciences Sociales de Paris, November 1976.

Granitsas, Spyridon. 'Government by the Press and for the Press, Aspects of Greek Communications.' Athens and New York, 1968–1974.
Greene, Sir Hugh. 'Report to the Under-secretary Mr. P. Lambrias on Greek Radio and Television.' January 22, 1975.
Jernaeus, Claes. *Pressfriheten I Grekland, Före under och juntatiden.* Thesis for Stockholm Universitet, Varen, 1979.
Krippas, George. 'Information Structures and Institutions in Council of Europe Member States; Draft Contribution for Greece.' Strasbourg, Committee of Experts on the Mass Media, Council of Europe, November 8, 1976.
– 'European Press Law.' Strasbourg, Committee of Experts on the Mass Media, Council of Europe, October 29, 1979.
Protheroe, Alan H. 'E.I.R.T.-T.V. News and Current Affairs Broadcasting, Final Report and Recommendations: April 1975.'
Raminger, Sepp. 'Report on the Mission to Greece from March 2–16, 1971' and 'Confidential Report only for Bureau members.' Brussels, International Federation of Journalists, May 1971.
Roubanis, Constantine. 'A Report [on] the Progress of the work of the Press Committees.' April 24, 1968.
Spicer, Joanna. 'Report to Mr. P. Lambrias, Television in Greece: E.I.R.T. Programme Output Organization and Operation.' April 25, 1975.
Stamou, Dimitrios. 'I Politiki Grammi tou Vimatos kata tin eptaetia 1967–1974.' Doctoral thesis for the Panteios Anotati Scholi Politikon Epistimon, Athens, 1981.

Publications with a continuing interest in Greek Press Matters
Athènes-Press Libre. Paris, October 1967–August 1974, 315 numbers.
Chroniko Typou. Athens, August 1974–December 1975, numbers 1–25.
Eleftherotypia. Athens, October 1963–April 1967, numbers 1–42; November 1974–December 1975, numbers 43–56; summer 1976, 'Eleftherotypia Chronicle '76', single issue.
I.C.A.P. Hellas S.A. *Ereyna Theamatikotitas tou Tileoptikon Programmaton.* Athens.
International Federation of Journalists. *Direct Line.* Brussels.
International Press Institute. *I.P.I. Report,* Zurich and London.
Institute for Research in Communications. *The National Media Survey.* Athens.
Unesco. *Statistical Yearbook.* Paris.
United Nations *Statistical Yearbook.* New York.
Writers & Scholars Educational Trust. *Index.* London.

INDEX